AF541513

BHARAT RATNA RADHAKRISHNAN :
A Quest for Being in Becoming

Surendra Nath Tripathi
Saket Bihari

Indian Institute of Public Administration

Prints Publications Pvt Ltd

Published by

Prints Publications Pvt Ltd
Viraj Tower-2, 4259/3, Ansari Road,
Darya Ganj, New Delhi-110002
Tel.: +91-11-45355555 Fax: +91-11-23275542
E-mail: contact@printspublications.com
Website: www.printspublications.com

Prepared by:
Surendra Nath Tripathi and Saket Bihari
Bharat Ratna Radhakrishnan: A Quest for Being in Becoming

Edition: 2024

ISBN 978-81-19972-44-9

Price Rs. 995/-

Published and Printed by Mr Pranav Gupta (Managing Director) on behalf of Prints Publications Pvt Ltd, New Delhi.

Preface

I express my sincere gratitude to the philosopher-statesman, leader of the Indian thought, intellectual light house, spiritual *Guru,* the voice of the east and west traditions, the prophet of humanity, Dr. S Radhakrishnan, the second President of India for his invaluable contributions that provided impetus to transform India into an inclusive landscape.

As a conscience keeper of truth, beauty and goodness (*Satyam, Shivam Sundram*), he raised the problems about the nature of man and his relation to the ultimate that always engrossed his attention by focusing on inner nature of reality. His ruling passion of life is expressed in the everlasting engagement with word, line and music. His deep feeling for harmony was born out of a fusion of truth and beauty that ought to be translated into intellectually motivated philosophical terms.

I would like to acknowledge the invaluable insights and encouragement I received from different sources for bringing out the book on such a towering personality who catalysed the national and cultural renaissance and Indian's quest for becoming. It really adds on to my satisfaction that the book has been complied in the premises of Indian Institute of Public Administration, New Delhi.

The book *Bharat Ratna Radhakrishnan: A Quest for Being in Becoming* is based on the writings of various scholars, administrators and contributors to the book where-in fathomless offerings remain to be highlighted from the works of *Bharat Ratna.* This is an endeavor to relive facets of Dr. S. Radhakrishnan's thoughts, values, ideology and nationalistic fervour they generated in the shaping of modern India. The modern changes and challenges rampant in the present-day social order may be addressed by taking into consideration the views of his resplendent personality. His engagement in the different phenomenal philosophical orientations provides a glimpse of modest noble president whose fame is co-extensive with the world's intellectual frontiers.

As a philosopher he advocated for *adaivatavad* (non-dualism) and as a teacher he envisaged to bring sync between a teacher and a taught. As a diplomat, he popularised Indian version of negotiation skills and as a president he wanted the democracy to reach out the grass root. In all his deliberations, he guided them with rare dignity and distinction. His optimism was of cutting edge level to the extent that he always stood to the promises made and assignments accepted.

As a visionary and *messiah* of poor, Dr. Radhakrishnan's thoughts provide rare attributes to nationalistic aspirations. His stimulating and erudite vision took up the helms of creating and curating the world of inclusivity.

The present book is premised on the scholarly contributions from well-known administrators and academics, on various facets of Dr. S Radhakrishnan. I am sure the papers compiled in the book would provide rare opportunities for the readers to consider the nationalistic values that Dr. Radhakrishnan upheld. The scholarly papers in the book have also implications for the state, market and society on move where ongoing journey between being and becoming continually evolves, experiments and changes itself. The underlying objective of the book is to present the works of Bharat Ratna Radhakrishnan to the readers as it was.

During the completion of the book, IIPA has received immense encouragement, inspiration and insightful suggestions from Dr. Jitendra Singh, Hon'ble Union Minister and Chairman, IIPA. I learned a great deal while selecting, analysing and including various works of Dr. Radhakrishnan. My sincere thanks and gratitude are due to all the learned contributors in this book, who have generously come forth with their ideas in line with the objectives of the book in the limited time frame, despite their tightly knit schedules.

Dr. Saket Bihari, Associate Professor, IIPA has been the initiator to compile the papers. He took the challenge of placing all the materials together. He also ensured that the book comes in the right size and retains the interest of the readers. He deserves all the appreciation for the work that has led to the fruition of the book.

I am thankful to Shri Amitabh Ranjan, Registrar, IIPA for providing inputs on the various contents of the papers received from the authors. I would like to place on record the communication support extended by Ms. Meghna Mani Chukath and her team for seeing the book through the press. Though every single effort has been taken to keep the facts and figures intact in the light of existing literature sources, my apologies for errors that may have crept in.

Surendra Nath Tripathi
Director General

Delhi
March 2024

Contents

Bharat Ratna Radhakrishnan: A Quest for Being in Becoming

SN Tripathi
Saket Bihari

Introduction

Bharat Ratna Dr. Sarvepalli Radhakrishnan was the first Vice-President (1952-62) and second President (1962-67) of India. His life and works exemplify the harmonious blending of scholarship, statesmanship and a profound commitment to promoting India as the indelible cultural capital of the world. A recipient of the Bharat Ratna Award in 1954, he made multifaceted contributions to philosophy, education and public service that led him to become a highly respected figure in Indian intellectual and political circles. As a man of versatile talent and multiple achievements, he served India and worked for the reconciliation of mankind. The thoughts, life and context of Dr. Radhakrishnan enable us to observe the changes and challenges of life in fixity. The attempt to find solutions in changing scenarios rightly ratifies the title of the book i.e. *Bharat Ratna Radhakrishnan: A Quest for Being in Becoming*. His quest for being in becoming posits that stability and agility are inextricably intermingled so far as development is concerned. Agility with the changes at the level of idea brings innovation whereas stability vouches for maintenance of the system. The rational blend of being and becoming makes the process real and ever-lasting. The 'becoming' without 'being' is instability. The 'being' without 'becoming' is stability.

'Being in becoming' does not necessarily represent a specific school of thought. In fact, it aligns with philosophical themes that emphasize the dynamic and evolving nature of existence. It reflects that identity and reality are not fixed but are continually shaped through actions, choices and the ongoing process of becoming. The broad counters of 'being in becoming' connote existentialism, a process of philosophy, Heraclitus, change and phenomenological orientations. Under the theme, the life world is seen as continuously evolving, changing and experimenting with phenomena with different stocks of cultural configurations. The recognition of the presence of change is closely associated with 'being in becoming'. As such, both the intent and content of the book's title become inclusive by negating fixity and housing a multiplicity of thoughts, ideas and actions to stay in harmony. To provide satisfactory answers to human quests, the philosophy of 'being in becoming' open the door for multiple responses through its very nature of being diffusionist. Therefore, the Indian cultural traditions on the one hand and the Indian knowledge systems on the other are embedded with diffusionism, as India's march to development has been accompanied by gross growth of cultural differentiations (both lowbrow and highbrow). However, assimilation and accommodation have been found at the core of Indian social and cultural realities from time immemorial. A man bestowed with all such qualities becomes lovable to all irrespective of his belonging to any cultural root. In fact, no one whose intellectual and public achievements have been so rich and diverse through changing contexts can escape from smears of deviousness, trimming and opportunism.

It is rightly said that thinking and acting do not occur in vacuum, they are the part and parcel of a social process within which an individuals is born and brought up. In a similar vein, the reins of Dr. Radhakrishnan's nationalistic doctrine came to the fore when the oppressive colonial and imperial systems received a sense of discontent from the people. The cultural inroads made by Christianity and Islam in South India were also found to be circumscribing with hegemonic superiority that was rightly scrutinized by a man from a humbler background, Dr. Radhakrishnan. His thoughts broadly captured that religion should be aligned with 'live and let live', encapsulating the principle of tolerance, respect, and coexistence. The arrival of other religions of the world on Indian soil not only became hegemonic custodians of culture and so called guardians of gratitude but also led to the marginalization of the existing native religions. Indeed, the arrival of new thoughts and ideologies may provide space for the native epistemological currents to refine and redevelop. But keeping them away from the people's faith and practice needs to be systematically examined beforehand. On the cost of ideal native practices, the alien practices should not illegitimately be allowed to expand. In other words, 'becoming' should not be countered by 'being' just for the hack. They should interact with each other in a way that refinement can take place and co-existence is ensured. Such time heralded innovative ideas to reinterpret the Indian worldview for which the philosophical insights of Dr. Radhakrishnan was the obvious choice.

Dr. Radhakrishnan was born on September 5, 1888. 'Tirutani to a very small temple town to the northwest of Madras City, the second son of a poor Brahmin couple, Sarvepalli Veeraswami and his wife Sitamma' . He had four brothers and a sister. Radhakrishnan joined the primary Board High School at Tirutani at the age of four and spent about four years in the school. He learnt elementary English, Telugu, arithmetic, geography and Indian history there. In 1896, he shifted to the Hermansburg Evangelical Lutheran Mission School at Tirupati. This school was run by German Missionaries till the outbreak of the First World War. In 1900, his parents shifted to Vellore where he got admission to one of the schools. After two years of study there, he passed out matriculation examination at the University of Madras and got a scholarship to Voorhee's College. Having a sharp memory, he was more influenced by a surreptitious reading of the letters of Swami Vivekananda and his eloquent appeal to India's youth to evince pride and self-respect. His avid readership and respect for Vivekananda's sermons aroused a profound sense of nationalistic aspiration in him. In fact, the circulation of VD Savarkar's *The First War of Indian Independence* catalyzed his nationalistic thinking process. His stay in Vellore inspired him to be an avid reader. His empathetic orientation and sense of providing help to the poor became vivid when he was found helping needy people from his scholarship amount.

In Vellore at the age of 16, Radhakrishnan married a distant cousin, Sivakamu. They had four daughters and two sons. He jelled well with his wife. He recognized his wife as the 'foundation of his life and genuinely believed that she was the only woman who had ever mattered to him and the greatest single influence on him. He was fond of quoting Hegel's remark that a man has made up his account of this life when he has work that suits him and a wife whom he loves. Marriage was to him a game seldom played according to the rules, and a happy marriage, as he saw it, did not require the husband's monogamous attitude. He always regarded himself as happily married. His wife was also a devoted wife by any standard' . In 1904, he passed out the first Arts examination in the First Class from Christian College, Madras, with distinctions in mathematics, Psychology and History which also fetched a scholarship for him. Keeping in view the availability and accessibility of text materials, despite his interest in Physical Sciences, he chose to study Philosophy. In 1949, to further sharpen his public life, he started learning philosophy with assiduity and sincerity.

From Vivekananda and Savarkar, Radhakrishnan transitioned to explore the works of other authors of a more general nature. His early interest in reading and the acquisition of books began to blossom during his years in Vellore. This marked the inception of a habit that would persist throughout his life. Despite being fundamentally, a reserved and solitary individual, Radhakrishnan cultivated his inner world and personal interests to confront the solitude he increasingly sought. During his time in Vellore, glimpses of his social side also emerged. Despite his essential introversion, he displayed a willingness to engage with others. Throughout his life, he maintained certain personal habits – abstaining from tobacco, alcohol and adhering to a simple vegetarian diet.

Dr. Radhakrishanan appreciated companionship. Allocating the remaining funds from his modest scholarship, after covering fees and book expenses, he either shared it with less fortunate peers or used it to entertain friends. His leisure activities included attending concerts and street theatre. Despite occasional indulgences, he was discreet about his financial constraints. Interestingly, during this phase of his life, there was no apparent interest in matters of individual exclusivity. However, a peculiar comment in his notes from 1943 suggests a potential shift in perspective. The intricacies of this aspect remain a subject of curiosity and exploration in Radhakrishnan's evolving narrative.

In the culmination of 1906, Radhakrishnan achieved the remarkable feat of earning a BA degree with First-Class Honours, emerging as the finest student in philosophy for that academic year. While contemplating a shift to the field of law, financial constraints stood as a formidable barrier. Radhakrishnan found himself responsible for supporting his mother and three younger brothers, who had joined him and his wife in Madras. The years following 1906 plunged him into a period of relentless, though dignified, financial hardship. This phase marked the onset of accumulating substantial debts. Faced with the imperative of providing for his family, Radhakrishnan was devoid of substantial financial resources, and had little choice but to embrace a studentship offering a modest stipend of Rs. 25 per month. With determination, he progressed into the MA classes in

Philosophy, navigating the challenges of financial strains with grace and resilience.

Radhakrishnan obtained his MA degree in January 1909. Thereafter, he was suggested to apply for one of the scholarships given every year by the Government of India for Indian students to study either at Oxford or Cambridge. Radhakrishnan had a domestic contingency and he chose to stay back and decided for going outside only for teaching and not for learning. However, teaching and learning are inseparable exercises. A job was also required for him. In this sequence, he was appointed to the substantive post of sub-assistant inspector of schools in an area far from the city but directed to fill a temporary vacancy as a Malayalam Master in the Presidency College at Madras. In partial fulfilment of the requirements of the MA degree, Radhakrishnan submitted his research work on *The Ethics of the Vedanta and its Metaphysical Presupposition.* His moral fortitude shines through his selection of a subject that lay beyond the conventional purview of established courses, demanding a reliance on his own intellectual resources. He expounded the fact that 'the Vedanta philosophy has not neglected the important sphere of ethics; but, on the contrary, we find ethics in the beginning, ethics in the middle, and ethics in the end, to say nothing of the fact that minds, so engrossed with divine things as the Vedanta philosophers, are not likely to fall victims to the ordinary temptations of the world, the flesh, and other powers'. It is a truism that the system of philosophy is generally verified and assessed by its ethical doctrines. A philosophy is also judged by its capacity to improve upon life. In that vein, Vedanta philosophy rightly satisfies the principles of morality consciousness. 'The ethics of the Vedanta is dependent on its metaphysics. According to the Vedanta metaphysics, the Brahman is the sole reality, and the individuals are only modifications of it. The Vedanta postulates the absolute oneness of all things. The metaphysics of the Vedanta, by default, leads to the ethics of love and brotherhood. Every other individual is to be regarded as your coequal, and treated as an end and not a means. This is very much embedded with the postulate of modernity. The Vedanta requires us to respect human dignity and demands and the recognition of man as a human being. To Vedanta, the whole universe is one family, a fascinating creation of God. No man has a right to isolate himself from the life of the whole, i.e. transcendental. The individual's life is not a means to the satisfaction of his desires but is a trust for humanity. This Vedantic ideal of love, fellowship, and self-sacrifice is not the vain fancy of a dreaming poet sighing after an impossible Utopia, but is the logical outcome of a rational reflection upon man's place in the cosmos' . Radhakrishnan enjoyed the freedom to explore unconventional themes.

Importantly, in 1910, he was deputed to a teacher training college at Saidapet. The money received from the practices was not satisfactory to him. Thus he took tuition and many examinerships. He compiled all his lectures in 75 pages culminating in a book, *Essentials of Psychology*. In 1911, Radhakrishnan returned to the hallowed halls of Presidency College, where he dedicated the next five years of his career. Initially appointed as an additional assistant professor, he later ascended to the position of assistant professor of philosophy in 1914.

Alongside his expertise in psychology, Radhakrishnan also delved into teaching European thought and political philosophy. His pedagogical prowess, characterized by clarity and comprehensiveness, garnered such acclaim that students from other colleges sought out his classes. Beyond the confines of Presidency College, his reputation as an exceptional educator spread far and wide. Particularly notable were his lectures on political philosophy, a course where Radhakrishnan's profound insights and engaging teaching style left an indelible mark, earning admiration and appreciation from students.

Dr. S. Radhakrishnan served as a Professor of Philosophy from 1918 to 1921 at Mysore University. During this period, he contributed assiduously to the academic and intellectual milieu of the University. His tenure as a professor marked a phase of his illustrious academic career, where he continued to impart knowledge and engage in philosophical discourses. He also solidified his reputation as a prominent philosopher and educator in India. He served as George V. Professor of Philosophy at Calcutta University during the years 1921-1931. His lectures and writings during this period continued to garner recognition and established him as a leading authority in the field of philosophy. This phase laid the groundwork for his later contributions to Indian and global philosophical thoughts. He headed the Indian Philosophical Congress (IPC) during the years 1925-1937. As a chairman of IPC, he contributed to the growth and development of philosophical thought in India, fostering dialogue and collaboration among scholars and intellectuals. His leadership during these years reflected his dedication to promoting philosophical inquiry and the exchange of ideas within the academic community in India. In 1928, he met Pt. Jawaharlal Nehru at the annual session of the Congress at Calcutta. Their meeting in 1928, marked the beginning of a close association between the two leaders. Over the years, their collaboration deepened, with Radhakrishnan becoming one of Nehru's trusted advisors. Their shared commitment to the nation's development, coupled with their intellectual acumen, played a crucial role in shaping the policies and direction of post-independence India. He took up the assignment of Hibbert lecturer at the University of London in 1929. The Hibbert Lectures are an esteemed series of talks on theological, philosophical, and ethical subjects. His selection for the distinguished position underscored his reputation as a leading philosopher and intellectual not only in India but also on the international stage. During his tenure as the Hibbert Lecturer, he delivered a series of lectures that explored various aspects of Indian philosophy, spirituality, and culture. His insights and interpretations served to bridge the gap between Eastern and Western philosophical traditions, contributing to a greater comprehension of Indian thought in the global context.

From 1929-30, he taught at Manchester College, Oxford. In 1930, he worked as a Jowett Lecturer, Marry Ward Settlement, London. He was appointed as Vice-Chancellor for Andhra University, Waltair during 1931-36. His appointment to this position marked a phase where his administrative skills complemented his academic prowess. As Vice-Chancellor, he raised the teaching and learning standards of the Andhra University. In 1931-1939, he was associated as a Member of the International Committee on Intellectual Cooperation, Geneva. The International Committee on Intellectual Cooperation aimed to foster intellectual exchange and collaboration on a global scale, promoting understanding and cooperation among nations. In 1936-52, he became Spalding Professor of Eastern Religion and Ethics at Oxford University. Later, he took up the charge of George V Professor of Philosophy at Calcutta University during 1937-41. In the year 1938, he became the Lewis Fry Memorial Lecturer at Bristol. In 1939, he was elected fellow of the British Academy. Dr. Radhakrishnan served as Vice Chancellor of Banaras Hindu University in 1939-48. He represented Oxford University at Santiniketan for conferring an Honorary degree on Rabindranath Tagore. He led the Indian delegation to UNESCO in 1946-52. He also served as a Member of the Constituent Assembly of India during 1947-49. In 1948, he became the chairman of the Universities Commission. He also served as Ambassador of India in the USSR during 1949-52. In 1954, he was awarded with country's highest civilian award, *Bharat Ratna.*

He took his last breath on April 17, 1975, at a nursing home in Madras. He passed away due to heart failure. But his teachings and preaching are still alive today. On the demise of Sarvepalli Radhakrishnan, many notable scholars and leaders expressed their condolences and paid tribute to his legacy. Late Smt. Indira Gandhi praised his contributions to Indian philosophy and culture, stating that his passing marked the end of an era. President V.V. Giri expressed sorrow at the loss of a great philosopher and statesman, highlighting his role in shaping India's intellectual landscape. Various political leaders, scholars, and intellectuals across India and around the world offered tributes and condolences, recognizing Radhakrishnan's profound impact on philosophy, education, and public life.

The book *Bharat Ratna Radhakrishnan: A Quest for Being in Becoming* has been compiled to pay a sincere tribute to the leader of the nation whose inspiring vision and mission stand as the guiding force in shaping transformative India based on economic growth, social welfare and technological innovation. His philosophy contains social sermons by emulating which the social life can be reformed, resurrected and rejuvenated. Armed with synergetic wisdom of West and East philosophical positions, he became a leading interpreter of our country's religious and intellectual heritage. He served as an integrating link between generations of India's leadership. His role in synthesizing the spiritualism of the East and the rationalism of the West stands out on the rare corollaries that modern India has ever witnessed. His lectures and writings were heard and read with interest in different countries. Inspired by the writings of *Gurudev* Rabindranath Tagore, Radhakrishnan went on to find satisfaction in simplicity, leading to freedom and democratic knowledge systems.

To him, religion was to be seen as the source of integration. He saw religion being interpreted as a dividing force through dogmatic claims and prejudice. The perseverance of the soul was central to all human victories. His philosophical foundation included Advaita Vedanta, spiritual humanism, harmony of religions, intuition of experience, ethics and morality, education and enlightenment. He emphasized on unity of existence and the underlying spiritual essence of reality. Spiritualism was considered to be the prerequisite for the development of the inner self.

Mutual respect for religious ideals can promote world peace. The rationalization of spiritual nature can only lead to self-fulfilment and progress where one can find true satisfaction and accomplishment. Radhakrishnan stressed the role of intuition and direct experience in understanding spiritual truths. He believed that philosophical inquiry should not be limited to intellectual analysis but should also involve personal experience and inner realization. For him, spirituality is the entry point to ethical behaviour in society. The transformative power of education in fostering intellectual growth and spiritual attainment was considered to be the ultimate goal of human life. He wanted education to be integrated with spirituality. Dr. Radhakrishnan's contributions to epistemological development can be summed up by delineation of four major elements: namely, his philosophy, education, diplomacy and statesmanship.

Radhakrishnan and Philosophy

As a philosopher, he bridged the gap between the East and the West. His lucid interpretation of Vedanta attracted the global audience. He emphasized spiritual values, ethics and synthesis of multiple philosophical traditions. His works, namely *The Philosophy of Rabindranath Tagore* and *Indian Philosophy* are significant. He presented a sympathetic account of the development of Indian thoughts from the Vedic poems to modern times. His legacy endures as a testament to the enduring power of philosophy to illuminate the human condition and inspire impactful positive change. He always expressed valid insights into all religions of the world. He showed his cultural affiliations by classifying himself as an Indian to realize heritage. He suggested that for Indians, the study of the Upnisadas is essential. He wrote, 'For us Indians, a study of the Upnisadas is essential if we are to preserve our national being and character. To discover the main lines of our traditional life, we must turn to our classics, the Vedas and the Upanishads, the Bhagavad-gita and Dhamma-pada. There is much in our past that is degrading and deficient but there is also much that is life-giving and elevating. If the past is to serve as an inspiration for the future, we have to study it with discrimination and sympathy' . But we must not be tied to the past, for 'the highest achievements of the human mind and spirit. The gates of the future are wide open. The fundamental motives, the governing ideas which constitute the essential spirit are not limited to the past. While the fundamental motives, the governing ideas which constitute the essential spirit of our culture, are a part of our very being, they should receive changing expression according to the needs and conditions of our times' . For cosmic development he wanted the spirit and matter (Purusha and Prakriti) to be separated. However, they are considered to be two poles of the same existence. In fact, 'both spirit and matter are real, as matter cannot be reduced to mind, nor mind to matter' .

He saw human freedom in a unified world in his philosophical discourses. He considered the existence of God. The importance of karma goes hand in hand with the existence of God. Karma is the simplest way to follow the doctrine of God that is based on love and perfection. Karma leads to consequences, not reward or punishment. 'Karma is not absolute. The supreme is love and knowledge, goodness and power. Thus, God redeems the world. He suffers with it since his nature is at odds with the evil that transpires in the world. Yet it must be thus, for human freedom must truly be real. Our present choices give a new form even to the past so what it depends on what we do now. Sin enters through our surrender to the restraint exercised by the play of mechanical forces. This is karma in operation. We can fill ourselves with the freedom of the eternal and overcome karma. Then we will work for the salvation of the world. As our knowledge and our love increase, the mortal becomes immortal in God' . He believed that modern mysticism based on the world is real and must be dealt with. The relationship between spirit and world is not of duality but polarity with mutual dependence. The existentialism of Radhakrishnan emerged out of his approach to Maya as positive, as the threat to nothingness that humanity faces. To mitigate the inertia of karma, the human spirit looks inward and can enter into being and experience mystic bliss through truth and goodness.

Dr. Sarvepalli Radhakrishnan, a towering man of Indian philosophy, left an indelible mark on the intellectual landscape of the 20th century. Globally recognized for his erudition, profound insights, and ability to bridge Eastern and Western philosophical traditions, his contributions continue to influence scholars and thinkers alike. The philosophical legacy of Radhakrishnan emphasized his role in interpreting Indian Darshan for the global audience thereby fostering dialogue between diverse philosophical traditions. His interpretations of ancient Indian texts, such as the Upanishads and the Bhagavad Gita, provided a fresh perspective on timeless philosophical questions. In fact, his philosophical scholarship transcended and trespassed geographical and cultural limitations. Drawing from both Eastern and Western philosophical traditions, he sought to reconcile apparent differences and uncover underlying harmonies. His comparative studies highlighted parallels between Advaita Vedanta and Western idealism, demonstrating the shared quest for ultimate reality and the unity of existence. As such, he facilitated cross-cultural dialogue and mutual understanding. He negated increasingly dominated materialism and scepticism in his philosophy. His vision of spirituality encompassed not only religious doctrines but also ethical principles grounded in compassion, non-violence, and selfless service. The current time marked by moral relativism and existential anxiety, his message resonates as a beacon of hope and wisdom. As a true scholar and academic, he embodied the ideals of intellectual integrity, moral courage, and compassionate leadership. His advocacy for peace, tolerance, and human dignity continues to inspire generations of scholars, activists, and policymakers. His philosophy centrally emphasized on oneness of mankind.

Radhakrishnan and Education

As a distinguished academic, he provided his leadership to the Banaras Hindu University as a Vice-Chancellor. He believed in the transformative power of education and vouched for its role in fostering and promoting design and critical thinking. His sense of respect for the teaching profession led to the institutionalization of the 'Teacher's Day' celebration in India on his birthday.

As a philosopher, distinguished academician and visionary leader, he revolutionized educational paradigms by emphasizing the role of education in shaping the social order. He espoused a holistic approach to education, viewing it as a means to nurture the intellectual, emotional, and moral dimensions of human development. His philosophy emphasized the integration of diverse disciplines, fostering critical thinking, creativity, empathy, sympathy, intuition and intentionality. Radhakrishnan believed that education should not merely transmit information but cultivate a deeper understanding of oneself for positive transformation. His vision was grounded in educational reforms aiming to promote holistic development and lifelong learning. Radhakrishnan expressed that the educational system must find its guiding principles in the aims of social order. The social philosophy of education must be clear. The social, natural and spiritual existence of mankind should be embedded with any educational attainment. The content of curriculum, teaching and learning outcomes should be designed around the above-stated elements. Indeed, education to be complete must be humane. It must include not only the training of the intellect but also the refinement of the heart and the discipline of the spirit. No education can be regarded as complete if it neglects the heart and the spirit. To keep the social values intact with the pupil, education in mathematics, arts and culture must be imparted. The method of learning should essentially be engagement of the taught with the teacher. Education consists of all those experiences which affect an individual from birth till death.

Education is also a process in which an individual develops his personality suitable to his nature. Education ensures an all-round development of the personality. It essentially deals with physical, mental, moral, social, vocational and spiritual aspects of life. The emancipatory power of knowledge becomes the greatest purifier of the human mind. Education capacitates a person to solve his problems. Education makes a man self-reliant and socially attuned. Education serves as a tripolar instrument for educators, education and the social environment. Education develops the ability to distinguish between right and wrong things.

He recognized teachers as the cornerstone of the educational process. Drawing from his own experiences as a teacher and administrator, he championed the cause of teacher empowerment and professional development. Radhakrishnan believed that teachers should be equipped not only with pedagogical skills but also with human and emotional skills. He considered teachers as the best minds in the country. He wanted investment to be made in the welfare and training of the teachers. He emphasized the moral dimension of education, advocating for the cultivation of ethical values and civic virtues. He believed that education should instil a sense of social responsibility, tolerance, and respect for diversity. His call for education was to address both intellect and character-building.

Radhakrishnan played a pivotal role in shaping the educational policy of India. As a Vice-Chancellor of Banaras Hindu University and later as the President of India, he leveraged his influence to advocate for educational reforms. He wanted educational initiatives to expand and provide responses to never-ending questions. He posited that educational brilliance can be established through customizing education to societal needs. In fact, synchronizing education with societal needs would make education relevant. It raises the need for skill development to be integrated into the Indian education system. A skill-oriented education can provide means to address social concerns. His efforts laid the groundwork for the establishment of premier educational institutions and the democratization of education in post-independence India. He wanted to have education for all. Education can provide liberty from clipped wings of dependence.

The legacy of Dr. S. Radhakrishnan in the field of education endures as a testament to his unwavering commitment to enlightenment and human progress. His vision of education as a transformative force for individual empowerment and societal renewal continues to inspire educators, policymakers, and scholars alike. As we navigate the chaos, crisis and contradictions of the 21st century, his wisdom reminds us of the profound potential of education to shape a more just, inclusive and fair society.

Radhakrishnan and Diplomacy

As an Indian Ambassador to the USSR (1949-52) and later as the Vice-President of India (1952-62) and subsequently President (1962-67) of India, he played an instrumental role in strengthening India's international relations and bolstering its interest on the world stage. He was respected for his intellect, statesmanship, peace and understanding among nations. Radhakrsihnan's diplomacy can be explained in terms of international relations, cultural call, promotion of peace and mutual understanding, & non-aligned movement. As President, he represented India on several occasions at international forums, fostering diplomatic relations with various countries. During the critical period between 1949 and 1952, he played a crucial role in strengthening Indo-Soviet relations and forging a strategic partnerships. It also led to the promotion of the cultural exchanges. His diplomatic efforts laid the foundation for enduring ties between India and the Soviet Union based on mutual and shared interests. This is how Radhakrishnan continued to wield influence in international affairs. His tenure as the Vice-President coincided with a period of significant geopolitical upheaval, marked by decolonization, the emergence of new nation-states, and the intensification of Cold War rivalries. Radhakrishnan utilized his diplomatic acumen to navigate the time of turmoil and social upheaval, advocating for non-alignment, disarmament and global cooperation. Radhakrishnan's elevation to the presidency in 1962 coincided with a period of heightened international tension, epitomized by the Cuban Missile Crisis and the Indo-China War. As President, he assumed the role of a statesman, representing India's interests on the world stage while championing the cause of peace and disarmament. His diplomatic overtures helped defuse regional conflicts and fostered a climate of dialogue and reconciliation. Radhakrishnan believed in the power of cultural diplomacy to strengthen connectedness between nations. He emphasized the importance of promoting Indian culture abroad and enhancing cultural exchanges with other countries. This endeavour contributed to the projection of India's soft power. Radhakrishnan engaged in extensive diplomatic outreach, hosting foreign dignitaries and visiting numerous countries during his presidency. His diplomatic efforts aimed to strengthen India's ties with both traditional allies and emerging powers, while also fostering relations with countries in Africa, Asia, and beyond. He advocated for a balanced approach in international affairs and steering India away from alignment with any major power bloc.

As such, Radhakrishnan's diplomacy was bestowed with the connotations of freedom and spirituality, attracting all the citizens of the world society to follow and emulate. He believed in smart negotiation skills while handling diplomatic matters. He wanted countries of the world to be on equal footing. His involvement in problem-solving and mitigating international conflicts made him respected. This led to the transformation of India as a soft power in the South Asian countries.

Radhakrishnan and Statesmanship

As a leader and statesman, his presidential regime was marked by his commitment to upholding democratic values, fostering cultural integration and love for harmony. He always cared for the welfare of the marginalized lot of the society. He encouraged dialogue between different religious and cultural groups. He expressed and practised an integrated approach for individuals, society and community. His humility, integrity and commitment to the nation inspire leaders and citizens the world over.

As a president, he followed the Gandhian spirit and tradition. 'Radhakrishnan's election in 1962, in accordance with the procedure laid down in the constitution, was endorsed by an overwhelming majority of the members of the Federal Parliament and the State Assemblies. It was a verdict amply justified by the distinguished record as the Vice President, both in Rajya Sabha of which he was the *ex officio* chairman and in many of the tours he undertook to different parts of the globe' . He conducted the proceedings of the Rajya Sabha with skill, tact and good humour during 1957-60. During these three years, he never exercised the power vested in him. "No presiding officer, whether in Lok sabha or the Upper House, relied less on the rules of procedure and the technicalities of debate than did Radhakrishnan. A member might on occasion prove persistent in urging a point of view-but never was it pressed to the point of challenging the authority of the Chair or in a defiant spirit. If tempers rose, as sometimes they did, at question hour or during debates, Radhakrishnan took liberties with recalcitrant members to say with a smile, 'That's enough, Mr. A., Now please sit down'. The reprimand was accepted with surprising meekness and the house proceeded without a ripple of excitement with the business of the day. The secret of the Vice-President's success was not mastery of the rules of procedure so much as the deep respect and affection with which all sections of the Houses regarded him' . His contribution to the effective functioning of the Rajya Sabha was much more than procedural. The members of the Rajya Sabha were confident that their rights would be protected. It is precisely because he shielded the officials from unfair comments. He was keenly interested in ensuring justice while conducting proceedings. These practices made inroads to step into Dr. Rajendra Prasad's place of being President in 1962. Pt. Jawaharlal Nehru also took advantage of Radhakrishnan while dealing with foreign policy, as Radhakrishnan already developed a platform for India on the global stage. Radhakrishnan also saw distress during his presidential times. Within a few days of the assumption of his office, China's aggression and the Kashmir problem crept in. 'Chinese armies began to move deep into both Ladakh and what was then the North East Frontier Agency. Radhakrishnan had no hesitancy about his role in this situation. He gave full support to the prime minister and with events shifting from day to day, his rapidly moving mind, which could reach and grasp intuitively what others followed very slowly if at all, could be an asset. That Radhakrishnan had no high opinion of Krishna Menon as defence minister, was made evident when he directed Menon to bring the three chiefs of staff with him to explain the situation to the conference of governors then meeting in Delhi. He also suggested that Menon should be moved from the defence ministry' .

'In five years as the President of India, Radhakrishnan without transgressing the letter or the spirit of the constitution, set healthy precedents and built for the office a role in confirming national purpose and unity. The people learned to look at him not only as the imperial guardian of the public interest, befriending and advising the government but also capable if need be of standing apart from it. Of his Prime Ministers, only Nehru welcomed an approach which led to a personal and, to this day, unique achievement' .

Indeed, the teacher, educationist, philosopher, orator, statesman, humanist and prophet of new Hinduism, Bharat Ratna Dr. Sarvepalli Radhakrishnan is no more today but his thoughts and works inspire thinkers and philosophers, the world over. The diamond of India, the gem of Tamil Nadu and the prince of humanity and Hinduism not only inspired Indian scholars, leaders and policymakers but also allured citizens of the world to emulate his ideals of inclusiveness. His apt use of concepts in philosophical doctrines unravels new thoughts for *Adbhut and Atulya Bharat.*

Contributions from Authors

The underwritten constitutes the bird's eye view of the contributions made. The authors have covered the relevance of Dr. S. Radhakrishnan's thoughts in relation to various aspects. The authors have not only collected the relevant information in making their paper factually precise but also interpreted the relevance of Dr. S. Radhakrishnan's work in the larger ambit of governance and direction within which India should take strides.

Dr. Mamta Anand in her paper 'Being and Becoming: S. Radhakrishnan on Spiritual Values to Attain *Shanti*' describes S. Radhakrishnan visualising India as a land where the spirit in human beings comes to the fore unbridled by fear or hatred, establishing unity with the entire creation in the love of God. India, since times immemorial, has seen the truth of being connected in a mysterious way to everything that constitutes the creation. She has exemplified the unity of things is central to his philosophical thoughts. The realization of a mysterious bond was termed as *Dharma*. This is why, as a mother, India welcomed every race, every religion, every culture and custom in her ambit, sheltered them, and nurtured them, adding glory to human existence on earth. Vanquishing others in the name of alien race, culture, and religion did not occur to her. Her *Dharma* extolling the virtue of realizing and living the mysterious connection with the entire creation empowered her to live organically and grow as a whole. Society, polity, economy, and households were not different units in her existence. These were the organs tied to the spine of spirituality serving the aim of human life in observing values while achieving *Artha (money), Kama (desires), Dharma (righteousness), and Moksha (salvation)*. It was held, that a human being's final goal is to attain salvation and union with God through the profession, desires and *swadharma* -the law of one's being. Citing several texts within the context, the author has demonstrated the idea of being and becoming in *Para* and *Apara*.

Shri Atulindra Nath Chaturvedi in his paper 'Visvamanav: The Philosopher as Statesman' delineates the thoughts of Radhakrishnan. He concedes that every culture has a vision of a philosopher and a statesman presiding over its destiny. The wisdom of the philosopher guides the statesman to govern the realm enhancing the prosperity and well-being of the people and ensuring their security. There is also the Platonian vision of the Philosopher-Statesman, in which the ruler combines in himself the strength of the statesman and the knowledge of the philosopher. These are two different categories—in the first, the philosopher is an advisor; in the second, the statesman is himself a philosopher. There is, however, a third, unique category, in which it is the philosopher who becomes a statesman, not necessarily the other way around. This rare category is exemplified by a rare individual—Dr Sarvepalli Radhakrishnan, a world-renowned philosopher and academic, one of the most influential public intellectuals of the 20th Century. He was widely read in the philosophies of East and West and was seen in his lifetime as a bridge builder between the two. It was Radhakrishna's explanation of Hinduism and Vedanta which greatly influenced the Western perception of what constituted religion in general and Hinduism in particular. Along with Mahatma Gandhi, Jawaharlal Nehru and Rabindranath Tagore, Radhakrishnan was one of the most recognizable Indians outside the country.

Dr. Jyoti Atwal in her paper 'Sarvapalli Radhakrishnan in the Soviet Union: The Philosopher–diplomat' describes the extraordinary contributions made by Radhakrishnan as ambassador to the Soviet Union. The paper engages with his life as a diplomat, particularly his only posting as the Indian Ambassador to Russia in 1949. This was a period when newly independent India had to deal with Stalin's difficulty with trusting the transfer of power to India. Radhakrishnan was initially reluctant but

Jawaharlal Nehru wanted him very much to take up the ambassadorship. He was promised six months in Cambridge every year. By taking citations, she establishes the phenomenal work done by him during his tenure. He believed that a truly religious man could only be a peaceful revolutionary. There was no space for violence. Soviet authorities did not appreciate his affiliation with Oxford and the Chair he held there. During the War, he delivered the Kamala lectures where he had established clarity between sympathy for Marxism as an instrument for social revolution and unacceptability of the Marxist philosophy of life, its atheism, its disregard of the sacredness of personality and its naturalistic view of man. He often repeated his commitment to democratic values and belief in the freedom of the individuals. To him, there was a 'knowledge solution' which was a way of approaching the opponent's position intellectually. He was not particularly close to the British or American diplomats, which made him less suspicious in the eyes of Russians. Not a curious museum/theatre or ballet goer, SR was mostly found after office time - in bed, reading and writing. Moscow was suspicious of any ambassador who was not interested in museums or performances. He fulfilled his duty of attending diplomatic receptions and dinners but he was well known for retiring early in the evening. Despite the fact that Moscow was the hotbed of global-political discussion as the Blocs had been created by the SR who was able to lead a life of solitude which is what gave him contentment. He held up Benjamin Franklin's formula for a diplomat 'sleepless tact, immovable calmness and a patience that no folly, no provocation, no blunders can shake'. Ironical as it may seem, in his speeches during his ambassadorship he clearly stated his apprehension about one-party rule and insistence on the party line.

Shri Kovuuri G. Reddy and Shri Uttam Prakash in their paper 'Dr Sarvepalli Radhakrishnan: The Tall Amongst the Tallest on Dharma and Democracy' highlight the whispered call of our scriptures. They mention the teachers' day, the payment to teachers, education in the Concurrent list of the Constitution, the Indian tricolour and motto, dharma Chakra and Ashok Chakra, adventitious philosopher and philosopher and philosophy. They find that the philosopher Radhakrishnan, without being politically active by aligning with the right and the left and the Centre of political parties, earned his place in the covetable positions of the country. His erudition and way of living were aligned with his commitment to the betterment of the country through education, in interpreting Indian thought and philosophy. In this way, he emerged as the complementary figure for Nehru, who presented India's statesmanship, Gandhiji and his people.

Radhakrishnan presented intellectual spirituality. His philosophy also enabled India to build bridges between Indian spiritualism and Western democracy. Radhakrishnan vociferously argued that political arrangements and economic ties are mere sandcastles against the tide of discord. To build a truly lasting world community, we must dive deeper, cultivating a shared psychological foundation. This, he proclaimed, is the transformative power of literature, the ability to awaken in us the unwavering realization that we are not isolated individuals, but interconnected threads in the vast tapestry of humanity.

Dr. Sunil Shukla and Ms. Vidhy Shetha in their paper 'Dr. S. Radhakrishnan: An Educationist Philosopher Whose Thoughts Guided the Indian Education Sector' explores Dr. Radhakrishnan's early life, educational path, and important contributions he made in the education sector and during also India's freedom struggle. No other academician with a worldly reputation advocated the British to end colonialism as eloquently as he did. The paper illuminates his futuristic vision for an inclusive India and his enormous focus on strengthening the country's educational system. Besides, his role as a philosopher-educationist, his life span covered a broad range of dimensions such as notable positions held, key thoughts and impactful contributions in the education domain. The paper has placed special emphasis on the Banaras Hindu University where Dr. Radhakrishnan's educational theories were put into practice which eventually led to the growth and prosperity of the University. He not only embraced Malaviya's vision of a University but he also saved it from crises in adverse times. His tenure as Vice-chancellor is credited with stellar work that reduced financial burden and increased student and faculty strength of the University. Dr. Radhakrishnan's extensive influence on the educational policies of India illuminated his expectations for the country's educational landscape. His clarity of thought in drafting the commission's report in 1950 still finds relevance in today's educational scenario. The unfolding of the University Commission Report 1950 is a walk through his model of the Indian Education system which encompasses topics such as aims of university education, inclusive and affordable education for all, women's education, professional education, students' welfare activities and programs, etc. The paper also sheds light on how his teachings were adopted by many, highlighting the long-lasting impact of Dr. S. Radhakrishnan on Indian education. The last segment of the paper is about the committees formed to reflect upon the educational scenario of the country and the emergence of National Education Policies. Although influences were drawn from several committees, the philosophical views and ideas of Dr. Sarvepalli remained central to the policy landscape of India.

Ms. Gunjan Pradhan Sinha in her paper 'Intuition as the basis for World Soul-Vasudhaiv Kutumbakam' delineates the ethical foundations of Hinduism as perceived in Dr S. Radhakrishnan's thought, largely dominated by Vedānta philosophy. As a master of comparative philosophy, he constantly defended the Hindu thought from mis-perceived criticisms from the West. But in doing so he outlined his own philosophical ideas that could shape the future of a nation or nations, if delved upon. He insisted on the union of *jñāna, bhakti* and *karma* for all human activity. He ascribed centrality and genuineness only to spiritual experience vis-à-vis the intellectual experience alone. In doing so he brought about an equal and uniform approach to the act of being human for mankind across caste, creed, nationality and religion. The contention of the paper is that his ethical views service the philosophy behind the dictum *'vasudhaiva kutumbakam'* or all the world is a nest or all the world is one home, which was also the motto for India's recent presidency of the G20 nations.

Dr. Manish Kumar in his paper 'Applying Radhakrishnan's Philosophical Ideas to Today's Challenges: Climate Change as a Case Study' underlines the relevance of Dr. S. Radhakrishnan's philosophical teachings with climate change. It addresses one of the most pressing issues of our time i.e. climate change. He was a prominent 20th-century Indian philosopher. He emphasised the synthesis of Eastern and Western thought. He advocated for a harmonious relationship between nature and culture. The paper seeks to offer new perspectives and solutions to the current climate crisis. It does this by analysing his three key ideas namely synthesis of Eastern and Western philosophy, practical Vedanta and spiritual realism. It demonstrates how Radhakrishnan's philosophy could inspire effective environmental stewardship. The paper also fosters global unity in the face of environmental challenges. Radhakrishnan's philosophy is deeply rooted in the idea of a harmonious universe. He believes in the interconnectedness of all life. This idea echoes through his extensive body of work.

Radhakrishnan explains the deep wisdom in Eastern spiritual traditions. The paper takes into its cognizance the themes such as synthesis of Eastern and Western thoughts, practical Vedanta, spiritual realism, and climate change mitigation trajectory.

Dr. Nishant Kumar in his paper 'Dr. Sarvepalli Radhakrishna: A Philosopher Par Excellence' has interpreted the thoughts of Dr. Radhakrishnan by emphasising the requirement of the synergetic correlation between a teacher and a taught. Radhakrishnan advocated for Indian social values, religion and wisdom. The 'teacher-taught', 'science-religion', 'individual-collectivity' and affection and love were found in his seminal writings. The paper traces his foundation as to why he became so precise as a master, philosopher, Vice-President and President. The paper attempts to find the upbringing of Radhakrishnan passing through different forms of trials and tribulations. To Radhakrishnan, the difficulty of life can largely be reduced through educational attainment.

Dr. Arnav Keyur Anjaria and Ms. Priynka Chugh in their paper 'Dr. S. Radhakrishnan Educational Ideology with New Education Policy (2020) Perspective' seek to explore the contributions of Shri S Radhakrishnan as a Philosopher and as India's Stalwart Academician. Dr. S. Radhakrishnan was a contemporary idealistic philosopher and an ardent preacher of Indic philosophy. An original thinker, spiritualist, philosopher, Professor, the Bharat Ratan awardee, the first vice-president of independent India, and a great philosopher who contributed immensely to the field of education. The paper presents a philosophical account of Shri Radhakrishnan's idea of Holistic Development, and it further highlights the adaptation of these ideas in the National Education Policy 2020, which unarguably is a tipping point in the history of the Indian education system. He not only theorised educational concepts, but also put them into practice in his teaching. As a result, in his philosophy of education, he synthesised idealism and realism, mysticism and pragmatism. Dr. Sarvepalli Radhakrishnan is considered a visionary primarily as the paper argues, he laid down the key framework of an Indic Education system suited to the Modern Era yet deeply grounded by the ethos and the exuberance of India's ancient traditions highlighting a historical trajectory of ideas of Dr. S Radhakrishnan that have had a transformative resonance, especially in the context of the National Education policy 2020. As such, the paper moves beyond being merely a glossary of ideas but rather through a discursive analysis, presents the nature of Indian Philosophy as an action-oriented entity unlike its other counterparts. Drawing parallels from different contexts, the authors argue to highlight Dr. S. Radhakrishnan's contribution as a Philosopher of the Indic perspective.

Dr. K N Mishra in his paper 'Sarepalli Radhakrishnan: Role of Education' traces the legacy of Dr. Radhakrishnan in the form of a Saint, Rishi, erudite individual, educator and philosopher. The paper finds that Radhakrishnan understood the essential duty and significance of a teacher. He was both highly thoughtful and a man of good moral character, dedicated to the teaching profession. He served India greatly since she needed him in her manner. Radhakrishnan showed his versatility as a teacher, administrator of the education system, and administrator to the people of our country. It is impossible to find a teacher who can be compared to Radhakrishnan in terms of the talents and virtues he showed during his lifetime. Dr. Radhakrishnan made a comparison between Western philosophical traditions and Indian philosophy. He exalted Hinduism and Indian thought in opposition to ignorant criticism from the West. He described the relationship between matter and spirit, stating that while matter demonstrates the supremacy of the human brain, humans also possess a non-natural factor called the spirit of man, which governs matter and surpasses both the quality and potential of matter. He underlined that while he truly believed in the benefits of religion, science and religion are not mutually exclusive in their pursuit of truth and the welfare of humanity. Indian philosophy's ethical precepts are vital to children's whole development.

Dr. Nibedita Priyadarshni in her paper 'Reflection of Dr. Sarvepalli Radhakrishnan's Philosophical and Educational Thought in Present Education System' examines Dr. Sarvepalli Radhakrishnan's philosophical and educational perspectives in relation to the National Education Policy-2020. A nation climbs to the heights of influence and achievements with proper education, which is the most important tool for the development of the individual and the enrichment of social life. The paper argues for providing training to young people in the necessary skills and giving them a new direction, a new goal, and a new vision for society. With the right education, we become efficient, professional and civilized citizens. Knowledge is a great tool that can be used to maximize human potential. Dr. S. Radhakrishnan is one of the Indian philosophers and educationists who have made significant contributions to the spread of knowledge and education. He was an eminent philosopher, educator, thinker, humanitarian and spiritualist, a man of values, a famous writer and an advocate of education. He had clear, simple and visionary ideas. The contribution of Dr. Sarvepalli Radhakrishnan greatly benefited the fields of philosophy and education. He was particularly known for his thoughtful, rational and constructive criticism of the philosophical views of Western philosophers. He brought the sacred light of Indian culture and philosophy to the Western hemisphere. Dr. Sarvepalli Radhakrishnan devoted his entire life to modern philosophy. He influenced the intellectual development of a civilization by comparing different philosophical schools. He made a remarkable and important contributions to modern philosophy. He influenced the intellectual development of civilization by comparing different philosophical schools. With his unique way of thinking, he visualized the ideas of knowledge, mission, awareness and development. He placed special emphasis on people and spiritual growth so that they could fully express their inner selves. According to him, it is impossible for human personalities to grow properly on all fronts without spirituality. Spirituality can strengthen a person's optimistic and constructive outlook and their inherent divinity. In his unique explanation, Dr. Sarvepalli Radhakrishnan argued that religion, philosophy and science are all interconnected.

Ms. Nidhi Katoch in her paper 'Dr. Sarvepalli Radhakrishna's Philosophical Legacy: Metaphysics, Ethics, Aesthetics and their Relevance to Public Administration' brings out the role of Dr. Radhakrishnan as a philosopher, par excellence. The paper highlights the fact that he made a great contribution to the field of philosophy and bridged the gap between Eastern and Western ideologies. Other than that, his contribution to education, religion, and ethics and his integrated approach to these subjects continue to have an impact and inspire people who work to promote moral and spiritual values in society. He chose metaphysics and religious philosophy for research purposes. He critically examined Indian philosophy and religion to determine what was alive and what was dead. *Advaita Vedanta* and the oneness of *Atman* and *Brahman* were focal points of his ideas on metaphysics. He emphasised the significance of moral principles that have a spiritual foundation in ethics. He praised Indian art and culture, spiritual and philosophical facets on an aesthetic level. This paper focuses on his contribution to metaphysics, ethics and aesthetics and their relevance in the field of Public Administration.

The fathomless intellectual depth and profundity of the contributors emerge as one turns pages through the book. The book *Bharat Ratna Radhakrishnan: A Quest for Being in Becoming* would be of special interest and use to the followers of diplomacy and Public Administration as much as to the general reader, as the book is entertaining, inspirational and enlightening. The influence of Dr. Radhakrishanan continues to be the key guiding principle in a people-friendly service-delivery system. Indeed, the pursuit of truth can be triumphed through love, compassion and spirituality, as they illuminate the path towards understanding, connecting hearts and minds in the journey towards enlightenment.

References

1. Diffusionism is a theoretical perspective in anthropology and cultural studies that explains cultural change and development through the spread of cultural traits, ideas, or technologies from one society to another. The central idea is that certain cultural elements originate in a particular cultural group and then spread or diffuse to other societies. This perspective contrasts with cultural evolutionism, which posits that cultures develop independently over time.
2. G. Sarvepalli. 1989. *Radhakrishnan: A Biography*, Delhi: Oxford University Press, p. 10.
3. Ibid, p. 14.
4. Radhakrishnan, S. 1914. *The Ethics of Vedanta*, Chicago: University of Chicago Press, The International Journal of Ethics, Vol. 24, Issue 2, pp.127-252.
5. Ibid. p.169
6. Radhakrishnan, S. 1953. *The Principal Upnisadas*, New York: Harper and Brothers, p. 9.
7. Ibid., pp.9-10
8. Lyon, Q. 1966. Mystical Realism in the Thought of Savapalli Radhakrishnan, in Philosophy East and West, July-Oct, Vol. 16, No. ¾, University of Hawai'I Press. pp. 221-233.
9. Ibid. pp. 227-228.
10. Dutt. K I. 1966. Sarvepalli Radhakrishnan: A study of the President of India, New Delhi: Popular Book Services, p. 72.
11. Ibid., pp. 72-73.
12. Gopal, S. 1989. *Radhakrishnan: A Biography*, Delhi: Oxford University Press, pp. 312-313.
13. Ibid. p.361.

Being and Becoming: S. Radhakrishnan on Spiritual Values to Attain Shanti

Mamta Anand

S. Radhakrishnan saw India as a land where the spirit in human beings comes to the fore unbridled by fear or hatred, establishing unity with the entire creation in the love of God. India, since times immemorial, had seen the truth of being connected in a mysterious way to everything that constitutes the creation. He writes in his glorious work, *Indian Philosophy Vol 1*, 'It is true that they were more intent on seeking the unity of things than emphasizing their sharpness and separation.' (*Indian Philosophy Vol 1* 80). The realization of this mysterious bond was termed as *Dharma.* This is why, as a mother, India welcomed every race, every religion, every culture and custom in her ambit, sheltered them, and nurtured them, adding glory to human existence on earth.

Vanquishing others in the name of alien race, culture, and religion did not occur to her. Her *Dharma* extolling the virtue of realizing and living the mysterious connection with the entire creation empowered her to live organically and grow as a whole. Society, polity, economy, and households were not different units in her existence. These were the organs tied to the spine of spirituality serving the aim of human life in observing values while achieving *Artha (money), kama (desires), dharma (righteousness), moksha (salvation).* It was held, that a human being's final goal is to attain salvation and union with God through the profession, desires and *swadharma* -the law of one's being.

She got energized by assimilating and building a living contact with everything. In this *dharmic* journey, she understood the real value of all (*The Heart of Hindustan* 12). She could see the entire life being metaphysically connected that could be mustered by love. Life in India thus became a celebration, not a struggle to redeem, restore, or reject.

More than a finite lifetime, she became interested in the soul's life and realized immortality as a worthy aspiration. Ideas, ideals and morality were more than mere philosophical issues to be debated, discussed and argued. They were seen as fundamental forces bringing the personality of human beings to fruition. Even today, in the 21st century, Indian homes rise to the chanting of eternalizing Sanskrit *shloka* from *Brihadaryanka Upanishad*,

Asto Ma Sad Gamaya
Tamso Ma Jyotirgamaya
Mrityor Ma Amritamgamaya

Meaning,

Lead me from unreal to real

Lead me from darkness to light

Lead me from death to immortality. (*Recovery of Faith* 94)

India's most significant contribution to the world of culture is the concept of non-cessation at death. It was then apparent for civilization and culture to pursue and invest in the glories of the spirit and tune their existence to the spiritual laws that govern it. Thus, even ordinarily, the Indians could dream of togetherness in non-violence. Life was to be cherished by making conscious choices asserting character. Success was not seen in gains, profits, money and abundance. But in transforming one's nature to reflect the indwelling spirit.

S. Radhakrishnan has explored these dynamics of India's rich, enterprising life. In his writings, we read the blueprint of the architects in great gurus and splendid rishis, saints and people of wisdom, who gave life to India and shaped her existence. This architecture has boldly stood the test of every time that challenged her life. He raised India by defending the Hindu religion and its vitalizing cultural complex built by its creative associations with cultures and faiths of the world. He taught, spoke and wrote for India to find glory in her discovery of truth and bejeweling wisdom. As a homage to his scholarly demeanour and contribution as a mentor who showed Indians the right path, his birthday, 5th September, is celebrated throughout India as Teachers' Day. In his most illustrious work, *The Hindu View of Life*, Radhakrishnan observes and reminds Indians of their strength that made them bear all onslaughts on their culture and civilization; he writes,

> The civilization itself has not been a short-lived one. Its historic records date back for over four thousand years, and even then, it had reached a stage of civilization which has continued its unbroken, though at times slow and almost static course, until the present day. It has stood the stress and strain of more than four or five millenniums of spiritual thought and experience. Though peoples of different races and cultures have been pouring into India from the dawn of history, Hinduism has been able to maintain its supremacy, and even the proselytizing creeds backed by political power have not been able to coerce the majority of Indians to their views. (Radhakrishnan 1)

Thanks to the recent developments in the field of brain sciences. The current century being the golden period for the brain sciences, many deliberations of the Upanishadic rishis have a ratification of the latest scientific research. Dr Jefferey Schwartz, in his signature work, *The Mind and the Brain* (2009), and Dr Daniel Seigel, in his work, *Aware* (2018), have recently discovered the mind as separate from the brain in the skull. Both are not synonymous. Mind, a mental force enveloping the human being, crafts the brain (Jefferey 295).

Radhakrishnan's writings are dedicated to understanding the operation of this complex mind, body and soul. There is an entire branch of medical sciences that could be benefitted from the works of Radhakrishnan, studying the impact of the mind on the body as Indian culture seeks to observe *deha* as *devalaya* – the body is the abode of God (*Faith Renewed* 7). Following from the Upanishadic thought; he is convinced that the spirit- the being, is veiled by a mind that needs to be made stable and pure. The mind is stabilized in control of *buddhi* (intelligence), lighted by the spiritual laws of existence emanating from the Universal Self- the *Atman.* In his most exalted work, *The Principal Upanishads,* he explores the importance of *buddhi* being guided by the being. He puts it as,

> If buddhi, vijnana, intelligence, has its being turned towards the Universal Self it develop intuition or true knowledge, wisdom. But ordinarily, intelligence is engaged in discursive reasoning and reaches a knowledge which is at best, imperfect, through the processes of doubt,

> logic and skilful demonstration. It reflects on the data supplied by manas or the sense mind with its knowledge rooted in sensations and appetites. (The Principal Upanishads 95)

Upon reaching stability of mind, which needs to be anchored and purified by spiritual laws, values, or truths, the human being lives in the light of the soul. In his illuminating work, *Indian Religious Thought*, he says,

> The yoga discipline is intended to train the mind to hear the mighty voice of the silence within. We then feel our identity with the universal self, the Atman (spirit) in us. (Indian Religious Thought 42)

In one of his books, he writes figuratively about the mind, imagining it to be like a stream capable of flowing towards negativity or positivity. If it mingles with the poison of negativity, it becomes poisonous. If it consumes *amrita* of positivity, it becomes fertile. He confirms with the illustration in *the Gita* about the mind that the mind is capable of constructing its own illusory world of *Maya*. If left free from the control of the *buddhi*, which is not illumined by the light of the soul, it becomes dark- ignorant. In that case, a human being lives a life lost in their illusory construct, bereft of reality. Thus, it is the mind which plays with the life of a human being. A *buddhi* lighted by the spiritual laws can restore the mind at the service of the spirit- the being. This state is famously addressed in India as *Shanti*. Radhakrishnan writes in *Indian Religious Thought*,

> The highest life enjoined by the dharma follows naturally from vital faith in the reality of God. If the indwelling of God in man is the highest truth, conduct, which translates it into practice, is ideal conduct...By the mastery of the soul over the sense, clouds of hate and mists of passion dissolve, and he will be filled with shanti or serenity. He will remain calm in moments of great peril, personal loss or public calamity. With tranquility of soul, a steady pulse and a clear eye he will do the right thing at the right moment. (Radhakrishnan 57)

The Gita has consistently held that the Supreme has a two-fold nature, that of the being- the spirit and the becoming, *para* and *apara*. Reason, revelation, realization and spiritual experience alike bear witness to the reality of a being. It is spiritual in its essence, which is the ground of all that is, 'whose shadow is immortality and death'. *Yasya chayamrtam yasya mrtyuh* (Rig Veda X, 121). It was experienced by Indian rishis that the being, the company of God could be had only in a *shant* state. That is why India as a country and culture has ever prayed for millennia for everyone on earth Peace! Peace! Peace! – *Shanti! Shanti! Shantih*! The prayer in Sanskrit goes as,

Sarve Bhavatu Sukhinah
Sarve Santu Niramayah
Sarve Bhadrani Pasyantu
Ma kascit Dukhabhag Bhavet
Om Santih! Santih! Santih!

Meaning,

Let all here be happy, let all be healthy, let all see the face of happiness, let no one be unhappy. Peace! Peace! Peace!

Without attaining the state of *shanti*, the entire system of the human being fails. Comprehension, perception, logic, and reasonable thinking all get obliterated, thus becoming a cause of error and, subsequently, of *dukh*. Such despair ends the existence of human beings into wretchedness.

Radhakrishnan comes up enchantingly in his speeches on his concept of spiritual laws that help in the process of becoming and *Shanti*. His collection of speeches delivered as the first Vice President and the second President of India, published by the Publication division of India, fills one with the strength of his great vision. Words in the speeches are crafted by his breath, giving veracity to the truth not taught but lived. Today, when we see ourselves beset by the chaos, insecurity, and destruction caused by wars in certain parts of the world, his words fill us with hope. While emphasizing the importance of operating through spiritual laws, he says, 'the true measure of a man is the truth in him'.

According to him, one of the primary reasons for the unrest, stress and tension in our times is that 'We have stopped being ourselves.' No doubt, at best, we just echo the powerful because we have not attained the singlehood of the mastery of our being. The human being is spiritual and natural at the same time. They have to undergo a process of becoming spiritual by taming the natural and making it reflect the divine within. Culture, therefore, is the taming of the animal within.

In his talk on the 'Need for Faith', he quotes Nehemiah, 'Neither was there any beast with me save the beast that I rode upon'. In Madras University speech, he cautions, 'No man of violence ever came to a good end.' His advice reckons with the wise dictum served by *the Mahabharata*, 'By unrighteousness man prospers, gains what is desirable, defeats his enemies but perishes at the root' *(Occasional Speeches and Writings, Third Series, 1959-1962* 159)

This root of the existence of human beings is investigated thoroughly in his writings filled with visionary appeal. In his inspiring work, *Recovery of Faith*, he brings the concerns of Geothe to the central focus, who emphasises the importance of 'belief and unbelief'. He says,

> Belief and behaviour go together. If we believe in blood, race and soil, our world will be filled with Belsens and Buchenwalds (concentration camps). If we behave like wild animals our society will be a jungle. If we believe in universal spiritual values, peace and understanding will grow. (Radhakrishnan 14)

He has investigated the problem of losing the sense of these spiritual values, laws or truths in his works. The main obstacle, as per his diagnosis, for a person losing contact with self is the imprisonment by the mesh of technology. It forces us to live life away from reality. It was visible to Radhakrishnan that technology that has devised newer ways of economic organization has led to the loss of 'our singleness'. We act as a mass. The horrific incidents of mass murders of innocent people due to fake WhatsApp messages rocked India and the world numerous times. The top courts are shocked that highly educated people are increasingly committing crimes. Surprisingly, people fall easy prey to technological havoc. The answer is in his warning issued to us in Sanskrit, '*sa arksaro viprit raksaso bhavati*', meaning, 'the reverse of a literate is a demon.'

Education has to be in the real sense. This is something India, in her New Education Policy 2020, should be aiming for. Knowledge gained must be reflected to be born into wisdom. Merely being educated enough to be able to earn a decent amount of money is not worthy of a human being. Education in disciplines of wisdom tradition peculiarly served by the training in humanities and arts makes a human being realize and live the 'Truth, Beauty and Goodness' within. These streams in the educational system train people to befriend themselves, enhancing the value of solitude. In befriending oneself, it is impossible one should lay prey to various debilitating tendencies, addictions or hurtful behaviour that is fast becoming the order of our day.

Becoming the being undergoes a struggle to do away with the non-being. This is often codified in Indic philosophy as *Maya*, the non-being. It has to be firmly dealt with through disciplined efforts. The first and foremost spiritual law humans deem to follow to curb *Maya* is adherence to truth. It sublimates the non-being. Radhakrishnan writes in his signature work, *The Bhagwadgita*, '*Satya Rakshati*', that truth protects. *Dharma* in India has recognized that there is something even above religion, and that is the company of God. It has been considered the essential truth of a human being's life. There is a tradition in India to seek the company of God in personal terms as a parent, a friend, a child, a spouse or a Guru. Religion is merely taken as a path to reform oneself to be capable of reaching to God for a company. It is not something to which one must necessarily belong to. No sense of creed, community, or institutional authority overrides the possibility of any individual seeking the company of God for oneself. For Indians, that is the ultimate goal they must attain.

For this reason, it was simple for Gandhi to pronounce, 'Truth is God and God is Truth'. Even Swami Vivekananda implored Indians to know the truth as the first and the last word of their religion. This perception of how truth leads us to the Ultimate comes from *Mundaka Upanishad*, where the rishis said,

Satyam Eva Jayate anartam
Satyena pantha vitato devayanah
Yenakramanty rsayo hy aota-kama
Yatra tat satyasya paramam nidhanam (Speeches and Writings, 64-67, 326)

Meaning,

Truth alone conquers, not untruth. By truth is laid out the path leading to the gods, by which the sages who have their desires fulfilled travel to where the supreme abode of truth is.

Mind the zone of thoughts and feelings as has been finally discovered by the sciences confirm the visionary statement made by Jesus Christ, 'Ye shall know the truth and truth shall make you free'. Nothing can rule over the mind of a person other than the truth. Human beings have an innate devotion to truth. Only a mind disabled by fear, anger, ego and illusions is incapable of accepting the truth. For ages, the rishis of India have taught '*Mano hi mahantam dhanam*' Mind is the greatest wealth (*The Present Crisis of Faith* 160). All education must aim at making the mind free and pure by truth.

Radhakrishnan blamed the absence of truth in thought owing to the caprice of the Indian mind as chiefly responsible for the loss of her freedom and wealth. Colonizing powers could rule over her not necessarily due to their own merits but the weakness of the Indian mind. He emphasizes that the ability to think by oneself is necessary to know the reality of being. Thoughts that go deep enough end in insight. Reason takes us deeper than reason, to the power and profundity of the human spirit. (*Speeches and Writings, 1964-1967* 326)

Radhakrishnan knows the clever ploy people adopt concerning truth to mislead the masses. Truth is today often referred to as 'Whose truth, yours or mine?'. We are damaging the culture with the impoverishment of thought- deep work and deep thought, a scarcity today that entertains such beliefs. This deformity has occurred in culture with the advent of technology that does not allow for comprehension by the individual due to a lack of focus. We are constantly forced to think in particular ways and impulsively dragged by gadgets. News that is circulated by the mass media is the only available information. As we cannot carry our own minds, we are losing the sense of uniqueness and unity with others. Self-mastery is the goal of no one today; facilities crowd our lives. (*Recovery of Faith* 20) A life moving away from truth never reaches the being. To bust the baseless argument of your truth or my truth, he quotes Adi Shankaracharya in *the Bhagwadgita*,

Yad visaya buddhir na vyabhicarati tat sat, yad visays vyabhicarati tad asat

In the above statement, Adi Shankaracharya defines real (*sat*) as that in regard to which our consciousness never fails and the unreal (*asat*) as that in regard to which our consciousness fails. Radhakrishnan cautions us that the most basic of spiritual laws or values, 'truth', if neglected, leads to disability of the human mind falling prey to illusory thinking devoid of reality. Such a mind is controlled by things, depersonalizing a human being. Discarding the spiritual value of truth leads to the loss of perfection, happiness and the highest goal of life, which is to initiate the process of becoming to be *shant* to perceive and be in the company of God within.

Once we focus on the truth, we naturally gain knowledge. Radhakrishnan feels that reflective people are not theoretical. They use the best of the theories to reach for the knowledge and truth merely as a raft, but the more capable ones do not depend upon it. Out of the knowledge of various disciplines, the knowledge of the self, the being, '*adhyatma vidya*', is the highest. It makes us contemplate the good. In several instances, he mentioned that the sciences that have gained an edge over the humanities in the world's education systems are best capable of giving us power, not vision, strength and not sanction. It is the role of philosophy, arts and humanities to shape the character, mind and heart of a person. Human beings are here to admire and wonder, not to collect dull facts and figures. (*Recovery of Faith* 62)

He further elaborates that this kind of knowledge makes a human realize how they are the microcosm participating in all strata of the universe. (*Recovery of Faith* 136) In his work *The Present Crisis of Faith*, he mentions a famous saying in India, '*anda and brahmanda*' the microcosm and macrocosm are akin to each other (*The Present Crisis of Faith* 187). He concludes in several of his masterpieces that this was the reason India could raise the notion of *Dharma* that fused the hearts and the minds of the people in the country equally. It could thus become the longest-living culture and civilization of the world, spanning over five millennia and still continuing. In his speech at the opening of Rabindra Bharti National Theatre at Hyderabad in 1961, he spoke about *Dharma*,

> Dharma in India is religion for the whole of society- its roots reach deep underground, but its top touches the heaven, and India has not contemplated the top apart from the roots- she has looked on religion as embracing earth and Heaven alike, overspreading the whole life of man, like a gigantic banyan tree. To realize the One in the universe and also in our own nature, to set up that One amidst diversity, to discover it by means of knowledge to perceive it by means of love and to preach it by means of conduct. (Occasional Speeches and Writings, Third Series, 1959-1962 148)

Thus, religion for India was not in arguments, speculations, or codes to be imposed to make for a creed. Ideals were nursed equally by the people, ranging all activities and spectrum of life, from social, economic, political and personal to spiritual. Ideas and ideals provided by the *Dharma* united the people of India as one mind. Adherence to a common set of ideas and ideals sets the life for a common realization of wisdom in the spiritual values of *Abhaya* (fearless), *Asanga* (non-attachment*) and Ahimsa* (non-violence).

In his awe-inspiring work on *Dhammapada*, Radhakrishnan writes about spiritual values as the roots of *Dharma.*

> The tree of civilization has its roots in spiritual values which most of us do not recognize. Without these roots, the leaves would have fallen and left the tree a lifeless stump. In the history of civilization, it has been the privilege of Asia to enrich the mind of the world with the noblest content of spiritual values. (Dhammapada Preface)

Even Buddha had observed that without spiritual values or laws, it was impossible to do away with ignorance and desire. *Shila* (good conduct) and *prajna* (wisdom) go together in Buddhism. In UNESCO Tagore centenary celebrations in Paris, 1960, he said about the values,

> whenever civilization decays and dies it is due to causes which produce insensitivity to human values. It goes down when our souls are deadened by greed and materialism. (Occasional Speeches and Writings, Third Series, 1959-1962 109)

India had clarity on the condition of the mind and its functioning where the spiritual values of *Abhay, Asanga* and *Ahimsa* played the chief role in reaching out to the being. Radhakrishnan explains their role in the becoming in the following words,

> The marks of genuine religion are Abhaya or freedom from fear, expressing itself in harmony, balance, perfect agreement between body and soul, between the hands and the brain, and Ahimsa or love. Abhaya and Ahimsa, awareness and sympathy, freedom and love, are the two features, theoretical and practical of religion. The free individual does not suffer from any conflicts. He does not give way to anger and depression- not even to what is called righteous indignation. For those who are opposed to us are our brothers from whom we happen to be estranged, and they can be won over by love and understanding. (Eastern Religions and Western Thought 46)

Radhakrishnan emphasized the role of A*himsa* in all of his writings as necessary to keep the mind free from the feeling of hatred. A mind polluted by hatred is incapable of correct reasoning. Hence, the spiritual anchor of A*himsa* born out of *Abhaya* and *Asanga* (non-attachment) leaves a person free to be a conduit rather than a constructor of situations. Indian *Brahmanic* religion has aimed to make every soul a Brahmin capable of perceiving God by making the mind pure to reflect the eternal (*The Philosophy of Hinduism* 19). Schweitzer had famously observed that 'Brahmanic mysticism has nothing to do with ethics. It is through and through supra- -ethical' (*Eastern Religions and Western Thought* 102)

It has been a belief of the Indian religions that there is no inconsistency between aiming to reach God and following the most exalted ethics, morality or spiritual laws. It is popularly described as contemplation and action, two sides of the same coin, the *yoga* of Krishna and the *dhanus* of Arjuna, two movements combined. However, interestingly, he observes in his great translation of the *Brahmasutra*, 'when one attains the spiritual level, he rises above the ethical, not that he repudiates it but he transcends it.' Shankar also said,

> This is indeed an ornament to us that, when there is the realization of Brahman, there is the destruction of all obligations and the accomplishment of everything that is to be accomplished. (The Brahma Sutra 165)

Radhakrishnan, therefore, hailed Mahatma Gandhi as the representative of the soul of India, an apostle of non-violence *Ahimsa, Asanga, and Abhaya.* A figure who truly represents the method of attaining *shanti* through spiritual values, thus reaching God, the being within, by becoming a conduit in the truest sense. All humanity recognized his greatness. He proudly quotes the London Times, 'No country but India and no religion but Hinduism could have given birth to a Gandhi' (Anand 61). Gandhi is the one who found out the immense role of *Ahimsa* in serving and maintaining the world order. Without it, we would have no good concerns to serve. Mystics, the ones who reach their being and become founded in the spiritual law of *ahimsa,* live for the welfare of all. Moreover, only in the welfare of all is the welfare of everyone possible. In his enlightening work *The Adaptive Indian,* he quotes Gandhi when he answered a question on how he would face an atomic bomb,

> How will I meet the atom bomb? I will not go underground. I will not go into shelters. I will come out in the open and let the pilot see that I have not the face of evil against him. (The Adaptive Indian Identity and Ethos 97)

To reach this level of understanding of ahimsa, one has to pass through the preliminary stages of Abhaya and Asanga. Though Gandhi found Ahimsa as the best medium to instruct the soul of the wrongdoer he advised the wise dictum of Mahabharata, 'sastrad api, sastrad api' (By scriptures or by arms), meaning the best method to meet a danger is to outrightly face it using the best principles of spiritual laws emphasized in the scriptures of the world. If that does not work the next best is to strike truthfully without allowing the mind to be made dirty by hatred for the wrongdoer. (The Adaptive Indian Identity and Ethos 97)

Lord Krishna in the Gita advises Arjun that if the mind longs to go by the desires which are not directed to truth or nobility, in that case, one must read what the scriptures say as they should have stood the test of times. Radhakrishnan writes in the Bhagwadgita,

> We generally act according to our personal desire, then regulate the course of our conduct by reference to prescribed social codes and ultimately attain a deeper intention of life's meaning and act according to its guidance. The prompting of desire, the guidance of the law (in the scripture) and the spontaneity of spirit are the three stages. (The Bhagavad-gita 391

Ethical conduct, which is an essential prerequisite of spiritual insight, is a significant investigation Radhakrishnan carries out in his writings. This leads us to his prescription for the right kind of education system. As wisdom wells in a human being on reaching the stage of *shanti*, where the mind is clear and stable and anchored by the spiritual laws, it becomes a mirror to the innermost being. Then, the mistaken belief that one is the source of action gets dropped. A realization that one is not more than an instrument connected to all life dawns. Radhakrishnan feels education must allow us this kind of growth.

Prof. Debashis Chatterjee, Director, IIM Kozhikode, in his recent release *Leadership Chronicles*, has explored how the indigenous system of education, *the Gurukul*, can bring morality and spiritual laws to reality rather than keep them as a mere content of the syllabus. He refers to the Gurukul system as the Active Learning Space. Having built it on the IIM Kozhikode Library grounds, the teachers and students are reminded of the old golden age of the Indian education system, which saw its last in 1835.

At IIM Kozhikode, the students and teachers sit under the Sun on the grass after removing their shoes, raising their emotions of worship. With this attitude to learning, where one is not the passive learner but an active participant in the learning process, a student becomes a free thinker, and a teacher is also a free thinker. At the same time, modern classrooms designed in the state of craft do not allow sunlight. The students sit together in one place, facing the teacher who acts under the pressure of authority; thereby, no actual teaching happens in the class. It is tragic imprisonment within their roles. The communication lacks, formulations dominate rather than deliberations. He writes,

> Schools of the future will look a lot less like police lockups and a lot more like conversation hubs where learning will happen through small group projects. Learning will move from painful rote memorization to the quest for creativity, problem-solving ability, higher-order thinking and the sheer joy of discovery. (Leadership Chronicles 133)

Radhakrishnan also says the same about education. Like Gandhi, he wants it to be activity-oriented and conducted in a natural environment. Some schools in New Zealand have already adopted the measure where the students plough, grow vegetables, feed themselves and live as a family with teachers, almost like the ancient Gurukul model of the education system in India. Spiritual laws can never appeal if the mind is always busy mastering facts without paying enough attention to listening to the God within. This aim requires the presence of nature and freedom of aspiration, not the disciplining of the class, where certain aspects go unquestioned and unexamined. Anything could not be believed just because someone with a higher education degree has uttered it.

In modern buildings, even teachers feel stifled in making the students explore their minds due to space and time constraints. Radhakrishnan himself had made such an arrangement where his PhD students lived with him in his own house as in Gurukul. India must understand that wisdom and spiritual laws cannot be understood in classrooms that inhibit the opening of the mind out of fear, ego or loss of communication. This is why even the courts in India mentioned that an educated person is perhaps more of a criminal than an uneducated one. This shows education is lacking in the real sense. In his work *The Present Crisis of Faith*, even Radhakrishnan mentioned, 'the great crimes against civilization are committed not by the primitive and the uneducated but by the highly educated and the so-called civilized.' (*The Present Crisis of Faith* 140)

To attend this malady, we need to adopt the ancient precept of India, *Gyanam Vigyanam Sahitam*, meaning wisdom and sciences must be learnt together. Radhakrishnan was a chief votary of this ideal in the education system. He did not see the world of Art as a mere hobby, he felt it had a much greater role to play in the evolution of the human being (*Search For Truth* 155). As a visionary educationist, he could see that art and the humanities were precursors to all the capabilities of human beings. He saw it to be a preparatory course for the people pursuing sciences. In his work, *Our Heritage*, he mentions art, literature and thought explorers shape the minds and hearts of people (*Our Heritage*, 21) His views are today proved to be true by the world of brain sciences. *Your Brain on Art*, an international bestseller written by Dr. Susan Magsamen, proves this belief of S. Radhakrishnan as she quotes the findings of the American Art Therapy Association,

> Artistic expression and the creative process enhance cognitive abilities, foster greater self-awareness, and help teens regulate their emotions. The arts help them with focus, problem-solving, decision – making skills, so when presented with health choices they make better ones as their brains are dramatically changing during critical developmental periods. (Your Brain on Art 109)

Brain sciences in the field of neuroaesthetics have done numerous studies that go on to prove the clear-witted statements of Radhakrishnan mentioned in his writings and speeches on the spiritual value of engaging with arts for spiritual development. Irish poet John O'Donohue once said, 'Art is the essence of awareness' (*Your Brain on Art* xiii). On the metaphysical importance of the arts in a speech at the Annamalai University in 1962, Radhakrishnan said,

> Art itself is a means for the realization of the Divine. It is a means by which you are able to grasp the mystery of the Eternal. Art is not merely for the purpose of your entertainment or even education. It is there to produce in you a spirit of satisfaction, to make you different from what you happen to be. Art is not divorced from religion in sense of the term.
> *(Speeches and Writings 1962-1964 1992, 191)*

Further, in his address at Kabul University in 1963, while talking about Science and Religion, he said,

> Artistic creation is something where you feel an experience, and you impregnate that experience with your own personal spiritual intensity and make it come alive-that is what art means. In our country it is said, art is that which transmits to you a sense of the eternal, a sense which is beyond the merely temporal. A sense of something which is non-temporal in this world conveyed to you by the achievements of the arts. (Speeches and Writings 1962-1964 1992 136)

It is indeed promising that scientists are discovering that the heart cells dance to music. They are also fascinated that art is responsible for meaning-making, where logic has a limited role. It informs us of the environment we are living in and our place in it. Thus, a sense of identity evolves, saving us from perishing in the pressures of life. Instead, in such a process of evolution, we find our roots and live purposeful lives, flourishing in our sense of the self. Thus, art has a very important role in our becoming and reaching the being. Nick, artist and founder of Art2Life, observes,

> Art-making is, really, about feeling more alive in your life. The creative path is unfolding process of becoming ourselves and it's a wonderful journey we get to take. (Your Brain on Art 185)

Out of all the arts, Radhakrishnan gives special importance to Literature, holding that all great literature is universal. Its purpose, according to Indian tradition, is *visva sreyas*, the good of the world. As there is just one real objective of all great literature, it is *karuna* or compassion. (*Occasional Speeches and Writings, Third Series, 1959-1962* 202) In his speech on presenting awards at Sahitya Akademi in 1966, he stated,

> Literature has so many functions to fulfil, the most important being to change the minds and hearts of people-vicara parivartana, hrydaya parivartana. If we want to make new beings, new human beings, we must give them right ideas and the zeal and the enthusiasm to implement those ideals. Today the whole world is suffering from spiritual disintegration. People are losing faith; they are

> lost and live in a world of uncertainty. They do not know what to do, what is right or wrong...(Purpose of Literature) is not merely to produce stability, but to produce a ferment, to produce a kind of confusion of mind from which they will be able to rise to the achievement of some proper goal and purpose. All through, literature has done that work. (Speeches and Writings, Second Series, 1964-1967 204)

The latest observations made by scientists on the creative art of writing show that the brain itself is a natural storyteller; it continuously tries to conceptualize an idea by building a narrative. In 2010, at Princeton University, the brains of storytellers and listeners were mapped using fMRI. It was found that the neuronal firing and brain activity of the storyteller is mirrored by the listeners, resulting in a phenomenon recently understood as neuronal coupling. We could easily imagine this could be the process happening in the brains of the writers and readers which the scientists conclude is responsible for the comprehension by the story listeners. (*Your Brain on Art* 205) This scientific study concurs with ideas about the literature of Radhakrishnan, where he suggests that literary writers are the parents of a nation and builders of culture and community by gifting the race with a mind. Their art crafts a mind. Dr. Magsamen concludes about the role of art in her book *Your Brain on Art* in these memorable lines,

> The arts by their very nature, reflect and inform the time in which they are created; they take the pulse of their time, but the artists have also been essential for forecasting the future, and serving as an early – warning system for society. (230)

There is an important suggestion that the scientists wish to give regarding the practice of art. They say all the crucial developments in a person's spiritual, emotional, social, and scientific personality through the practice of art result from one's free venture into it. It may not necessarily be training in the arts that would give a person root to the centre of their being. They strongly recommend art for everyone by everyone. That is how we as a culture, community and society can share common values, ideas and ideals and practice them. Scientists have observed how art forges bonds of humanity,

> We are ultra-social creatures who biologically evolved to belong to something greater than ourselves. We need one another, and without strong and lasting connections to family, friends, colleagues and neighbours, without the relationships we create over a lifetime, we cannot survive, let alone thrive. Supporting this core human imperative to live in a community is our unique ability to creatively share our thoughts, ideas and emotions. The success of our species comes down to this: Art creates culture. Culture creates community. and community creates humanity. We created stories. We sang. We danced. We developed myths and metaphors that passed on the moral and ethical values of the group. (Your Brain on Arts 202-203)

Thus, we see the evolution of the understanding of moral forces and ethical values through the practice of art. Radhakrishnan makes a fascinating comment, 'though morality commands conformity, all moral progress is due to nonconformists' (*Sarvepalli Radhakrishnan* 96). His views interestingly meet the exalted standards set by humankind in various periods in history. He says our great moral heroes have been like the artists working on the intuitive power of the soul, which is worked upon differently by scientists and artists. While the sciences discover a quantitative principle working universally, an artist gives birth to art through creative subjective contemplation which is a process of the travail of the spirit, a crystallization of a life process. (*Sarvepalli Radhakrishnan* 91) However, he warns that art becomes mechanical without the intuitive experience. It merely becomes a rehearsal of the old themes. Such art is an exercise in reproduction rather than a communication of the artist's intuitive encounter with reality.

> Technique without inspiration is barren. Intellectual powers, sense facts and imaginative fancies may result in clever verses, repetition of old themes, but they are only manufactured poetry…difference in the kind of source itself' (Sarvepalli Radhakrishnan 91)

What true art meant for Radhakrishnan aligns with the recent scientific evidence. He believed it to be an expression of the whole personality where reflective powers are subdued by intuitive powers. (*Sarvepalli Radhakrishnan* 91) These intuitive, artistic powers can see the workings of the spiritual laws that build the ultimate vision. This is so much akin to Aristotle's theory. Art purges us of the impure, transforming a wicked into a nobler soul. *Katha Upanishad* also opines,

> He who has not ceased from immoral conduct cannot obtain God through intelligence. Immoral conduct (duscharita) and spiritual life are incompatible since the eternal is pure and free of all evil (apahatapapma). The pure being can be apprehended only by those whose nature is purified (visuddhasattava, vitaraga)...the motive of the ethical practices is that of purging the soul of selfish impulses so that it may be fitted to receive the beatific vision...The perfecting of self is to pass from the narrow, constricted, individual life to the free, creative, spiritual life. (Eastern Religions and Western Thought 104-105)

In the modern education system, the arts have not been given importance akin to the sciences. This was evident in the times of S. Radhakrishnan. Therefore, in his book *Religion, Science and Culture*, he has stressed the equal development of both streams as necessary for the betterment of human beings. In the absence of one, we become handicapped. He says,

> We have to reckon with the spirit of science, understand its limitations and develop an outlook which is consistent with its findings. Science will triumph over ignorance and superstition, and religion over selfishness and fear. (Religion, Science and Culture 108)

Not encouraging arts in education had a very negative impact. We are increasingly seeing conversations between people becoming coercive. Men and women are not able to recognise each other as companions. There is unwanted competition, struggle and insecurity between them. We see an unprecedented rise in crimes against women and girls child. The level of barbarity in such crimes is horrifying. We are now more than ever reminded of the great observation made by Radhakrishnan, 'it is when thought becomes perfected in intuition that we catch the vision of the real. The mystics the world over have emphasized this fact' (*Indian Philosophy, Vol 1* 176)

Arts themselves are getting dominated by the sciences. They need to be more intuitive. They have become mechanical and scholastic. In mimicking sciences, arts have discovered tools and theories that give them the penchant of working like the sciences, as if they are a kind of formula sciences use, but this tendency results in a loss of insight development. They have succumbed to the pressure of being commercially viable and wish to become money churners. We see this impact on the latest releases in the world of cinema and OTT series. Sex and violence that affect the reptilian part of the human brain, which is habit forming, is becoming a trend that is a big money grosser. Art in such works is not about 'truth, beauty and goodness'. It does not influence the brain and mind's higher thinking abilities. This is something that leaves the human culture damaged. In his magnum opus, *An Idealist View of Life*, Radhakrishnan talks about the use of intuition in both the sciences and the arts.

> Creative work is not blind imitation or mechanical repetition. It is synthetic insight which advances by leaps. A new truth altogether unknown, startling in its strangeness, comes into being suddenly and spontaneously owing to the intense and concentrated interest in the problem. When we light upon the controlling idea, a wealth of unco-ordinated detail falls into proper order and becomes a perfect whole. Genius is extreme sensibility to truth. Scientific discovery is more like artistic creation in its reaching out after new truth. (An Idealist View of Life 126)

The intuitive ability used at this level shall solve most of our social, political, economic, environmental, and other crises. A famous writer Chinua Achebe said, 'Art is man's constant effort to create himself a different order of reality from that which is given to him.' (*Story of Consciousness* 7). Art cannot remain limited to habit-forming pleasures. It must be explored. Today, popular art is more sensual than soul-touching and searching.

Radhakrishnan thus leads us to a significant emphasis in his writings, which is the ultimate solution to most of our problems. This is about the treatment of women. Hindus have realized since the beginning that 'respect for women' is a significant spiritual value. Women have been seen as a bridge to reality, the ultimate spirit, a '*sahadharmini*' of man (*Occasional Speeches and Writings 1952-1959* 575). In his book *Search for Truth*, he writes, 'Women, after all, are much nearer to the roots of Reality than men' (87). He has held in his writings that women, by the gifts given by nature, are more sensitive, emotional and spiritual. The same is perfectly proved by the brain sciences today. In his book, *The Hindu View of Life*, he calls their life '*tapahpradhanya*', meaning a life capable of reaching great heights of self-control and self-denial, chief of spiritual merits. Further in the book, he mentions that women are naturally superior to men (63).

In his book *Unleash the Power of the Female Brain*, Dr. Amen has written that the emotional part of the brain, the Limbic region, is larger in women. The prefrontal cortex- the crown of the human brain, responsible for thought, decision-making, and focus acts as a brake on the reptile brain, is also bigger in women (31). This makes her genuinely interested in spiritual, religious, cultural and philosophical things. He writes that the restraint that women are capable of is a compliment to them; Tagore also has mentioned in his essay 'Woman and Home' that her 'cadence of restraint' are the poetry of life (*Creative Unity* 82). Thus, women become much more responsible for cultural matters. In his general introduction to a special edition of Kalidasa's works sponsored by Sahitya Akademi, he writes, 'The wife does not belong to the husband but makes a whole with him. The wife is the root of all social welfare (*Speeches and Writings, 1952-1959* 575)

In his essay, 'Woman' in the collection *Personality*, Tagore said, 'For woman's function is the passive function of the soil, which not only helps the tree to grow but keeps its growth within limits. (*Personality*, 1464). Similarly, Radhakrishnan also opines, the main contribution of women on earth shall always be that she makes us. She is the mother of the human race. Therefore, we must understand that what she receives will be served to generations. If we treat her well, her presence shall nourish us, and her refined abilities will shape us. If she is ill-treated, then everyone in the society suffers; she is the one we have our roots in. Crimes against her are crimes against humanity. This is the reason why he says that Hinduism has accorded women an exalted position. To the extent that we name the goddess first out of respect before the gods, like Sita- Ram, Radha-Krishna, and Uma -Mahesh.

Radhakrishnan regrets there have been times in India when women were not treated well, as men took pride in power and subjugated them. More than the injustice done to them by men, Radhakrishnan is anxious that women must not devalue their immense importance and mimic men. In his excellent book, *Religion and Society*, in the essay, 'Women in Hindu Society' he writes,

> Women as mothers are more directly sensible of the inequity and injustice of the present order and can bring about far-reaching change of spirit, and work into the new style of life. Then will the new Man be born. (Anand 89)

Like Tagore, Radhakrishnan hopes that women may someday help God by delivering His message of love, thereby activating the spiritual laws, making it more important than power, which has engulfed the lives of human beings and thrown it into misery and cruelty. Her capacity to love shall enable her to act as the guardian of the individual, saving lives for the worth of their life and heart and not because of their usefulness. She might thus prepare the ground for the work of the nobler, saintly souls who burn to enact the spiritual laws, thus saving the world. By enacting the spiritual laws, they create models for us so we could imbibe them. While paying homage to Swami Sivananda in 1963 at Hyderabad, he recited a *Sanskrit Shloak*,

Santo bhumim tapasa dharyanti,

Meaning,

The saints, by their tapas, sustain this world…A saintly life is the highest expression of eternal truth. People may discuss it, may talk about it, but only they are entitled to teach it to others who have known it for themselves and who have practiced it. (Speeches and Writings, 1962-1964 157)

In the 21st century, if we hope to live by the beautiful dream of the Rig Vedic rishis who said, 'Walk together; seek in concord; Let your minds comprehend alike, let your efforts be united; let your hearts be in agreement. Let your minds be united, that we may all be happy' (Rig Veda, X, 191), then we must realize that this is possible through only spiritual values. The *buddhi* (intelligence) must face the *Atman*, the being, and seek the light of spiritual values, truths, or laws from there. Only then can the mind be anchored and stabilized to be harnessed in the process of becoming establishing *shanti* on getting infused by the being, leading humanity on the path of Peace through understanding. Albert Einstein, while reflecting on the importance of understanding between human beings, wrote in his work *Ideas and Opinions*,

> Understanding of our fellow -beings is important. But this understanding becomes fruitful only when it is sustained by sympathetic feeling in joy and sorrow. (Ruhela 1)

References

1. Amen, Daniel. *Unleash the Power of the Female Brain.* Hachette Digital, 2013
2. Anand, Mamta. *Missing Girl- Geometry of Creation Essays and Poems.* Delhi, Authorspress, 2021
3. Anand, Mamta. *S. Radhakrishnan His Life and Works,* Second Edition. New Delhi, Atlantic Publishers, 2019
4. Bhattacharjee, Govind. *Story of Consciousness.* New Delhi, Vigyan Prasar, 2019
5. Chatterjee, Debashis. *Leadership Chronicles.* Gurugram, Penguin Random House India, 2023
6. Goel, Vijay. *Sarvepalli Radhakrishnan-Second Edition.* Delhi, Vijay Goel, 2009
7. Magsamen, Susan. Ivy, Ross. *Your Brain on Art How the Arts Transform Us.* New York, Penguin Random House, 2023
8. Radhakrishnan, S. *Recovery of Faith.* Delhi, Orient Paperbacks,1994
9. Radhakrishnan, S. *Recovery of Faith.* Delhi, Orient Paperbacks, 1994
10. Radhakrishnan, S. *Indian Religious Thought.* Delhi, Orient Paperbacks, 2011
11. Radhakrishnan, S. *Occasional Speeches and Writings, Third Series, 1959-1962.* Delhi, Publications Division, 1992
12. Radhakrishnan, S. *Speeches and Writings, Second Series, 1964-1967.* Delhi, Publications Division, 1992
13. Radhakrishnan, S. *Eastern Religions and Western Thought,* (Delhi, Oxford University Press) 1996
14. Radhakrishnan, S. *The Adaptive Indian, Identity and Ethos.* Delhi, Orient Paperbacks, 2013
15. Radhakrishnan, S. *The Bhagwadgita.* New Delhi, Harper Collins, 2002
16. Radhakrishnan, S. *The Hindu View of Life.* Noida, Harper Collins, 2009
17. Radhakrishnan, S. *Speeches and Writings, 1962-1964.* Delhi, Publications Division, 1992

18. Radhakrishnan, S. Occasional *Speeches and Writings, Combined Edition, 1952-1959.* Delhi, Publications Division, 1992
19. Radhakrishnan, S. *The Dhammapada.* New Delhi, Oxford University Press, 2008
20. Radhakrishnan, S. *Religion, Science and Culture.* New Delhi, Orient Paperbacks, 2016
21. Radhakrishnan, S. *The Heart of Hindustan.* New Delhi, Rupa Publication, 2007
22. Radhakrishnan, S. *Our Heritage.* Delhi, Orient Paperbacks, 1994
23. Radhakrishnan, S. *Faith Renewed.* Delhi, Hind Pocket Books, 2000
24. Radhakrishnan, S. *The Philosophy of Hinduism.* Delhi, Niyogi Books, 2015
25. Radhakrishnan, S. *Search For Truth.* Delhi, Hind Pocket Books, 2000
26. Radhakrishnan, S. *The Brahma Sutra The Philosophy of Spiritual life.* New York, Harper and Brothers. 1960
27. Radhakrishnan, S. *The Present Crisis of Faith.* Delhi, Orient Paperbacks, 1994
28. Radhakrishnan, S. *Indian Philosophy, Vol 1.* New Delhi, Delhi, Oxford University Press, 2000
29. Radhakrishnan, S. *The Principal Upanishads.* Noida, HarperCollins Publishers, 2012
30. Radhakrishnan, S. *The Principal Upanishads.* Noida, HarperCollins Publishers, 2013
31. Ruhela, S.P. *The Emerging Concept of Education in Human Values.* New Delhi, Regency Publications, 1996
32. Schwartz, Jefferey. *The Mind and The Brain.* Harper Collins ebook, 2009
33. Seigel, Daniel. *Aware.* Mumbai, Jaico Publishers, 2018
34. Tagore, Rabindranath. *Personality,* (New Delhi, Rupa and Co) 2002 Kindle
35. Tagore, Rabindranath. *Creative Unity,* (New Delhi, Vishv Books)

Visvamanav: The Philosopher as Statesman

Atulindra Nath Chaturvedi

Introduction

Every culture has a vision of a philosopher and a statesman presiding over its destiny. The wisdom of the philosopher will guide the statesman to govern the realm enhancing the prosperity and wellbeing of the people and ensuring their security. There is also the Platonian vision of the Philosopher-Statesman, in which the ruler combines in himself the strength of the statesman and the knowledge of the philosopher. These are two different categories—in the first, the philosopher is an advisor; in the second, the statesman is himself a philosopher. There is, however, a third, unique category, in which it is the philosopher who becomes a statesman, not the other way around. This rare category is exemplified by a rare individual—Dr Sarvepalli Radhakrishnan, a world-renowned philosopher and academic, one of the most influential public intellectuals of the 20th Century. He was widely read in the philosophies of East and West and was seen in his lifetime as a bridge builder between the two. It was Radhakrishna's explanation of Hinduism and Vedanta which greatly influenced the Western perception of what constituted religion in general and Hinduism in particular. Along with Mahatma Gandhi, Jawaharlal Nehru and Rabindranath Tagore, Radhakrishnan was one of the most recognizable Indians outside the country.

Radhakrishnan: A Vishvamanav

Radhakrishnan became a member of the Constituent Assembly of India, India's representative at UNESCO, India's second ambassador to the Soviet Union, the country's first vice-president and chairman of the Rajya Sabha, and its second president. The conventional understanding is that the president and vice-president, in the Indian constitutional scheme, are expected to be mere rubber stamps of the government of the day. The experience of Dr Radhakrishnan, then, should have been on these expected lines. But a reading of the years during which Dr Radharishnan held office shows that he was far more proactive behind the scenes than is usually assumed while maintaining all constitutional norms. But before we venture to examine the 'political' years, we need to first have an understanding of his life to that point, and the philosophical perspective that created the contours of his worldview.

Sarvepalli Radhakrishnan was born in 1888 in Tirutani, in modern-day Andhra Pradesh. He went to a school in nearby Tirupati, a pilgrimage town. The religious devotion that permeated the very air of these two towns, with their emphasis on personal experience of the divine, was clearly a great inspiration and influence on his young mind. Another formative factor was the fact that he studied in a missionary school. He saw the devotion shown on a daily basis to their Christian faith and came for the first time across denunciations of Hinduism.

The milieu in which Radhakrishnan grew up was that of an India reawakening, rediscovering its past, and the first stirrings of nationalism. He noted later that his influences at the time were the writings of Swami Vivekananda, VD Savarkar's account of the 1857 uprising, and the activities of the Theosophical Society.

At Madras (now Chennai), he studied at Madras Christian College. It was here that he first encountered the philosophers of the West, and came under the spell of AG Hogg, who differentiated between theoretical knowledge and knowledge derived from personal perceptions. Another influence was the systemic castigation of Hinduism he came across, which led to his earliest forays into an understanding of Hinduism which lasted throughout his life.

After completing his thesis in 1908, Radhakrishnan began his teaching career and ultimately moved to Calcutta where he took up the George V Chair in Philosophy, became Vice Chancellor of Andhra University and later on of Benares Hindu University. In 1936, Oxford University appointed him to the HN Spalding Chair of Eastern Religions and Ethics. His rapid and enormous scholarly output made his reputation both in India and abroad, and in 1931 he was knighted. During this time Radhakrishnan did not take any overt political stand, but it was impossible for him to avoid the turmoil that the nationalist movement unleashed, and be left unaffected by it. While met and maintained relations with both the nationalist leaders and British officials, and made plain where his preferences lay, he did not himself descend into the political trenches. Radhakrishnan moved into the political realm shortly after the Second World, and he remained in it for twenty years. The first move in this regard was when he became the chairman of the University Education Commission, which presented its report in 1949. Radhakrishnan's influence can be seen in the sections devoted to the aims of university education and religious education.

At this point, we need to explore whether Radhakrishnan had anything that amounts to or is close to a comprehensive political outlook, viewpoint or philosophy. Radhakrishnan did not present his political ideas and ideals in a comprehensive manner, but they can be reconstructed based on what he wrote and said throughout his career.

The first point to note is that Radhakrishnan was an idealist. He explained it thus: "An idealist view finds that the universe has meaning, has value. Ideal values are the dynamic, the driving power of the universe. The world is intelligible only as a system of ends, it finds life significant and purposeful. It endows man with a destiny that is not limited to the sensible world. Idealism today has to reckon with our problems and help to solve them."[1]

Radhakrishnan insists that man can exist only within a society: "No one can stand in proud isolation with contempt for the common herd. We can rise in the scale of being only by drawing all into ourselves. While the individual has to cultivate his own garden and integrate his own self, the self is not sharply marked off from the world, the garden is not fenced off from the rest of the universe. The world is our garden and we cannot become self-sufficient until the world is so."[2]

Radhakrishnan is not concerned with the typology of a state as it exists, but with the purpose of the ideal or best state: "The importance of any nation is estimated not by its territory, population, or commerce, but by the values it has brought to the world and the degree to which they have been embodied in its life."[3]

But what is this ultimate value which needs to be achieved? To Radhakrishnan, it was spiritual freedom. He noted, "Freedom has many implications, the chief one being to provide scope for the expression and development of the individual human being. All other freedoms—political, economic and social–are an indispensable end to this."[4]

For Radhakrishnan, if a man is to reach his best, it means that a modern state must intervene to provide certain standard conditions for such a development to take place. For Radhakrishnan, it is not enough for the state to avoid interference in individual lives. It has to do more: "We must help to bring up the buried treasures in each individual without breaking any of it. For this, certain minimum cultural and economic conditions must be provided. That is why we have universal education as a target in our Constitution. We talk often of a socialistic pattern of society. This does not mean regimentation of the individual. In the drama of human evolution, the chief actors are the individuals, the individuals of genius. We should not allow the individuality of human beings to be crushed or even diminished by the assaults of science and technology, by the mechanization of life."[5] He adds, "When we say that it is necessary for us to feed, clothe and shelter all human beings, we are emphasizing what may be called the economic aspects of the democratic ideal. We wish to diminish wealth and poverty and to raise the living standards of the ordinary man. So long as there are people in our country who do not have a square meal a day, who sometimes do not have a roof over their heads, who sleep on the pavements of our cities, it is a challenge to us. We should combat them, abolish them if our country is to be called democratic."[6] He went on to note that all this would be impossible until and unless industrial and agricultural increased manifold. Then, and only then, could economic democracy be said to have been achieved.

For Radhakrishnan, democracy was a sin qua non, and a faith. "When we emphasise the ethical character of democracy we mean that every human has an element of rationality that it is possible for us to appeal to it. We must believe that we may not always be right, our opponents may sometimes be right. We should be modest enough to believe that there may be some virtue in our opponents also. It's this sense of humility, the sense of restraint, that democracy imposes upon us. Dissent is not treason; opposition is not rebellion. We must try to settle our problems with reason, without bitterness. Democracy and violent action are inconsistent with each other."[7] We can see that Dr Radhakrishnan had full faith in democracy in the modern sense and its ability to sustain human beings to achieve their best.

Dr Radhakrishnan led the Indian delegation to the United Nations Educational, Scientific and Social Council (UNESCO) from 1946 to 1952. He was also the chairman of the Executive Board in 1948-49. Earlier, Radhakrishnan had called for a strong international organization to be created after the end of the Second World War. But the establishment of the new United Nations ended up as a disappointment to him: "The lessons of the Second World War seem to be lost on the politicians who are trying to perpetuate their old policies of greed and hatred, which will again make a menace of the world. If this process goes on uninterrupted, this world will cease to be the home of the human species and become its grave. "[8]

Radhakrishna's attempt at UNESCO was to ensure that it did not fall prey to the vagaries of the Cold War and become an instrument of the rivalries between the Western powers led by the USA, and the Soviet Bloc. He also emphasized that the culture of the West was not to dominate UNESCO and its work, and a truly international cultural spirit needed to be fostered. Needless to say, this stance of his did not win him, friends, in either bloc, but raised his and India's international visibility.

Radhakrishnan's understanding of UNESCO was that it should promote intercultural understanding between different parts of the world, an issue that was his constant refrain. Just before the establishment of UNESCO, he wrote, It will not do, if we merely establish the machinery which will deal with disputes as they arise; we have to examine and change, where necessary the ideas and institutions which periodically produce catastrophes. We must endeavour to establish a new social harmony in which conflicts will not arise."[9]

Dr Radhakrishna was elected a member of the Constituent Assembly from the United Provinces (today's Uttar Pradesh), on the ticket of the Indian National Congress, though he was not a formal member of the party, testifying to the great respect in which he was held. Radhakrishnan spoke for the first time in the assembly on December 11, 1946, shortly after the session began. He pointed to the destruction that had been wrought by partition. The interventions that he made were few and infrequent and did not amount to anything much.

He resigned from the Constituent Assembly upon his appointment as the Indian Ambassador to the Union of Soviet Socialist Republics (USSR) in 1949. He spent half the year in Moscow and the other half teaching at Oxford, where he was still the Spalding professor--a most unusual arrangement, to say the least. Radhakrishnan arrived in Moscow at the height of the Cold War. The Soviet leaders were very suspicious of India and believed it to be an ally of the Western poers, notwithstanding India's claims of non-alignment. Radhakrishnan met the Soviet leader, Joseph Stalin, on January 15, 1950, for a rare personal audience which lasted three hours. Radhakrishnan wanted India to have closer relations with the Soviet Union, but the Indian Prime Minister was wary of his proposal of a friendship treaty between the two countries.

However, when the Korean War broke out in 1950, Radhakrishnan was instrumental in conducting private parleys between the Soviet Union and the American ambassador, which led the Soviets that India had a role to play in bringing about a ceasefire on the Korean peninsula. But Radhakrishnan was not happy with India's stance at the United Nations, labelling North Korea as the aggressor. Radhakrishnan left Moscow in 1952 after being nominated for Vice-President of India under the newly-promulgated Constitution. He met Stalin a second time, in which a surreal incident took place. Radhakrishnan patted an ill-looking Stalin on the cheek and back, and rubbed his head. The soon-to-be-dead Stalin told him that Radhakrishnan was the first person to treat him as a human being, and not a monster.

Dr Radhakrishnan was elected the first Vice-President of India by both Houses of Parliament for the first of two terms—he was in office from 1952 to 1962. In 1957 he expressed his desire to step down. He was persuaded to stay on with the understanding that the President, Dr Rajendra Prasad, would step down halfway through his second term, and Radhakrishnan would succeed him. In the event, Radhakrishnan had to wait till Prasad completed his presidency.

Most of Radhakrishnan's two terms as Vice-President were spent on tours abroad and in India, giving speeches that placed India as an ancient nation in the garb of a new state, taking its rightful place in the comity of nations, and placing its ancient culture front and centre as a necessity in the modern world. However, the most important part of his vice-presidency lay in the creation of norms by which the Rajya Sabha was to conduct its business, in his role as its Chairman. He was adamant that India should develop its conventions as regards parliamentary procedure and not just rely on British precedents. It was Radhakrishnan who asserted that Parliament consisted of two equal Houses. It was Radhakrishnan who ensured that members of the Rajya Sabha were part of the most important parliamentary committees—the Public Accounts Committee and the Committee on Public Undertakings.

Radhakrishnan was elected the second President of India in 1962 upon Prasad's retirement. The relations between Prasad and Nehru had been frosty, with Prasad wanting more of a role in governance than Nehru felt was warranted under the Constitution. Prasad had not even been his first choice for President, that being C Rajagopalchari, who did not find favour with the rest of the Congress Party. Radhakrishnan envisaged the presidency more on the lines that were acceptable to Nehru. It was a retreat from the activist role of Prasad to a more symbolic position. It has been observed that "When one reads Radhakrishna's speeches as Vice-President and President one might be tempted to think of them as echoes of Prime Minister Nehru's ideas. But an important difference is discernible, and it grows much stronger in the later years, in that Radhakrishnan's advocacy of democracy and socialism has an important detachment about it. He is advocating these policies not as a member of the political order but of the ideological order…"[10]

Radhakrishnan did not comment publicly on policies and events, except at least twice. The first was when the Chinese attacked India, and he praised the people for their unity in the face of the enemy. The second was when violence occurred in South India over the government's language policy, and he publicly wondered what been the necessity for it. It is said that he had been instrumental in privately convincing congressmen that Indira Gandhi should succeed Prime Minister Lal Bahadur Shastri on his death.

Dr Radhakrishnan's was an active but private retirement. At the time of his death in 1975, he still stood by the optimistic words he had said about the future of humankind. He believed "Ä world without fear, without anger, may seem to be impracticable. But all historical experience confirms the view that man would not have attained the possible unless time and again he had not reached out for the impossible. What man has achieved so far is immense, yet it is very small compared to what he may yet achieve. History has many surprises in store for us."[11]

References

1. S. Radhakrishnan, An Idealist View of Life (George Allen & Unwin, 1932), pg 16
2. Ibid, pg 15
3. President Radhakrishnan's Speeches and Writings, May 1962-1964 (Publications Division), pg 14
4. S Radhakrishnan, Occasional Speeches and Writings, Third Series (Publications Division), pg 3
5. Ibid, pg 286
6. Ibid, pg 286
7. Ibid, pg 287
8. S Radhakrishnan, Moral values in Literature (ibh) pg 100
9. S Radhakrishna, Is this peace (Kalyani) pg 64
10. Paul Younger, Indian Political Tradition and Radhakrishnan (Indian Philosophical Annual 1977-78), pg 128
11. President Radhakrishnan's Speeches and Writings, May 1962-1964 (Publications Division), pg 13

Sarvapalli Radhakrishnan in the Soviet Union: The Philosopher - Diplomat

Jyoti Atwal

"Until philosophers are kings, or the kings and princes of this world have the spirit and power of philosophy, and political greatness and wisdom meet in one, and those commoner natures who pursue either to the exclusion of the other are compelled to stand aside, cities will never have rest from their evils -- no, nor the human race, as I believe -- and then only will this our State have a possibility of life and behold the light of day."

Plato, *The Republic*, 4th century B.C.

Introduction

Dr Sarvepalli Radhakrishnan (1888-1975) was an extraordinary philosopher, educator and statesman whose ideas and work had evolved in the socio-political milieu of colonial India. Dr Radhakrishnan (henceforth SR) believed that political subjugation interfered with the inner freedom of an individual. The outer cry for Swaraj was an expression of the need for this inner freedom. For him, progressive thinking and culture were required to include science and technology. His scholarly publications included *Indian Philosophy*, 2 vol. (1923–27), *The Philosophy of the Upanishads* (1924), *An Idealist View of Life* (1932), *Eastern Religions and Western Thought* (1939) and *East and West: Some Reflections* (1955). In his lectures and scholarship, he tried to interpret Indian thought for the Westerners. He was knighted in 1931 for his contribution as a philosopher but he abjured the title after independence.

He served as the President of India from 1962 to 1967. Despite wearing different hats, he held a strong affiliation with the academic world at all times during his lifetime. He worked as a Professor of Philosophy at Mysore (1918–21) and Calcutta (1921–31; 1937–41) universities and as Vice-Chancellor of Andhra University (1931–36). He was a Professor of Eastern religions and ethics at the University of Oxford in England (1936–52) and Vice-Chancellor of Banaras Hindu University (1939–48).

He was appointed as Chancellor of the University of Delhi from 1953 to 1962.

In 1949 he was appointed as the Indian ambassador to the Soviet Union. On his return to India in 1952 he was elected vice president. In 1962, he was elected as President of India. SR was elected to the Constituent Assembly from the United Provinces on a Congress Party ticket. In the Assembly, he intervened in minority issues and objectives resolution debates. He led the Indian delegation to the United Nations Educational, Scientific and Cultural Organization (UNESCO; 1946–52) and was elected chairman of UNESCO's executive board (1948–49).

Despite the various capacities in which he served, one fact remained–he was essentially a philosopher. His patriotism stood out both in his stress on the vitality of Indian thought and in his non-philosophical addresses. He underlined the wider aspects of his appointment: 'You may rest assured that my own work will be direct to propagate philosophy and indirectly to convince all that India is not a subject to be administered but is a nation seeking its soul' (S. Gopal, p145).

Text within the Context

However, this paper engages with his life as a diplomat, particularly his only posting as the Indian Ambassador to Russia in 1949. This was a period when newly independent India had to deal with Stalin's difficulty with trusting the transfer of power to India. SR was initially reluctant but Jawaharlal Nehru wanted him very much to take up the ambassadorship. He was promised six months in Cambridge every year.

Here too, SR initiated a philosophical enquiry to understand Marxism and social revolution. He was reading *'God that Failed'* on his way to Moscow. This 1949 book was written at the beginning of the Cold War. Contributors André Gide (France), Richard Wright (the United States), Ignazio Silone (Italy), Stephen Spender (England), Arthur Koestler (Germany), and Louis Fischer, an American foreign correspondent, all tell how their search for the upliftment of humanity led them to egalitarian values, and how they rejected it owing to revulsion and personal agony. Arthur Koestler was a Hungarian-born author and journalist. The editor of the book, Richard Crossman, worked as an editor of the *New Statesman* and *Nation* and was a Labor MP. The book was an outcome of his engagement/dissent and debate with Arthur Koestler. In 1931,

Koestler joined the Communist Party of Germany, but he resigned in 1938 after becoming disillusioned with Stalinism. According to Grossman the purpose of the book was 'to study the state of mind of the Communist convert, and the atmosphere of the period—from 1917 to 1939—when conversion was so common'. Silone and Wright were identified as victims of exploitation, the former with the peasants of Central Italy and the latter with the Negroes of the United States. Fischer and Koestler were well aware of the insecurity of their class in society. Gide and Spender belonged to privileged groups and were moved almost exclusively, as the others were moved partly, by pity and a sense of guilt. Koestler was son of a *déclassé* Hungarian Jew. He belonged to no disadvantaged group such as Silone, who had grown up amongst peasants and whose heart and soul belonged to the Italian peasants. The book philosophically argued that what communism offered the intellectuals could be described, in religious terms. Communism offered them redemption from sin, the fellowship of true believers, and an all-inclusive theology. Redemption from sin is a running theme of the book. Moreover, the feelings of guilt seem to derive from the intellectual's awareness of the imbalance between his well-being and the exigencies of society.

SR believed that a truly religious man could only be a peaceful revolutionary. There was no space for violence. Soviet authorities did not appreciate his affiliation with Oxford and the Chair he held there. During the War, he delivered the Kamala lectures where he had established clarity between sympathy for Marxism as an instrument for social revolution and unacceptability of the Marxist philosophy of life, its atheism, its disregard of the sacredness of personality and its naturalistic view of man. He often repeated his commitment to democratic values and belief in the freedom of the individuals. To him, there was a 'knowledge solution' which was a way of approaching the opponent's position intellectually.

SR discussed how great was the silence for a diplomat. He held up Benjamin Franklin's formula for a diplomat 'sleepless tact, immovable calmness and a patience that no folly, no provocation, no blunders can shake'. Ironical as it may seem, in his speeches during his ambassadorship he clearly stated his apprehension about one-party rule and insistence on the party line.

He was not particularly close to the British or American diplomats, which made him less suspicious in the eyes of Russians. Not a curious museum/theatre or ballet goer, SR was mostly found after office time - in bed, reading and writing. Moscow was suspicious of any ambassador who was not interested in museums or performances. He fulfilled his duty of attending diplomatic receptions and dinners but he was well known for retiring early in the evening. Despite the fact that Moscow was the hotbed of global-political discussion as the Blocs had been created by the, SR was able to lead a life of solitude which is what gave him contentment.

The successor of SR, Mr KPS Menon was after independence, India's first Foreign Secretary from 1948 to 1952, then Ambassador of India to the Soviet Union, Hungary and Poland from 1952 to 1961. He was the last foreigner to see Stalin in person in 1953. He reminisces about SR that he was the 'most unconventional diplomat who ever served in Moscow'. He would receive his fellow Ambassadors in his bedroom. He spent most of his time in bed, reading writing and translating the *Brahmopanishad.* In a lighter vein, Menon recalls that after he succeeded him in Moscow he found on the back of the bed in the Embassy, the stain left by the hair oil on SR's head. According to Menon, SR kept himself 'above the dust and din of diplomacy and the drudgery of office work.' He was privileged to have as his Minister-Counsellor, Yezdi Gundevia, who was known to be a very efficient Foreign Service Officer. His wife, Rokshi, who had accompanied him, looked after the social side of his diplomatic life.

Another highly significant development in the global balance of power and weaponisation took place the same year when SR arrived in Moscow. The Soviets had successfully yet secretively tested a nuclear bomb. On 9 September 1949, Director of Central Intelligence, Admiral Roscoe Hillenkoetter handed to President Harry Truman a report that "samples of air masses" collected in the Northern Pacific included evidence of "abnormal radioactive contamination." This report was published later by the National Security Archive, but the intelligence community was not sure whether the contamination was evidence of a Soviet nuclear test or if it was a nuclear accident. By 21 September, Truman was advised that the Soviet Union had staged a nuclear test. On 23 September 1949, Truman announced that the Soviet Union had tested a nuclear device several weeks earlier. This was a huge development as the U.S. strategists and intelligence had expected this test to be completed at least five years later.

The Soviets were alarmed by the announcement by the US and the capability to isolate and identify the signs of a nuclear blast.

As a reaction, the Soviets issued a counter-statement on 25 September, claiming they had not performed a weapons test. The U.S. had probably detected "blasting" caused by construction work. Soviet Union's entry into the nuclear club may have had a direct impact on encouraging Stalin to support Kim Il-sung's plan for a North Korean invasion of the South.

In his first speech at Moscow, SR offered a peculiar course of action. He said that it would be worthwhile to hold a meeting of six heads of government, two from Asia; two from Europe and the rest from the United States and the Soviet Union. It was not important that any immediate political results could be derived but for him, it was important to remove the misunderstanding and prejudices. This public statement was Radhakrishnan's own and had not been approved by the headquarters.

However, there were matters which required special attention such as the status of democracy and freedom in the Soviet Union. It was claimed by the Indian ambassador that India was willing to learn from the Soviet Union in her search for progress.

Menon writes that the Russians were pleased with the appointment of a prestigious philosopher as India's envoy. He was well-recognised as a nationalist. While SR was teaching at Calcutta University, Irwin who was the Viceroy, before recommending him for a Knighthood, asked the Governor of Bengal for his opinion. His reply was: *'All the police reports are against him, but I like him.'* He had been knighted by the British Government for his eminence as a philosopher /scholar.

By 1949 relations between the Government of India and the Soviet Union were not too cordial. The main reason was, that the Soviet Union was directing the Indian Communist Party to rebellion and condemning the Government of India policies.

Jawaharlal Nehru flagged his perception of the Russian misconceptions about India after independence. He reiterated that India wanted friendship and cooperation with Russia in many fields, but India was a land of sensitive people and would react strongly to be cursed at and run down. The whole basis of Russian policy appeared to be that no essential change had taken place in India, and it was presumed by the Russians that India after 1947 continued to be camp followers of the British. Nehru said that this was complete nonsense and that if a policy is based on nonsensical premises, it is apt to go wrong. India's foreign policy under Nehru had a good understanding of the two leading groups of the times -the Russian bloc and the Anglo-American bloc. There was a need to be friendly to both and yet not join either. Both America and Russia were extraordinarily suspicious of each other as well as of other countries, which made India's choices difficult, as India was suspected to be leaning towards the other.

Mrs Vijayalakshmi Pandit as the first Indian Ambassador in Moscow was not able to build good communication and contacts or find an audience with Stalin. Stalin avoided her as he probably considered her aristocratic. SR stepped in to take charge of such a chaotic diplomatic situation between India and the Soviet Union. Nehru had cautioned ambassadors to move cautiously. India was too mindful of the reaction of the United States and Britain.

The overall perception was that SR had successfully broken the ice with Stalin. There are 'top secret' telegrams detailing their meetings of 1950 and 1952 in Moscow, now archived in India and overseas.

Maharaja Krishna Rasgotra , in his memoir 'A Life in Diplomacy' published in 2016, notes that *'Stalin had to be convinced of the genuineness of India's Independence, of the depth of India's concern over Cold War tensions and its desire for peace and Russia's friendship and cooperation. The usual diplomatic approach would be of no avail, and Radhakrishnan was just the man for the complex task.'*

On 15th January 1950, Ambassador accompanied by Counsellor interviewed Generalissimo Stalin at Kremlin. Vyshinsky was present at the interview. Pavlov who was Head of the North Europe Division of the Soviet Foreign Office and former Counsellor in London acted as the interpreter. SR expressed the hope that good relations between the two countries would be strengthened and affirmed. India's anxiety to do everything possible to work for peace which was essential to enable her to build up the country and improve living standards. India's policy of neutrality was real and positive and in Colombo, Nehru had reaffirmed India's anxiety to avoid Cold War tactics and anti-Communist pacts. SR conveyed that India expected that the big powers would do their utmost to put an end to the Cold War and to place embargo on propaganda against each other. Expressed the hope that Generalissimo Stalin should take the lead in the larger interest of humanity. Stalin'replied that doing so did not depend on him alone. The ambassador replied that Stalin should take the initiative and thus help suffering humanity. Stalin said that two days ago he was informed that when Pandit Nehru was in London he wanted to return to India via Moscow but he was not sure Moscow would favour this trip. SR answered that he knew Pandit Nehru would be glad to visit Moscow if time and opportunity permitted.

Stalin asked several questions regarding India's position in the Commonwealth and seemed anxious to know if she was more or less independent than, say, Canada. The ambassador explained the position, especially in light of India's forthcoming declaration as a Republic. Stalin asked if India was entitled to have her army without any restriction and also if there was a navy. He consented and approved when informed that was the case; the Commander-in-Chief was Indian and there was also an Indian Air Force. He enquired if relations with Pakistan were still bad and about the language they spoke there. He was told that relations were rather strained as Pakistan was of the view that wherever there were Muslims they must be with them. Of the languages of India he enquired, which was dominant and expressed satisfaction that Hindi was phonetic and not hieroglyphic. He enquired if the Government proposed to carry out agrarian reforms and added something had to be done as peasants were in very poor condition. The ambassador assured that landlordism was being abolished and essential land reforms were being carried out. India had a hard time solving all problems in these two years when she had to clear up remnants of feudalism and the devastating effects of partition. Stalin asked if Ceylon was a separate State and whether its separation was so necessary and laughed. The interview lasted for half an hour. The report mentioned that during the interview Stalin smoked cigarettes continuously and laughed occasionally; appeared in quite good health and was alert and attentive. The report ended with the note that there was a pleasant and relaxed atmosphere.

The other meeting with Stalin just before departing from Moscow is even more significant.

The record of this conversation is titled as of Ambassador Radhakrishnan's interview with Generalissimo Stalin on April 5, 1952. They discussed India's internal politics and stance on foreign policy. SR told Stalin of India's recent elections and emphasized that India shares the Soviet Union's stance against capitalism. Radhakrishnan also put forth the question of peaceful co-existence between capitalist and communist spheres, and the possibility for a neutral commission to replace the Cominform (Communist Information Bureau) and UN.

SR expressed his gratefulness and thanks to the Generalissimo for receiving him at such short notice on the eve of his (Ambassador's) departure.SR went on to say that his stay of two and a half years in Moscow was most useful and he had every courtesy and assistance from the Foreign Minister and his Deputies. He recalled the prompt and ready assistance that the Foreign Office and the Soviet Government had rendered last year in the matter of the despatch of wheat to India. When the Ambassador stressed that he was grateful for the promptitude and readiness with which the Soviet Union had come to our aid in this, Stalin said: "There is nothing to be grateful about. We have only fulfilled our duty." The Ambassador remarked that many States did not have a proper conception of their duty, nor did they discharge it when they had.

The Ambassador then referred to the various Soviet delegations that had recently visited India and said that he felt that the Indian people got some idea of the Soviet achievements – what could be done by a people with determination and will.

Focusing on the Indian internal matters, SR said that the country (India) was indeed 'passing through critical times. We had got rid of various forms of exploitation. We had rid ourselves of foreign domination and we had got rid of the princely rule. We hoped to tackle the problem of our landlords equally successfully'. "It would be good", said Stalin, "if you succeed in doing it."

The Ambassador then generally referred to recent elections in India and claimed that for the first time in history, 175 million people were enfranchised of whom 105 million had voted. But Stalin expressed doubt saying, "The women did not vote in your country". The Ambassador corrected the Generalissimo by pointing out that not only did women vote in the elections, but the women voters had, if anything, shown a more progressive spirit. SR pointed out that we had a lady Governor, a lady Cabinet Minister, and his own predecessor in Moscow, the Generalissimo would doubtless recall, had also been a lady. The elections he claimed had been free and fair. There was no official interference of any sort and many Ministers were defeated.

On the political and economic situation in India, SR said that India was as much against capitalist exploitation as Russia and it had a similar economic goal. "*But we wish to adopt peaceful parliamentary methods to achieve our aims, because our whole history has taught us that enduring progress should be of a peaceful character.*"

Referring to India's foreign policy, SR pointed out that India was pursuing the same policy as the Soviet Union in several matters – China, Japan, Korea or, for that matter, the admission of other nations to the UN. He claimed "*We are not with America and we are not with any power", he stressed, "We act according to our sense of right and do not yield to any political or economic pressure.*"

Stalin was at one time reported to have said that if Capitalism could adapt its production not to getting maximum profits, but to the systematic improvement of the masses of the people, then there would not be any crisis, but then that would not be Capitalism. In a reconfirming tone, Stalin said that it was difficult for a Capitalist to do without profits and it was a pity that the capitalists could not do without profits. If the Capitalists gave up profits, he said, they would be giving up themselves.

Furthering posing more difficult questions, SR - referring to the desirability of the peaceful co-existence of the two systems, asked Stalin if the Soviet Union would be prepared to "give up the Cominform", as it had at one stage given up the Comintern. Stalin responded by saying that this was of no importance whatsoever to the question of the co-existence of the two systems; the Cominform had not been created by the Soviet Union alone – there were other countries involved too.

SR raised the question of and added that if the Soviet Union looked upon a UN Commission as necessarily pro-American, could they not agree to some sort of a neutral commission to see if conditions for free and fair elections existed in that country? The reply was that representatives of the four powers could appoint any commission they wished. The UNO had nothing to do with Germany and only the four occupying powers according to the POTSDAM declaration could do these things. The Ambassador posed a question about the possibility of a neutral commission investigating the allegations of the use of bacteriological weapons in Korea. Stalin said that he had not given thought to this. As far as they were concerned, he said, "To us, it has been proved that they (Americans) have attempted to try this out in Korea", and said that a body of international lawyers had seen the evidence of this.

Another issue regarding a Russian correspondent was raised by Stalin. He turned to Vyshinsky and asked what "this complaint" was. Vyshinsky explained that we had felt that Borzenko's articles were unfair and unnecessarily critical of the Government of India, Prime Minister Nehru had also complained to Novikov about this. SR immediately was heard and understood. Stalin ordered "That is all right, recall him," to Vyshinsky. "We will recall him", Stalin assured the Ambassador, 'If you don't like him, you tell us frankly. We assure you that he will be recalled.' SR expressed that he aimed to reconfirm good relations and friendship that we had built up here in Moscow should not be damaged by Soviet representatives in India saying things that offend our national dignity. SR spoke about Borzenko and the Moscow Radio. At that point, Stalin gave definite orders for Borzenko to be called back. This was an important win for India and personally SR. Stalin also reassured that "Both you and Mr. Nehru are persons whom we do not consider to be our enemies. This will continue to be our policy and you can count on our help… and 'the United States and Britain look on Asian peoples as backward and look down upon them. We treat all Asians as equals. It is this which helps us to conduct a correct policy.

SR agreed with the sentiments expressed by Stalin and added that Malaya, Indo-China, Morocco, Tunisia, Egypt, Iran and South Africa were examples of a very different policy towards, what may be called, backward peoples. "Is this democracy?" he asked. Stalin smiled and said: "This is what they call democracy?"

Undoubtedly the conversation with Stalin was a turning point in the history of diplomacy of Indo-Soviet relations and for strengthening the vision of India's balance and neutrality. KPS Menon in his reflection on this period recalls how SR used to spend half the year at Oxford and the other half in Moscow. But, Menon thought that the day was coming when it would no longer be possible to combine philosophy and diplomacy, Oxford and Moscow (he had written so in one of his letters to the Government of India).

Another important watershed in the diplomatic history of India was the visit of Radhakrishnan to the United States in 1953 as the second President of India . During the toast at the dinner reception in honour of

President Radhakrishnan, President Kennedy said that the USA has never gone as far as making a Professor the President of the United States.

At the invitation of President Kennedy, SR paid a State visit to the United States from the second to the eleventh of June 1953. During his stay in Washington, both Presidents met and along with members of the United States Government, including members of Congress. In their discussions, both Presidents reaffirmed that relations between the United States and India, the world's two largest democracies, were based on a large measure of agreement on basic values and objectives. The Presidents of the United States and India agreed that the striking advance in science and technology has put enormous power in the hands of men which can be used either for the benefit of humanity or for its destruction. It is, therefore, necessary for all concerned to see that international cooperation in accordance with the Charter of the United Nations was held up; that peace is maintained and that the enormous power which science and technology have given is used for the betterment of humanity. Both Presidents expressed the hope that the governments and citizens of the world will commit themselves to economic and social betterment, particularly those in the countries of Asia, Africa and Latin America.

The President of India spoke of the determination of the Government and the people of India to preserve India's territorial integrity and of their efforts to improve the living standards of the people within the framework of a liberal parliamentary democracy. President Kennedy reiterated the deep interest of the Government and the people of the United States in these endeavours and reassured President Radhakrishnan that India could count on the sympathy and assistance of the United States in its development and defense. They agreed that the two countries share a mutual defensive concern to thwart the designs of Chinese aggression against the subcontinent. Both Presidents recognized the vital importance of safeguarding the freedom, independence and territorial integrity of India for peace and stability not only in Asia but in the world as well. President Kennedy conveyed the admiration of the American people for the great accomplishments already achieved and for the spirit of sacrifice and dedication displayed by the people of India.

SR expressed the gratitude of his nation for the generous assistance provided by the United States to the Indian people in support of their development and defense. The two Presidents reaffirmed the dedication of their people to the cause of peace and freedom in the world. They are confident that their two countries will continue to cooperate in the future, as in the past, in the attainment of these common objectives. President Kennedy and President Radhakrishnan were highly satisfied with the meetings and agreed that it has contributed to a closer understanding between their two countries and peoples.

To sum up the international scenario under Nehru and SR – the foreign policy of newly independent India had a name—it was called Non-alignment—which meant, as he had outlined in the radio address, 'keep away from power groups aligned against one another', and defining its practical agenda for the immediate future. India was able to develop its threefold programme of Liberation of Colonies, One World United for Peace and Cooperation, and Opposition to Racism, and General and Complete Disarmament, a ban on Nuclear Tests and the Elimination of Nuclear Weapons, which was an extension of the Gandhian commitment to non-violence. The resources for defense of the new nation of India were to be invested in but the proliferation of weaponisation leading to the arms race was to be resisted. Devastation from Wars had made negotiations and treaties a must in the post-War world.

Indo-Russian ties strengthened after Nikita Khrushchev and Nicholai Bulganin visited India in 1955. By then, Radhakrishnan was Vice President of India and took over as President subsequently. The foundation was laid for the unique balance and foreign policy through efficiency in diplomacy during the initial years when SR was India's ambassador in Moscow.

Conclusion

In conclusion, it is important to revisit some perceptions of SR as a statesman and diplomat. A highly distinguished diplomat himself, K Natwar Singh writes that when he joined the Indian Foreign Service in 1953, S. Gopal, Dr Radhakrishnan's son, was director of the Historical Division of the Ministry and as a part of their training, he as a probationer had to spend a week in various divisions of the Ministry including Historical Division. With a high sense of humour, he pulled Natwar's leg about going to the "other place", i.e., Cambridge. Gopal was himself Oxford-educated. Before leaving for Peking, which was his first posting, he asked Gopal, "What books should I read on China?" Not many books on China were available in Delhi. He suggested Edgar Snow's 1936 book called *Red Star Over China.* None of the bookshops in Delhi had the book. But Natwar bought it in Hong Kong on his way to Peking in July 1956. Snow was the first Westerner to meet Mao Tse-tung and the Chinese Communist leaders in 1936, Snow wrote the first authorized account of Mao's life. The book tells the history of the famous Long March and the men and women who were responsible for the Chinese Revolution.

He recalls that one of the highs of his stay in China was Vice President Dr Radhakrishnan's visit to China in September 1957, when Gopal had come along. Chairman Mao Tse Tung received him in the courtyard of his house, which was situated in Chungnanhai, the most exclusive part of Peking that was well guarded and secluded with only the members of the Political Bureau who resided there. Philosophers bear a reputation for lacking in humour. Natwar tells us about this unforgettable and unbelievable moment when after shaking hands with Chairman Mao, Radhakrishnan did the unthinkable. He patted on Mao's left cheek. Mao was taken aback as no one had taken such a liberty. Natwar and the Indian delegation were embarrassed. SR as Vice President announced that *"Mr Chairman, don't be alarmed, I did the same thing to Stalin and the Pope."* This statement perhaps brought relief to everyone.

In another instance when the King of Greece came to India on a state visit. President while welcoming him commented that *"Your Majesty. You are the first King of Greece to come to India on invitation. Alexander the Great came uninvited."*

One cannot more than agree with S. Gopal, that it is the intellectual confidence of Radhakrishnan, that astonishes. One can also conclude that philosophy was for him an intellectual tool with which one could construe and de-construe society, religion, nation and the globe.

Picture courtesy :
https://www.financialexpress.com/business/defence-dr-s-radhakrishnan-played-stellar-role-in-helping-nehru-shape-non-alignment-policy-3232657/

Picture Courtesy:
https://commons.wikimedia.org/wiki/File:President_John_F._Kennedy_with_President_of_India,_Dr._Sarvepalli_Radhakrishnan_(1).jpg

References

1. Maharaja Krishna Rasgotra joined the Indian Foreign Service in 1949. In his career, held several important posts in Indian diplomatic missions abroad and in the Ministry of External Affairs. From 1958 to 1962, he was India's representative on the United Nations' Trusteeship Council, the Fourth Committee and the De-colonization Committee of the UN General Assembly.

2. Record of the Conversation of J.V. Stalin and Sarvepalli Radhakrishnan, January 15th, 1950.

3. The rank of Generalissimos was established by the Presidium of the Supreme Soviet on 26 June 1945, and awarded to Stalin (who had held the rank of Marshal since 1943) on 27 June by the same body "for especially outstanding services to the Motherland in leading all the armed forces of the state during the war".

4. He was a Soviet politician, jurist and diplomat who was a state prosecutor of Joseph Stalin's Moscow Trials and Nuremberg trials. He was the Soviet Foreign Minister from 1949 to 1953. He served as Deputy Foreign Minister under Vyacheslav Molotov. He also headed the Institute of State and Law in the Academy of Sciences of the Soviet Union.

5. Record of the Conversation of I.V. Stalin and Sarvepalli Radhakrishnan, April 5, 1952, *Wilson Center Digital Archive,* N.M.M.L., J.N. (S.4) Vol. No. 123 Pt. II, 294-297. Available on Revolutionary Democracy website on 11 December 2010. https://digitalarchive.wilsoncenter.org/document/119265

6. John F. Kennedy, Joint Statement Following Discussions with President Radhakrishnan of India. Online by Gerhard Peters and John T. Woolley, The American Presidency Project https://www.presidency.ucsb.edu/node/236566

7. 3rd June 1963 Audio archive, White House https://www.jfklibrary.org/asset-viewer/archives/jfkwha-188-003

8. K Natwar Singh, My memories of Gopal and Radhakrishnan, April 25, 2020 https://sundayguardianlive.com/opinion/memories-gopal-radhakrishnan#google_vignette

9. Article by KPS Menon on diplomatic journey of SR 1976 (https://india.mid.ru/en/history/memoires_/k_p_s_menon_on_dr_radhakrishnan_as_diplomat_1976/

10. K Natwar Singh, My memories of Gopal and Radhakrishnan, April 25, 2020 https://sundayguardianlive.com/opinion/memories-gopal-radhakrishnan#google_vignette

11. John F. Kennedy, Joint Statement Following Discussions with President Radhakrishnan of India. Online by Gerhard Peters and John T. Woolley, The American Presidency Project https://www.presidency.ucsb.edu/node/236566

12. A Philosopher's Journey: President Radhakrishnan of the Republic of India Visits the United States, 3 June 1963 (short documentary)

13. https://www.jfklibrary.org/asset-viewer/archives/usg-01-q

14. Record of the Conversation of I.V. Stalin and Sarvepalli Radhakrishnan, April 5, 1952, *Wilson Center Digital Archive*, N.M.M.L., J.N. (S.4) Vol. No. 123 Pt. II, 294-297. Available on Revolutionary Democracy website on 11 December 2010. https://digitalarchive.wilsoncenter.org/document/119265

15. *Maharaja krishna Rasgotra : A Life in Diplomacy* (Penguin Books LTD , Delhi, 2016)

16. S Gopal, *Radhakrishnan: A Biography* (Oxford University Press, Delhi, 1989)

Dr. Sarvepalli Radhakrishnan: The Tall Amongst the Tallest on Dharma and Democracy

Kovuuri G. Reddy
Uttam Prakash

Introduction

Like a luminous thread woven through Indian thought, dharma, the path of righteousness, ignites the sacred flame of humanity within. By steadfastly walking this path, we illuminate the way for truth's eternal victory, *Satyameva Jayate*. In this journey, as Dr Radhakrishnan exhorts, we fulfil the whispered call of our scriptures, our lives becoming a melody of human saintliness.

To uphold dharma, does education help? Sure, education equips us to uphold dharma, but is that all? Dr Radhakrishnan reminds us that mere academic prowess or physical health falls short. It is the awakening of our 'spiritual sensitivity' that imbues our actions with purpose and connects us to a deeper reality. This, he believes, is the goal of education. Spiritual sensitivity is a deliberate and thoughtful attitude that guides one's actions, being aware. To this effect, he ardently emphasized the importance of spirituality in humanity.

Addressing the Karnataka University convocation, Radhakrishnan offered a practical recipe for success: read, read deeply, and read with focus. He argued that amid life's challenges, great books and good company are the "incomparable fruits" we should seek out. To ensure that scientific and technological advancements serve humanity, he urged students and teachers to embrace the wisdom of literature, philosophy, and religion. He said, "There is a great verse which says that in this poison tree of *samsara* are two fruits of incomparable value. They are the enjoyment of great books and the company of good souls."

Teachers' Day: 5 September

One and a half decade after India's political independence from the imperial British Raj, India has been observing September 5 as the

Teachers' Day. Teachers' Day forever bears the mark of Sarvepalli Radhakrishnan, scholar, statesman, and educator. His impact on nascent India shines through his roles as first Vice President and Chairman of Rajya Sabha, the upper house of the Indian Parliament (1952-1962), and even rising to second President, succeeding Babu Rajendra Prasad.

Across educational institutions, in India, it is not uncommon to find portraits of Sarvepalli Radhakrishnan gazing out alongside Pt Jawaharlal Nehru or Mahatma Gandhi. His stern demeanour, accentuated by spectacles and a traditional South Indian headgear, reflects his scholarly background and priestly lineage. Yet, beyond the outward image, his name evokes a guiding spirit in Indian education and an erudite voice for interpreting the nation's unwieldy philosophical tapestry. Radhakrishnan's intellectual prowess encompassed not only the teachings of Buddhism, Jainism, Christianity, and Islam, but also delved deep into the Hindu texts of the Vedas, Shastras, Upanishads, Brahma-sutras, epics like the Mahabharata and Ramayana, and the profound Bhagavad Gita.

When Sarvepalli Radhakrishnan was the President of India, once "he was visited by a few students of him with a request of celebrating his birthday. Instead, Dr Radhakrishnan asked them to dedicate it to teachers. Thus, celebrations of September 5 as Teachers' Day started in India," reported *The Hindustan Times.* By this time in his career, he had gathered vast experiences in the educational sector across India serving as the Vice Chancellor of Andhra University, Banaras Hindu University and Kolkata (Calcutta) University. He had also become an eminent educationist and interpreter of ancient Indian philosophy to the West and the East emphasizing the universality of humanity.

While at the University of Calcutta, Radhakrishnan was invited to give a series of lectures at Manchester College, Oxford, in 1926. He returned on a tour in 1929-30 to give the Hibbert Lectures at University College, London, Open University in the UK mentions. Radhakrishnan was knighted (Sir) in 1931 and invited to take up the Spalding Professorship of Eastern Religions and Ethics at All Souls College, Oxford from 1936 to 1952. Radhakrishnan also served as an Indian delegate to the League of Nations during the 1930s. The university credits his success in comparing Eastern and Western philosophies and in interpreting Indian philosophy for Western audiences by providing rationality to it.

Teachers Should be Paid Well

With the experiences of being a student and teacher, Radhakrishnan campaigned for the betterment of teachers. Dr Kavita Sharma, an educationist, said in an interview with Sansad TV for a documentary film on Sarvepalli Radhakrishnan, "He never romanticized the teaching profession like everybody says, it's a very noble profession. It is a noble profession, but he consistently said that your teachers need to be paid properly. They need to have a particular social status so that they can deliver. Because no profession can be just made to, not get a return, if, if you want good talent to be attracted towards it."

Although Teachers' Day is celebrated on September 5 across schools and colleges, universities and educational institutions in India with performances and remembrances in memory of Sarvepalli Radhakrishnan, there is another day in a year that has little pedagogic value and more cultural significance rooted in ancient heritage: Guru Purnima.

Unlike Teacher's Day, Guru Purnima has no fixed day in a year as it is celebrated annually on the full moon day in the month of Aashaadha (June-July) based on the Hindu calendar. For example, Guru Purnima is observed on 21 July 2024, was observed on 3 July 2023 and would be observed on 10 July 2025.

However, Guru Purnima has transnational and trans-religious importance for it is celebrated in Nepal and Bhutan, and by the Hindus, Jains and Buddhists within the country and beyond, diaspora. Guru Purnima, also known as Vyasa Purnima, the tentative birthday of the sage Veda Vyasa, author of Mahabharata and compiler of Vedas, is more of a religious festival to offer respect to a spiritual guru.

Additionally, there is World Teachers' Day, observed annually on 5th October. It is a day to celebrate how teachers are transforming education but also to reflect on the support they need to fully deploy their talent and vocation, and to rethink the way ahead for the profession globally. His vision for teachers was truly universal, extending far beyond borders even before the concept of globalization truly took hold. However, a question lingers: Why didn't India champion September 5th as World Teachers' Day instead of October 5th?

"He symbolized what one of our Upanishads has said that teaching is nothing but a dialogue between the teacher and the taught," said Dr Kavita Sharma. In the country, Radhakrishnan himself stressed that the students should be taught the history of the different nations, the elements of modern science and technology, and glimpses into world literature so that the minds are sharpened and feelings refined. He earnestly desired that 'our children are treated as human beings and not as automata'.

Education in the Concurrent List of the Constitution of India

As a member of the Constituent Assembly, he played a pivotal role in the framing of the Indian Constitution and in establishing the University Grants Commission, a body that maintains and coordinates standards in the country. He envisioned that education should be decentralized in India: not the sole prerogative of the Government of India, but the state governments should have an equal say. To this effect, he succeeded in creating a balance between the central government and the state governments over education. This resulted in placing education in the Concurrent List of the Constitution of India.

Indian Tricolour and Motto: Satyameva Jayate

At the time of framing the Indian Constitution, in the Constituent Assembly, the proposed national flag's saffron colour faced criticism. Undeterred, Radhakrishnan eloquently presented his case before the flag committee. He emphasized that the three colours were not mere emblems of division, but unifying symbols steeped in profound meaning. Saffron, or *bhagwa*, he explained, transcended its religious connotations, instead representing the ideals of sacrifice and indifference to material gain, qualities he deemed indispensable for politicians. White, he continued, shone as the guiding light of truth, while green served as a constant reminder of our shared bond with the soil, the source of all sustenance.

Dharma Chakra the Ashoka Chakra: The Wheel of The Law of Dharma

Dharma is one of the untranslatable Indian words rooted in Sanskrit, Prakrit, Pali and Dravidian languages loaded with meaning and echoes code of conduct. The Ashoka Chakra wheel in the centre of the middle white stripe of the national flag is the Wheel of the Law of Dharma, also called Dharma Chakra. It signifies motion, or movement, and truth, satya, and virtue. In the fiery crucible of independence, a new flag was forged. Radhakrishnan, its ardent advocate, argued that India must cast aside the inertia of the past and forge ahead. The Ashoka Chakra, he emphasized, was not a mere emblem, but a dynamic wheel of peaceful change, propelling the nation from colonial shadows into the bright sunshine of democracy. This potent symbol, he pointed out, whispered of the ancient Ashoka Lion Capital, a majestic reminder of India's heritage, and subtly echoed the spinning wheel, the banner that had spun threads of freedom throughout the struggle against British rule. The 24 spokes in the Dharma Chakra depict the qualities that should be in a person. The spokes are attributed as the pathway for humans and will lead the country on the path of progress. The 24 spokes represent Chastity, Health, Peace, Sacrifice, Morality, Service, Forgiveness, Love, Friendship or cordiality with the citizenry, Fraternity, Organization or Strengthening the unity and integrity of the nation, Welfare, Prosperity, Industry, Safety, Awareness, Equality, Artha, Policy (have faith in the country's policy), Justice, Co-operation, Duties, Rights and Wisdom.

All the spokes talk about the holistic development of an individual in the country of democracy. These are also a constant reminder to all the countrymen about their rights and duties irrespective of caste, religion, or language. "Our motto is, truth alone prevails. Truth is the name which we give to God," Radhakrishnan said. The national emblem of India contains the phrase Satyameva Jayate: 'Truth alone triumphs', a mantra from the Hindu scripture Mundaka Upanishad but a timeless phrase of universal value. Satyameva Jayate was adopted as the national motto on 26 January 1950, the day India became a Republic.

The philosopher Radhakrishnan, without being politically active by aligning with the right and the left and the centre of political parties, earned his place in the covetable positions of the country. His erudition and way of living were aligned with his commitment to the betterment of the country through education, in interpreting Indian thought and philosophy. In this way, he emerged as the complementary figure for Nehru, who presented India's statesmanship, Gandhi its people, and he presented intellectual spirituality. His philosophy also enabled India to build bridges between Indian spiritualism and Western democracy.

Radhakrishnan vociferously argued that political arrangements and economic ties are mere sandcastles against the tide of discord. To build a truly lasting world community, we must dive deeper, cultivating a shared psychological foundation. This, he proclaimed, is the transformative power of literature, the ability to awaken in us the unwavering realization that we are not isolated individuals, but interconnected threads in the vast tapestry of humanity.

The Adventitious Philosopher

Sarvepalli Radhakrishnan studied philosophy because of an external factor of chance rather than by inherent nature in the land of unborn India under imperial rule. He studied philosophy at a time when its career path was mainly teaching and a Western subject. A student of philosophy, however, can branch out as a politician, paralegal, marketing or research consultant, data analyst, administrator, journalist, or psychologist among others. In the case of Radhakrishnan, he also taught psychology after he had graduated from Madras Christian College and when he was a student preparing to teach philosophy at Madras Presidency College.

Philosopher and Philosophy

A philosopher is a person who is a learner in philosophy, or studies philosophy. In ancient Greece, philosophy was the love of wisdom, exploring aspects of existence, knowledge, language, mind, and reason for this and that with critical inquiry. It is the study of the processes governing thought, the conduct of life, morals, character, and behaviour; the mental balance of calmness and composure; investigation of the universal laws of regulation; and underlying knowledge and reality including aesthetics, ethics, logic and metaphysics.

Philosophy is also the study of a field of acknowledgement or activity such as the philosophy of politics, polity, and economics among others. Indian philosophy has its roots in its pre-ancient times alongside Western philosophy rooted in Greece, Arabic-Persian and Chinese philosophies. Indian philosophy, however, has been emphasizing abstract and concrete themes as varied as sorrow and samsara, meditation and renunciation, nirvana and moksha, karma and dharma. Over time, philosophy branched out as epistemology, (what is knowledge, how to acquire it), ethics (code of conduct) logic (reasoning, exploring by arguments on why something is right or wrong), and metaphysics (reality, existence, properties, objects). The subfields are aesthetics, and philosophies related to language, mind, religion, and politics among others.

After completing his schooling in his tiny native town of Tiruttani and the temple town of Tirupati, he joined Voorhees College in Vellore for his high school education called First of Arts. Then he joined the Madras Christian College. In an interview for a documentary produced by Films Division, established under the Ministry of Information and Broadcasting, Government of India, a year after independence, Radhakrishnan revealed that he did not have a spectacular background but was a rigorous student. "When I passed my intermediate what was then called the first of arts examination…It was open to me to have taken up mathematics or history for my BA degree but the accident of my getting a few books on philosophy from my cousin of mine who just passed the BA degree examination made me select philosophy…Not that I had any predilection for it or eagerness to solve the problems of the world. An accident of getting the books free that decided my career as a student of philosophy."

As a student of philosophy, he was completely absorbed in the subject because of the social milieu and by the subject. He recalled, "The way in which Indian philosophy was criticised by the teachers in Madras in those years led me an interest in Indian thought and find out what is alive and what is not alive in Indian thought, how much it has changed and how much it should change for the betterment of our own culture. I tried to make a clear study of Indian thought (ethics, aesthetics, Indian philosophy, Hindu philosophy), whether the criticisms are justified or not, what is wrong with it and what it has to shed off and what is right with it and what has to be preserved."

As a student, he started to write for the college magazine on aspects of philosophy which is invariably linked to religion and rituals among others. His thesis was "The Ethics of the Vedanta and its Metaphysical Presuppositions", which was to be a reply to the charge that the Vedanta system had no room for ethics. Later published titled 'The Ethics of the Vedanta', he argued by stating that philosophy is a criticism of life and it is judged by its capacity to improve, and the Vedanta philosophy satisfied the demands of the moral consciousness and with ethical interest.

His thesis invited commendation from his professors, Rev. William Meston and Dr. Alfred George Hogg. Since then, it almost became his mission to study Indian philosophy and religion critically and objectively. He went on to emerge as the apologist of Hinduism and ancient philosophy of the land against 'uninformed Western criticism' and as the resonant voice in interpreting Indian thought to the West and the country.

Books

Radhakrishnan's works include Indian Philosophy (1923–27), The Philosophy of the Upanishads (1924), An Idealist View of Life (1932), Eastern Religions and Western Thought (1939), and East and West: Some Reflections (1955). He edited Mahatma Gandhi: Essays and Reflections on his Life, which was presented to Gandhi on his seventieth birthday, 2 October 1939.

He is credited for his interpretation of the Hindu scripture: Bhagavad Gita. Journalist Kuldip Nayar said in an interview, "I think the book he wrote on the Gita was more a philosophical book than in any case religious book. Here is a comparative study of religion, traditions, cultures, and civilizations. So, he gives a larger kind of interpretation, varied kind of an interpretation, to the book Gita."

His best work, hailed as a masterpiece, is Indian Philosophy. "This work gives a clear and rational account of the highest conceptions of Hinduism. The happy blend of Eastern conceptions with Western terminology makes the book intelligible even to the inexpert and it need hardly be added, instructive. Professor Radhakrishnan has shown that in their perception of the goal, in the acuteness of their reasoning, and the boldness of their conceptions, the Indian thinkers are second to none," noted Times Literary Supplement. "Comprehensive and authoritative. No such adequate account of Hindu thought has appeared in English. The spirit, motive, and method of this great book are admirable," Church Times reviewed. Indian Philosophy embarks beginning with the situation in India, characteristics of Indian Thought charges against Indian Philosophy, the Vedic Period and its hymns, theology, monotheism verses monism, cosmology, religion, ethics, eschatology, the philosophy of the Upanishads, the pluralistic realism of the Jainas and the ethical idealism of Buddhism, Brahmanism, epics Mahabharata and Ramayana, codes of Manu and Bhagavad Gita. His philosophical diagnosis in the book mentions the unity of all systems and the decline of philosophy in the recent past and the present. His observation is, 'there is a cordial harmony between god and man in Indian thought, while the opposition between the two is marked more in the west'.

One of the constant barbs of the Abrahamic faiths of Christianity and Islam against Hinduism has been idol worshipping in the country. To that his response in the book was that Gods in India are closer to the devotee – they are friends, they are lovers, they are the near and dear. In contrast, in the Judeo-Christian gods seem to be distant and vengeful. Zeus is bent on destroying the human race, and Prometheus and Hercules have to defend mankind against divine vengeance. The main tendency of Western culture is an opposition between man and god. Whereas in India man is a product of god. The whole world is due to the sacrifice of god. The Purusha Sukta (spiritual unity of the universe) speaks of such an eternal sacrifice that sustains man and the world. In it, the whole world is pictured as one single being of comparable vastness and immensity animated by one spirit, including within its substance all forms of life.

Recognition and Responsibility

Pt. Jawaharlal Nehru the first Prime Minister of India detected the philosophical powers of Radhakrishnan and called upon him to contribute to a free and independent India. He was one among the three to deliver a historic speech in the Constituent Assembly at midnight on August 14, 1947. He led the Indian delegation to the Educational, Scientific and Cultural Organization (UNESCO, 1946–52) and was elected chairman of its executive board (1948–49). From 1949 to 1952, Nehru appointed Radhakrishnan as the ambassador to the Soviet Union, India's second ambassador to Moscow. When Stalin finally agreed to meet him in January 1950, he was impressed with the philosopher-ambassador of India. It should be noted Stalin had not received Radhakrishnan's predecessor even once! During their meeting, Radhakrishnan answered Stalin's questions (why Ceylon was not a part of India, whether India still employed British officers in its army and navy) before suggesting that the USSR take the initiative to end the Cold War. Stalin answered by saying that it takes two hands to clap and that there was another side responsible for the Cold War too. Radhakrishnan replied with a sentence that left Stalin at a loss for words. "As a peace-loving country, the Soviet Union should withdraw its own hand as it takes two hands to clap." When he was returning to India, Joseph Stalin commented: "You are the first person to treat me as a human being and not as a monster. You are leaving us and I am sad, I want you to live long."

Radhakrishnan possibly saw the fallibility in a human being, however powerful he might be and should be treated as a human, which reminds us why some lawyers defend the indefensible. One of his quotes is: "The worst sinner has a future, even as the greatest saint has had a past." On his return to India in 1952, he was elected the Vice President. During his vice-presidency, his reputation was firmly established as a spiritualist and philosopher, too. Jan Myrdal, the 'enfant terrible' of Sweden, poet, political columnist and art critic, writes about him in his book *India Waits*, a travelogue that documents and interprets the human details of contemporary reality: "In the newspapers, I read that the Vice President said what we had expected him to say. Vice President Emphasizes Spiritual Values: Dr Radhakrishnan quoted the Upanishads and stressed that the amassing of wealth must not be the goal of human labour. He has recently visited Holland, Germany and Hungary, and the leaders of these countries had *confessed* to him with *uncommon unanimity* that their people were better off than ever but were not at all happy. *This proves that man needs more than just material well-being.*"

As the Vice President of India, he had come to aid the Indian foreign policy, especially with China, when Prime Minister Nehru found Mao in China intractable and antagonistic. Ramachandra Guha writes, "In 1960, Chinese Prime Minister Chou En-Lai spent a week in New Delhi, meeting Nehru every day, with and without aides. A photograph reproduced in the Indian Express after the second day of the talks suggested that they were not going well. It showed Chou raising a toast to Sino-Indian friendship, by clinking his glass with Mrs Indira Gandhi's. Mrs Gandhi was stylishly dressed, in a sari, but was looking quizzically across to her father. On the other side of the table stood Nehru, capless, drinking deeply and glumly from a wine glass while avoiding Chou En-Lai's gaze. The only Indian showing any interest at all was the vice-president, S. Radhakrishnan, seen reaching across to clink his glass with Chou's." Guha writes that along with G. B. Pant, he complained to Chou, 'more in sorrow than in anger, of China's lack of appreciation for all India had done to gain its communist government legitimacy in the eyes of the world.'

While India's internal boundaries shifted and solidified, new states blossoming and territories finding their place, Radhakrishnan emerged as a guiding hand. He navigated domestic complexities, filling diplomatic gaps when Prime Minister Nehru could not tread. Nagaland's 1963 inauguration in 1963 is one such example. With Nehru hesitant, Radhakrishnan stepped in, offering a calming presence. This reassuring voice served India equally well during external conflicts, bolstering national spirit during wars with Pakistan and China as the nation safeguarded its territory.

Presidential Years: 1962-1967

With the explicit support of Prime Minister Nehru, after the retirement of Dr. Rajendra Prasad as the President of India, Vice President Dr S. Radhakrishnan won the 1962 presidential elections by an overwhelming majority. On his appointment, Bertrand Russell, a famous philosopher said, "It is an honour to the philosophy that Radhakrishnan should be the President of India, and I, as a philosopher, take special pleasure in this." Because even in the USA and UK, no philosopher had the opportunity to become the Head of the State. Plato stressed and inspired philosophers to become kings. It is a tribute to India that she should make a philosopher her President.

At the invitation of President Kennedy, USA, in 1963, Dr Sarvepalli Radhakrishnan, President of the Republic of India, paid a state visit. President Kennedy admiringly remarked about their first encounter, "The president is a noted philosopher. When I commented on the weather this morning, he said, we cannot always control events, but we can always control our attitude towards events. This is only the beginning I'm sure, president, of a good deal of the wisdom that we will derive from your visit so that I know that I speak on behalf of all of my countrymen in welcoming the distinguished president of a great country to the shores of the United States."

The striking outward personality of Radhakrishnan was that he 'never concealed his own Indian identity while he visited foreign countries and this made him an ideal President. His personality reflected different sides of his nature-physical, intellectual, moral and spiritual. As the President of the nascent Indian republic, Radhakrishnan administered oath of office to Prime Ministers four times between 13 May 1962, 13 May 1967 beginning with the demise of Jawaharlal Nehru. It was not an easy period for the young country, which saw some of the biggest challenges to India's integrity.

During this period, he saw the deaths of two Prime Ministers, Nehru in 1964 and Lal Bahadur Shastri in 1966. On both these occasions, he administered the oath of office to Bharat Ratna Gulzarilal Nanda, in 1997, as interim Prime Minister of India for two 13-day tenures. On Shastri's death, he administered an oath of office to India Gandhi as the Prime Minister of India.

Dr Radhakrishnan's presidency coincided with pivotal moments in India's history. While wars with China and Pakistan posed immediate threats, the loss of Nehru and Shastri added to the national anxieties. Yet, under his leadership, India witnessed smooth transitions of government and remained firmly committed to democracy. His neutral stance, respect for the Constitution, and ability to bridge divides proved crucial in steering the nation through uncharted waters, a young democracy with a diverse parliament representing a newly independent nation. Unifying a young nation riddled with fault lines – caste, creed, region, religion, language, ideology – was Radhakrishnan's monumental task. With unwavering faith in the people, he championed democracy as both a spiritual duty and a political system. His tenure as President saw him navigate these tumultuous times with the combined wisdom of philosopher, statesman, and sage. His intellect, dignity, and warmth embodied his philosophy – one must reach peaks of achievement, but true fulfilment lies in returning to the embrace of society.

Having fulfilled his commitment to a full term as President, Radhakrishnan, in 1967, chose to retire from public life, much to the admiration of those who longed for yet another term. He said, "Left to myself, I wish to get out of the present office." He showed disinterest in another term and paved the way for Dr Zakir Hussain, who was then the Vice-President of India, as the Congress nominee for the Presidency of India.

To this day, he is one of the best-liked public figures of his time across the country.

The Farewell to Sarvepalli Radhakrishnan

Radhakrishnan, born in 1888 in Tiruttani, returned to his storeyed art deco residence Girija, in Madras (now Chennai) in 1967. Though retired, he continued writing through the 1960s. However, declining health, marked by a stroke and a hip fracture in the 1970s, confined him to bed. Yet, the music of Carnatic tradition remained a source of comfort and serenity in his final years.

In 1975, Dr Radhakrishnan was awarded the Templeton Prize, established in 1972. The prize was a philanthropic initiative of Sir John Templeton, who wanted to recognize discoveries that yielded new insights about religion, and he set the award amount above that of the Nobel Prizes in order to recognize the importance of what he called 'progress in religion'. Radhakrishnan was awarded the Templeton Prize 'for his vital contributions to bridging the understanding between cultures and religions of the Eastern and Western hemispheres. In coming to their conclusion, the Templeton Prize judges decided that he 'led the rediscovery of the understanding of God and his contributions to modern Hinduism is one of the most outstanding features in world religion today.'

Due to his age and illness, he was not able to attend the Prize ceremony held in London's Guildhall with HRH Prince Philip, Duke of Edinburgh, who then was presiding over it. The award was accepted by The Indian High Commissioner Shri B. K. Nehru on his behalf. Unable to speak at that time, Radhakrishnan gladly expressed his feelings with a broad smile. The Bharat Ratna Vice President of India, peacefully passed away in Chennai (then Madras) on 17 April 1975 at the age of 86. The philosopher, who was called upon to serve the country, balanced religion and politics. He revealed throughout his life that dharma, spirituality and democracy are important in life, especially in politics.

The Treasure of the Country: Democracy

Radhakrishnan envisioned a world united by 'Vasudhaiva Kutumbakam' where humanity transcended borders and divisions to stand as one family. This universal connection, he believed, held the key to eradicating conflict and inequality. In the realm of politics, he stood firmly against superstition and irrationality, embracing a rationalist approach. For him, the future of independent India lay in a robust democracy, one that offered every citizen the chance to flourish and express their individuality. His interpretation of democracy, bold and inclusive, might have raised eyebrows at the time, but he saw it as essential for granting legitimacy and stability to a fledgling nation. He believed that national symbols and emblems should serve as constant reminders of this core message.

Democracy in India affords opportunities for all, he reckoned. He called upon India that it should persevere to create opportunities for the betterment of one's soul, spirit, and individuality: betterment of oneself. He looked at politics through religion and regarded democracy as the highest religion as it guaranteed liberty of thought and freedom of conscience to every citizen. He said," I am a great believer in democracy, not because it is a fine political arrangement but because it is the highest religion." He asserted that the freedom of the individual should never be suppressed. In a society, the individual should be able to develop his mind and spirit.

As the Vice President and President, he never bowed in front of narrow-minded politicians albeit never developed any political philosophy but gave utmost importance to individual liberty. He believed in economic betterment and equality in social status for all in democracy, which should be a way of life. Addressing the convocation ceremony of Karnataka University, Radhakrishnan stressed that the teachers and students form a family and in a family, one cannot have the spirit of a trade union. He urged, "We must strive to become democratic not merely in the political sense of the term but also the social and economic sense. It is essential to bring about this democratic change, this democratic temper, this kind of outlook by a proper study of the humanities including philosophy and religion."

Dharma: The Enduring Legacy

Dharma is the refrain of Indian philosophy and democracy is the melody of Indian citizenry. Both dharma and democracy form the collective leitmotif of the young social democratic republic of the world rooted in more than two millennia-old civilisation. But the competitive melody of the country is democracy. Together, dharma and democracy form the quintessential soul of the country since independence.

Dharma is indeed one of the directly untranslatable Indian words rooted in Sanskrit, Prakrit, Pali and Dravidian languages foundational to

Hinduism, Buddhism and Jainism and loaded with multiple meanings relatable to codes of human conduct. It means the eternal and inherent nature of reality, cosmic law underlying right behaviour and social order, universal truth, universal law, righteousness, law, doctrine, teaching, truth, duty, natural law, social duties, and good qualities that are the constituent elements of all existence. Dharma enables one to overcome *duḥkha* and escape from the cyclic existence of samsara. Dharma the moral values-righteousness is one of the P*urusharthas,* the four goals of a human life among *Artha, Kama* and *Moksha.* However, *Dharma* is considered more important than Artha or Kama, which are obtainable by upholding Dharma, which could lead to *Moksha,* the ultimate goal of human life.

Sanatana Dharma signifies the everlasting set of ethical duties and spiritual practices expected of all, regardless of background or belief. Honesty, non-violence, purity, kindness, compassion, patience, self-control, generosity, and self-discipline are among its core values.

The term has also more recently been used by Hindu leaders, reformers, and nationalists to refer to Hinduism as a unified world religion. *Sanatana dharma* has thus become a synonym for the "eternal" truth and teachings of Hinduism, the latter conceived of as not only transcendent of history and unchanging but also as indivisible and ultimately non-sectarian.

What is Indian philosophy? Is Indian philosophy Hindu or Vedic philosophy? Is Indian philosophy a syncretisation of Hinduism, Buddhism, and Jainism? Or something more, Islam and Christianity? The answer to this could be one word that underlies all religions: righteousness: dharma, both abstract and concrete, the eternal and inherent nature of reality, cosmic law underlying right behaviour and social order, universal truth. He said:

"Dharma is to be performed by all of us", he said, quoting the Sanskrit aphorism in the *Mahāsubhāṣitasaṃgraha: Anityani sarirani vibhavo naiva sasvatah | nityam samnihito mrtyuh kartavyo dharmasamgrahah ||* (Our bodies are perishable, wealth is not at all permanent and death is always nearby. Therefore, we must engage in acts of merit, good conduct.)

'Performing dharma' became Radhakrishnan's clarion call, a potent mantra devoid of religious dogma. He envisioned dharma and democracy as a luminous tapestry, woven with threads of service and empathy, stretching beyond any single faith. This, he believed, was the spirit that would weave India's socialist democratic future into a vibrant, inclusive reality. "Dharma is helping others, and adharma is causing harm. It's that simple. Why elaborate with volumes of books? If you understand that hurting is wrong and bringing joy is right, then you are on the path of dharma." stressed Radhakrishnan. Dharma and democracy sans religious connotations have universal appeal and form the leitmotif of socialistic democratic India.

References

1. Agarwal, D. (2016). Words To Live By: The Best of Indian Non-fiction for Children. Hachette India.
2. Are we aware of the true significance of the tricolour? (2015). The Times of India. [online] 28 Sep. Available at: https://timesofindia.indiatimes.com/india/are-we-aware-of-the-true significance-of-the-tricolour/articleshow/49131112.
3. Encyclopedia Britannica. (n.d.). Sarvepalli Radhakrishnan | president of India. [online] Available at: https://www.britannica.com/biography/Sarvepalli-Radhakrishnan.
4. Films Division (2020). Sarvepalli Radhakrishnan - President of India. YouTube. Available at: https://www.youtube.com/watch?v=NUJ24KuSh8Y [Accessed 20 May 2022].
5. Free Press Journal. (n.d.). Sarvepalli Radhakrishnan, Philosopher & Scholar; Know Unknown Facts Here on His Birth Anniversary. [online] Available at: ttps://www.freepressjournal.in/education/sarvepalli-radhakrishnan-philoshper-scholar-know-unknown-facts-here-on-his-birth-anniversary [Accessed 1 Dec. 2023].
6. Guha, R. (2017). India After Gandhi: The History of the World's Largest Democracy. Pan Macmillan.
7. Hindustan Times. (2020). Importance, Significance, And History Of Teachers' Day. [online] Available at: https://www.hindustantimes.com/more-lifestyle/teachers-day-2020-importance-significance-and-history-of-teachers-day/story-eIOH8135uPLNKE7xdV1RAP.html [Accessed 15 Dec. 2023].
8. India Today. (n.d.). How S Radhakrishnan managed to win 1962 presidential elections with Nehru's support. [online] Available at: https://www.indiatoday.in/fyi/story/1962-elections-sarvepalli-radhakrishnan-president-nehru-1023593-2017-07-11 [Accessed 15 Dec. 2023].
9. Lakshman, N. (n.d.). 'Indira played politics with the ease of a sleepwalker'. [online] Rediff. Available at: https://www.rediff.com/news/interview/she-played-politics-with-the-ease-of-a-sleepwalker/20170713.htm [Accessed 15 Dec. 2023].
10. Myrdal, Jan. (1980). INDIA WAITS. P. A. Norstedt and Soners, Stockholm, Sweden and English edition published 1984 by Sangam Books (India) Pvt Ltd, Madras (Chennai), India.

11. Pal, S. (2017). Remembering Dr. Radhakrishnan: 8 Little-Known Facts About India's Legendary Teacher and Philosopher President. [online] The Better India. Available at: https://www.thebetterindia.com/114184/sarvepalli-radhakrishnan-teacher-day-philosopher-president-india/ [Accessed 12 Dec. 2023].
12. Radhakrishnan, S. and JSTOR (1914). The Ethics of the Vedanta. [online] Internet Archive. International Journal of Ethics. Available at: https://archive.org/stream/jstor-2376505/2376505_djvu.txt [Accessed 17 Dec. 2023].
13. Tribune, I.H. (2017). 1967: Mrs. Gandhi Is Hit in the Face by a Rock. [online] IHT Retrospective Blog.
14. Available at: https://archive.nytimes.com/iht-retrospective.blogs.nytimes.com/2017/02/08/1967-mrs-gandhi-is-hit-in-the-face-by-a-rock/ [Accessed 11 Dec. 2023].
15. www.cse.iitk.ac.in. (n.d.). Book Excerpts: Indian Philosophy, Volume 1 by Sarvepalli Radhakrishnan. [online] Available at:
16. https://www.cse.iitk.ac.in/users/amit/books/radhakrishnan-1931-indian-philosophy-volume-v1.html [Accessed 17 Dec. 2023].
17. www5.open.ac.uk. (n.d.). Sarvepalli Radhakrishnan | Making Britain. [online] Available at: https://www5.open.ac.uk/research-projects/making-britain/content/sarvepalli-radhakrishnan [Accessed 9 Dec. 2023].
18. www.unesco.org. (n.d.). World Teachers' Day | UNESCO. [online] Available at: https://www.unesco.org/en/days/teachers.
19. www.youtube.com. (n.d.). Documentary on Dr. Sarvepalli Radhakrishnan. [online] Available at: https://www.youtube.com/watch?v=UjwhXOqfBJY [Accessed 15 Dec. 2023].
20. www.youtube.com. (n.d.). Dr Sarvepalli Radhakrishnan's speech at prize distribution function of National awards to Teachers. [online] Available at:
21. https://www.youtube.com/watch?v=IGBHeUx97cQ [Accessed 15 Dec. 2023].

Dr. S. Radhakrishnan: An Educationist Philosopher whose Thoughts Guided the Indian Education Sector

Sunil Shukla
Vidhy Shethna

Introduction

Dr. Sarvepalli Radhakrishnan (1888-1975) was a prominent Indian scholar, philosopher, and statesman who influenced academic circles during the 20th century. He has contributed immensely to the education sector and Indian philosophy. He was particularly well-known for his thoughtful and nuanced criticism of the philosophical theories of Western intellects. He introduced Indian philosophy and culture to the Western world, bringing Eastern and Western ideas together. Dr. Sarvepalli Radhakrishnan passionately advocated the education of youth and women, for the complete development of society. His extensive writing career and influential speeches have shaped societal thoughts towards progression. The sociological, political, economic, and cultural concerns of the nation motivated him to transform his theoretical ideas into useful teaching strategies.

This article explores Dr. Radhakrishnan's early life, educational path, and important contributions he made in the education sector and during India's freedom struggle. No other academician with a worldly reputation advocated the British to end colonialism as eloquently as he did. The article illuminates his futuristic vision for a freed India and his enormous focus on strengthening the country's educational system. Besides, his role as a philosopher-educationist is examined thoroughly covering a broad range of dimensions such as notable positions held, key thoughts and impactful contributions in the education domain.

A special emphasis is placed on Banaras Hindu University where Dr. Radhakrishnan's educational theories were put into practice which eventually led to the growth and prosperity of the University. He not only embraced Malaviya's vision of a University but he also saved it from crises in adverse times. His tenure as Vice-chancellor is credited with stellar work that reduced financial burden and increased student and faculty strength of the University. The article delves into Dr. Radhakrishnan's extensive influence on the educational policies of India, illuminating his expectations for the country's educational landscape. His clarity of thought in drafting the commission's report in 1950 still finds relevance in today's educational scenario. The unfolding of the University Commission Report 1950 is a walk through his model of the Indian Education system which encompasses topics such as aims of university education, inclusive and affordable education for all, women's education, professional education, students' welfare activities and programs, etc. The article then sheds light on how his teachings were adopted by many, highlighting the long-lasting impact of Dr. S. Radhakrishnan on Indian education. The last segment of the article is about the committees formed to reflect upon the educational scenario of the country and the emergence of National Education Policies. Although influences were drawn from several committees, the philosophical views and ideas of Dr. Sarvepalli remained central to the policy landscape of India.

Dr. Radhakrishnan's Early Years, Education and Training

Dr. Sarvepalli was born in a modest Telegu-speaking Niyogi Brahmin family on September 5, 1888, in Thiruttani, Madras (now Tamil Nadu). His father, Sarvepalli Veeraswami, was a subordinate revenue officer and his mother, Sarvepalli Sitamma was a homemaker. The religious culture of Tiruttani and his parents' strong inclination towards Hinduism, had a profound and enduring influence on young Radhakrishnan. It shaped his entire perspective and outlook on life. He demonstrated an early aptitude for learning which gradually led him to enroll for schooling. Dr. Radhakrishnan graduated from Madras Christian College with honours in philosophy. Later, he acquired his post-graduation in 1908. His academic excellence was marked by his voracious reading habits. Throughout his academic journey, he was awarded several scholarships which fully supported his higher studies. His thesis titled, 'The Ethics of the Vedanta and its Metaphysical Presuppositions', was published when he was just 20 years old (Murty & Vohra, 1990). Throughout his life, he never let poverty come as an excuse in the way of his achievements. Instead, he embraced a resilient and enterprising mindset of overcoming obstacles. He was a firm believer in the idea that success is measured by how one utilizes the resources, regardless of the circumstances of the origin. He tutored to sustain himself and leveraged his knowledge and skills to meet his financial needs.

Dr. Radhakrishnan's academic career started with an impressive array of accomplishments. He began teaching as an assistant professor at Madras Presidency College in 1909. Later in the year 1918, he was promoted to a greater designation and was awarded a full-time professorship in Indian philosophy at Maharaja's college. Dr. Radhakrishnan made a lasting contribution to academia by publishing academic works in prestigious journals. In 1921, Dr. Radhakrishnan took up King George V's Chair of Mental and Moral Science. Throughout the 1920s, Dr. Radhakrishnan's academic reputation remained prolific and gained more traction in India and beyond (Deshpande, 2016). His book, "An Idealist View of Life" is regarded as Dr. Radhakrishnan's most outstanding, stellar and mature work. It garnered significant scholarly attention and solidified his status as a well-known thinker. His influence started gaining momentum internationally. His lectures transformed the perceptions of Western intellects about Indian Philosophy. Besides academia, he served as an Indian ambassador to UNESCO, networking a diplomatic bridge between the nations. In late 1939, Dr. Radhakrishnan began his vice chancellorship at Banaras Hindu University (BHU).

After a fulfilling academic career, Dr. Radhakrishnan began his political career. His influence in foreign countries got him involved in politics. In the years that followed independence, he served as a member of the Indian Constituent Assembly for two years. He was able to implement his political and philosophical convictions after being elected to Rajya Sabha. In 1952, he was appointed as India's first Vice-President which he served for two terms and in 1962, he became the nation's second President. Renowned philosopher Bert Russell responded by stating that it was an honour to philosophy worldwide that the great Republic of India chose him for the position of its President. He was conferred with many awards and recognitions for his stellar contribution to the field of academics and politics (Figure 1). Almost all of his books gained significant traction worldwide. His all-time renowned books include Indian Philosophy, The Philosophy of Upanishads, Eastern Religions and Western Thoughts. His book 'An Idealist View of Life' popularized him as a very powerful and influential writer.

AWARDS & HONORS of Dr. Sarvepalli Radhakrishnan

Figure 1: Awards and Honors of Dr. Radhakrishnan

Carrying Malaviya's Legacy and Vision for Bhu

Upon assuming the leadership as the second Vice-Chancellor in 1939 after Malaviya, Dr. Radhakrishnan ensured a seamless transition into the role. He played an impressive role in upholding and advancing the legacy of Shri Madan Mohan Malaviya. In the times when the institution faced financial crises, he took several initiatives to save it from closing. This led to the growth of the institution. At the outbreak of World War II, he was restricted from visiting Oxford so he devoted his time productively to assess the financial problems of the university. He evaluated the reports and attributed the shortfalls to unplanned expenses. As a long-term remedy, he suggested abstaining from expenses that required further funding unless those were supported by specific donations. Due to the strict control over spending, the university's income account for the 1940–1941 fiscal years had a surplus, a first in its history. Additionally, he started a fundraising effort that led to the collection of four lakh rupees by April 1941 (Murthy & Vohra, 1990). This move helped to clear the existing overdraft and marked his unwavering commitment to achieving economic stability for the University.

Dr. Radhakrishnan also integrated his educational philosophy into the administration of the BHU. He stressed the holistic development of individuals and hence placed significant importance on developing intellectual growth along with moral values. He successfully integrated Indian philosophical traditions into the education framework. This resulted in a profound understanding of the nation's rich culture and spiritual heritage among students.

After assuming the mantle of Vice-Chancellor, he ensured that Malaviya's vision for the institution was carried out seamlessly. He reflected the spirit of a true Hindu through his lectures, a quality that Malaviya was fully aware of and impressed with. He had also gained popularity among the students of BHU. Besides, he showcased unwavering patriotism and was a strong supporter of Indian nationalism, the right to self-rule and Gandhian philosophy. He was quite familiar with Banaras Hindu University because of his honorary professorship in philosophy. He joined the university's senate, a well-known body of people tasked with setting the direction of the institution. He was an integral member of the University's decision-making processes. In 1928, he was elected to the university's court to supervise its operations. At the university's twenty-first convocation, he was awarded an honorary Doctor of Laws where he also gave a memorable speech on "Religion and Politics." Because of this extended affiliation, he was well-versed in the academic and administrative structures of the university and had a thorough awareness of its difficulties. He was more than just a professor at BHU. Besides, his proven record as a Vice-Chancellor of Andhra University testified to his fun-raising abilities. He played an active role in core committees that made decisions. During the war, he not only prevented the institution from closing permanently, but he also restored its finances. In the year 1939, when he took over the office, the overdraft was Rs. 13,43,548 and on April 1, 1947, it had reduced to Rs. 7,54,485. Besides his dedicated efforts in the developmental activities of the University, he also introduced new subjects like Engineering, Technology, Ayurveda and Commerce and ensured physical education was also incorporated into the curriculum. During this time, the number of students rose from 3,603 to 5,233, and many new faculties joined the university. He was also given particular appreciation for his work at a grand ceremony at the University. It's interesting to note that Gandhiji himself recommended Malaviya to consider Dr. Radhakrishnan for the vice-chancellorship at Banaras Hindu University (Murthy & Vohra, 1990).

After resigning from BHU, Dr. Radhakrishnan took up the position of chairman of the University Education Commission. The report of the 'University Education Commission 1948-49' provided great insight into what Indian leaders and esteemed thinkers foresighted about University Education at the time of Independence. The report had a whole chapter dedicated to 'The Aims of University Education and Religious Education'. The Commission's 1950 Report functioned as a thorough assessment of the current condition of higher education in India and provided recommendations for improving it in the newly formed India. Even though the report had been jointly written by many people, Dr. Radhakrishnan's unique influence was most apparent in the chapters that addressed The Aims of University Education and Religious Education (Deshpande, 2016). These important components of the report were greatly influenced by his visionary thoughts and insights, which demonstrated his unwavering dedication to the progress of education in the post-independence age.

The Future Education of India: Reflecting Upon the Indian Model of Education

The British form of education introduced by Lord Thomas Babington Macaulay irked Dr. Radhakrishnan and many prominent scholars of India as they had minimalized traditional Indian education. The introduction of mass and modern education along with an excessive emphasis on the English language gradually killed all four periods of Indian education and ushered in the 'rat race' format of an education system. Soon enough the Indian government realized the shifting focus from prominent subjects like mathematics and science to English language in the curriculum. To address the situation of crisis, many commissions were formed and among them, the first was the University Education Commission chaired by Dr. Radhakrishnan Sarvepalli in 1948-49. His idea of the Indian education system was based upon a model that moved away from the British structure. Acknowledging the linguistic diversity within the country, he advocated for education to be in vernacular languages to make it more accessible across the regions of India. Besides, his model promoted technological advancements balanced by a creative, spiritual and philosophical approach. The entire report is divided into 18 sectors spanning topics such as "Professional Education"(115), "Engineering and technology"(145), "New Professions"(186), "Women's Education"(270), "Finance"(302), "Rural Universities"(387). The report highlights his goal of broadening the educational landscape. His thoughts reflected the new educational dream of post-independence India. He stressed imparting professional education aimed at skilling the youth across diverse sectors such as agriculture, engineering, technology, commerce, law and medicine. He was committed to driving a shift from traditional commerce courses to the delivery of professional business education. He pressed upon preparing individuals to practice high-quality business administration. He criticized the traditional focus on improving only craftsmanship and promoted the holistic development of individuals through proper business understanding. Besides, the report also reflected his commitment to widening the scope of education across the economic and social sections, irrespective of the gender and religion of people. He was a firm believer and promoter of gender equality.

The report offers his perspective on the significance of women's education. The section on 'Primacy of Woman Education' emphasizes striking a balance between men and women by encouraging women's education. He advocated that educational opportunities for women should not be limited, but rather increased significantly. Women should be provided intellectual support and guidance to lead them to reflect upon their educational interests. Besides empowering women through education, he also reflected a deep interest in developing rural universities. He had immense faith in the potential of the rural youth of India. He believed that educating rural India would remove social and economic disparity and enable the youth to hone their skills and develop expertise. The report also stated the key responsibilities of an educational university. He considered university as the place for the creation of knowledge, training of minds and driving radical shifts. He believed that it is the responsibility of a university to show new paths nurture the minds of the students and promote freedom of thought to think independently and coherently (Rodrigues, 1992). He wished for universities to be a repository of culture and pressed upon members to bind cohesively. He believed if the culture is alive, it will be able to respond to challenges in unity. A university must advocate the involvement of intellectual individuals and seek guidance from scientists, poets, artists and inventors who are great at driving societal changes. He considered the purpose of education to extend beyond providing facts that aimed at awakening innate abilities and nurturing minds with knowledge and wisdom. The educational university must cultivate humane relationships, create social harmony, promote leadership and proper administration and foster an environment full of justice, liberty and equality in education (Murthy, Vohra 1990). To him, one of the main goals of university education is to prepare students for leadership roles in the workplace and public life. This goal is difficult to achieve but essential for advancing society. He pressed universities to become more socially conscious, prioritizing character and personality development over quantity. He laid immense importance on the quality of education. Dr. Radhakrishnan regarded teaching and research as complementary pursuits. He believed that in the void or lack of anyone, there would be a dearth of well-trained students. Unlike those who regarded imparting intellectual excellence as the primary role of universities, Dr. Radhakrishnan advocated building a character of disciplined intellect, will, integrity, vision and courage (Rodrigues, 1992). The Report 1950 also emphasized instilling a basic set of values, passing along cultural heritage, and creating a unifying force in young people. He resisted over-specialization in places where the focus is only on specialization without imparting holistic knowledge. He believed that other aspects of international affairs which include the origins and evolution of other civilizations, the relationship between nationalism and internationalism, the causes of conflicts and how the world functions, should be studied in universities.

The 1930's and 1940's

During these years, the escalating tensions around the question of nationalism caught Dr. Radhakrsishnan's attention. The rise of the Hindu Mahasabha further intensified the communal differences he had witnessed in the 1920s. Along with that, Muhammad Iqbal's poetic vision of 1930 encouraged Muslim self-assertion and provided Muhammad Jinnah with an ideological platform to advocate for an independent Pakistan. Early in

1930, in London, this sentiment was also acknowledged during the Round Table Conferences. Additionally, The Government of India Act of 1935 brought more political complexity and widened the already existing rifts between rival factions while promising increased self-government.

The intertwined issues of education and nationalism became the most central to Dr. Sarvepalli. He advocated that the most responsible and realistic way to create Indian unity and a distinct national vision was through university education that promotes the full development of individuals. In his many speeches about an independent India in the 1930s and 1940s, Dr. Radhakrishnan pictured a country moulded and directed by people who were educated, had a vision for the future, and was dedicated to raising Indian consciousness (Murthy & Vohra, 1990).

Dr. Radhakrishnan became more and more involved in Indian politics and global issues in the years after Indian independence. The last few years of the 1940s were extremely critical. Serving on the Executive Board of the newly formed United Nations Educational, Scientific, and Cultural Organization (UNESCO) as well as heading the Indian delegation from 1946 to 1951, Dr. Radhakrishnan was tirelessly working. In addition, he was a member of the Indian Constituent Assembly during the two years that followed India's independence. He expressed strong criticism towards organizations like the League of Nations which had the potential to exert divisions and exhibited dominance. He rather promoted, 'creative internationalization', which is formed on the grounds of spiritual principles. This approach suggested the connection of nations beyond political and economic interests. He believed that true international cooperation can be achieved only by developing understanding between nations and fostering a deeper level of compassion.

After India attained its independence and citizens recovered from the immediate aftermath of the division, a determined attempt was made to improve the educational system in India. Acknowledging its critical role in the advancement of the economy and the general populace, the government established the University Education Commission in December 1948. The commission headed by Dr. Radhakrishnan and other eminent educators, toiled hard to improve higher education in India. Dr. Radhakrishnan led the commission to expeditiously submit its findings in August 1949. The committee report outlined that education should lead people from darkness to light and free them from all forms of oppression.

The content of teaching must lay thrust on three things how- we relate to values or the spiritual realm, how we relate to people or society, and how we relate to things or nature. Further, the report called for education as an equal right for all to access regardless of race, religion, sex, occupation and economic status. The report also recommended closer cooperation among the educational institutions keeping in view diverse cultures. In the case of providing government grants to the universities, the report strongly asserted granting full autonomy on educational policies, thereby keeping state grants and state control separate. This report left an indelible mark on the trajectory of higher education in the country.

Contributions to the Indian Education System

As a philosopher educationist, Dr. Rashakrishnan reflected his key thoughts on several aspects of life. He stressed the value of education that takes into account students' intellectual, moral, and spiritual growth as well as their development in totality. And hence, he laid immense focus on the quality of education. He would accredit teachers with the responsibility of ensuring that education remains diverse, holistic and inclusive, irrespective of student's background. He promoted teaching in vernacular languages for the smooth delivery of knowledge, contributing to inclusivity. He also worked towards fostering cross-cultural exchange and educational collaboration by setting up the Indian Council for Cultural Relations. Additionally, he encouraged open distance learning programs to reduce barriers to education, especially for those who faced socio-economic challenges. His philosophical beliefs in the education domain influenced scholars to devise policies that prioritized well-rounded and inclusive education that goes beyond mere academics. In addition, he believed that philosophy was the guiding principle that needed to be smoothly incorporated into teaching methods. He saw education as a tool for developing a moral character that aimed to raise people with a strong sense of social responsibility. He also underlined the importance of integrating spiritual values the way it is rooted in Advaita Vedanta. He made a strong case for universities' autonomy so they could maintain academic policies and carry out educational practices free from state control. While fervently promoting educational equality, he advocated voraciously for the equality of education and assistance to the backward communities. Dr. Radhakrishnan distinctively characterized philosophy as the logical exploration of ultimate reality and also captured it in the phrase, "दर्शन यथार्थ के स्वरूप की तार्किक विवेचना है" (Mishra & Shresth, 2022) i.e. Philosophy is the logical inquiry into the nature of reality. This phrase revolved as a cornerstone to his philosophy wherein he asserted that "Education should be men making and society making". He emphasized the potential of holistic youth development. Driven by this determination that a nation's progress depends on the quality of education it delivers, he highlighted the influence of the state's ideology on education outcomes. He asserted that complete education must be humane covering aspects such as intellectual training, discipline and heart refinement as these reflect the true nature of holistic education (Majumdar, 2021). The National Education Policy 2020 echoes Dr. Radhakrishnan's ideas on spiritual, democratic, constitutional, value and character development as a key to achieving economic and intellectual goals.

Dr. Radhakrishnan and Education Policies of India

Dr. Sarvepalli Radhakrishnan has been a great influence on Indian Education Policies. As the second president of India and a great philosopher, his focus was always on the holistic development of individuals. He had always advocated for an education system that included the refinement of hearts and discipline of spirit. As a strong Indian philosopher, his principles were guided by Adwait Vedant, and hence, the main aim of education is to raise one's spirit to find the ultimate truth of the world (Mohanty, 2021). He has not set down specific guidelines but certain ideas stressed his work. For instance, he regarded a considerable amount of importance in establishing a strong connection between the teacher and the students. He attributed the role of a teacher as a gadfly who facilitates discussions and tutors at the undergraduate level and seminars at the post-graduate level. He believed the success of educational processes depends upon the teacher for it is a teacher who implements the aims and builds the character of a student. He would say, "At the bottom, the quality of a university is always in direct proportion to the quality of its teachers" (Rodrigues, 1992). It is impossible to achieve the goals of intellectual, industrial, technological, and economic growth without providing students with a rich education that instils morality, democracy, spirituality, and good character (Mishra & Shresth, 2022). Dr. Radhakrishnan provided an appropriate road map for accomplishing these objectives in the University Education Commission's 1948–1949 draft. In the University Education Commission draft, Dr. Sarvepalli Radhakrishnan stated that moral, religious, and spiritual development should not be overlooked while focusing on technological advances. Without these, education isn't complete.

Besides, Dr. Radhakrishnan was a fervent supporter of universal free and compulsory education for all children, regardless of gender, caste, creed, or socioeconomic background. He placed a strong emphasis on education's role in children's complete development. In addition, he encouraged the inclusion of the teaching subjects like languages, mathematics, literature, grammar, geography, history, philosophy, and religion. In his view, games are essential for a child's social and physical development, and physical education, yoga, and other activities like tree planting, NCC (National Cadet Crops), NSS (National Service Schemes), and related social welfare initiatives should be included in the curriculum. This is highlighted in the National Education Policy-2020 document as well. The fundamentals of the NEP 2020 are in line with his long cry for free and compulsory education for all students, irrespective of socioeconomic status.

Dr. Radhakrishnan's progressive perspective on Indian education stresses a method that goes beyond only providing intellectual training, based on preconceived beliefs. In his opinion, education should be a transformative process that feeds individuals' souls and hearts in addition to their minds. His theoretical framework holds that compassion and humanity are integral parts of a holistic education. Character development and the instillation of principles should be prioritized while delivering education. His view of education extends beyond merely getting students ready for jobs. Instead, he believed that education helps people live meaningful lives and have a constructive social influence. He recommended vocational training at the secondary and university levels as he held that preparation of livelihood meant preparation for life (Rodrigues, 1992). In some works, he has mentioned professional education where the stress was upon disciplined scholarship and services besides profit. Professional education entails a sense of social responsibility and respect for moral values which is in addition to gaining knowledge and skills. According to Dr. Radhakrishnan, education should be the guide for individual development and the advancement of society as a whole (Mohanty, 2021).

Dr. Radhakrishnan was more likely to endorse educational policies that supported a well-rounded curriculum, given his emphasis on holistic development. To him, an educational curriculum must cover cultural, ethical, and physical education in addition to the standard academic disciplines. Such a thorough approach is consistent with his view that education ought to address the various facets of human development. Creating responsible, empathetic, and inquisitive people was at the centre of Dr. Radhakrishnan's vision for education in the future. He believed people trained in this manner would make significant contributions to the advancement of both the country and the international community because they would have received a well-rounded education. His ideas provide direction for an educational model that goes beyond the acquisition of knowledge to produce people who are both personally and socially conscious.

Inspiring thoughts and Indian Education System

The revolutionary ideologies of Dr. Sarvepalli Radhakrishnan served as an inspiration for many visionary leaders to lay a strong foundation for the Indian educational system. There were 20 Universities and 500 Affiliated Colleges in India at the time of Independence. The Commission 1948-49 recommended the setup of the University Grants Commission (UGC) followed by which the Secondary Education Commission (1952), the National Policy on Education (1986) and other allied commissions were established. These were all set for formulating plans in higher education. Serving as the nation's first Minister of Education, Maulana Abul Kalam Azad played a significant role in shaping the educational framework of independent India. The establishment of the University Grants Commission (UGC) was greatly aided by Azad's efforts. It is committed to providing high-quality education and aligns with Dr. Radhakrishnan's aim of maintaining a high and excellent standard for education. The Kothari Commission was established in 1964. The Commission headed by D.S. Kothari (1964–1966) set out to conduct a comprehensive evaluation of the country's educational system. Among many topics covered by the commission, the creation of a more thorough and integrated educational system was the greatest re. The panel ruled that, in keeping with Dr. Radhakrishnan's philosophy, education should foster intellectual growth as well as moral and spiritual development. It suggested radically reorganizing Indian education to fulfil constitutional objectives and deal with the problems it faced on many fronts. According to the Commission, this rebuilding has to be completed with three main goals: a) internal change; b) quality improvement; and c) building more educational facilities. Later, in the formulation of The National Policy on Education in 1986, the plan paid great emphasis on developing a framework that promotes secular notions, national solidarity, and a scientific style of thinking, all following the teachings of Dr. Radhakrishnan. Although educating all sections of the population was its primary objective, it paid particular attention to women, SC, ST, and other lower castes since they had been denied access to school for generations. The National Policy on Education (1986) strongly emphasized opening new schools and colleges, employing instructors from minorities, providing adult education, and providing fellowships to the impoverished. Additionally, it prepared the groundwork for the integration of IT into the field of education. This demonstrated a dedication to providing a thorough education that went above and beyond the call of duty when it came to teaching. Afterwards, in 2016, the TSR Subramanian Committee developed the New National Education Policy. A progressive educational philosophy that transcends the views of one person is shown by the NEP 2020. The panel discussed how the community's requirements are evolving and underlined the need for an educational system that is more adaptable, multidisciplinary, and skill-focused. To enable students to flourish in a dynamic and constantly changing world, the committee set out to establish a framework that would promote adaptation, multidisciplinary learning, and a concentration on practical skills. Furthermore, no one is prevented from pursuing a job of any kind by the Indian government. Thousands of people from all castes have achieved success today. The emergence of contemporary competition has made success exceedingly difficult. However, under the current government, no man is forbidden from pursuing any career path. This has led to fierce rivalry, with thousands of people searching for and achieving their ideal goal of success.

Conclusion

Dr. Radhakrishnan Sarvepalli- a name synonymous with versatility, wisdom, vision and growth stands as a beacon of education and Indian ethos. The essence of a man is not only etched in his doctrine philosophy but also through the impactful speeches he delivered. As he would say, "When we think we know, we cease to learn", lays down a strong emphasis on the perpetual journey of learning. He is a man known all over the world as an achiever, scholar, educationist, statesman and able parliamentarian. Not only did he exhibit stellar leadership but also remained the most humble and grounded person throughout his career. He devoted his entire life to addressing issues concerning modern civilization, international peace, colonialism, education, and, most importantly, India's secularity and growth. No other academic scholar in India has had such a broad canvas of interest. He researched issues assiduously and wrote very passionately. If analyzing and criticizing modern society and making recommendations for its improvement counts as philosophical work, Dr. Radhakrishnan is without a doubt the most prominent modern Indian scholar philosopher. As an educator, he advocated very strongly for establishing centres of knowledge and institutions where education could be freely pursued. When he got the chance to formulate the Indian educational system as the chairman of the University Education Commission he did stellar work by reflecting his widely accepted educational philosophies into the report. Dr. Krishnan had a holistic approach to curriculum, educational goals, and school management to foster spiritual personality through education. He also wanted to incorporate all disciplines within the curricula of education at all educational levels. Dr. Sarvepalli Radhakrishnan was a fervent supporter of education and was regarded as one of the finest intellectuals and educators of all time. His birthday on September 5th is celebrated as Teacher's Day across the nation as a tribute to this extraordinary educator. It honours the dedication and year-round effort of teachers all over the country. His legacy is not just about achievements but about the path he opened for others to follow. His chronicles of bringing transformation in the education sector have brought along other myriad possibilities. He has left a 'way forward' for the world where knowledge transcends boundaries reinforcing peace, respect and understanding among everyone.

References

1. Deshpande, V. N. (2016). *Educational Philosophy of Dr S Radhakrishnan.* Manipal: Manipal Universal Press.
2. Mishra, A. & Shresth, S. (2022). A Study of Philosophical and Educational Views of Dr. Sarvepalli Radhakrishnan with Reference to National Education Policy-2020. *International Journal of Research in Humanities & Social Sciences, 10*(11), 33-37.
3. Murty, K. S., & Vohra, A. (1990). *Radhakrishnan: his life and ideas.* New York: State University of New York Press.
4. Mohanty, B. B. (2021). Salute to Sarvepalli Radhakrishnan. *Odisha Review,* 74-78
5. Rodrigues, C. (1992). *The social and political thought of Dr. S. Radhakrishnan: an evaluation.* Greater Noida: Sterling Publishers Private Limited.
6. Majumdar, K. (2021). Ideology of Dr. Sarvapalli Radhakrishnan on education. *International Educational Scientific Research Journal,* 7(1), 74-75.

Intuition as the basis for World Soul- Vasudhaiva Kutumbakam

Gunjan Pradhan Sinha

Introduction

This paper attempts to delineate the ethical foundations of Hinduism as perceived in Dr S. Radhakrishnan's thought, largely dominated by Vedānta philosophy. As a master of comparative philosophy, he constantly defends the Hindu thought from mis-perceived criticisms from the West. But in doing so he outlines his own philosophical ideas that can shape the future of a nation or nations, if delved upon. He insists on the union of *jñāna, bhakti* and *karma* for all human activity. He ascribes centrality and genuineness only to spiritual experience vis-à-vis the intellectual experience alone. In doing so he brings about an equal and uniform approach to the act of being human for mankind across caste, creed, nationality and religion. The contention, here is, that his ethical views service the philosophy behind the dictum *'vasudhaiva kutumbakam'* or all the world is a nest or all the world is one home, which was the motto for India's recent presidency of the G20 nations.

Philosophy is often judged by its capacity to improve life (Radhakrishnan, 1914, p168). Human advancement is dependent not on social, economic or political progress but on the height of moral consciousness. Even though the Vedanta does not articulate a clear theory of ethics, the philosophical foundations of this school of thought can help develop the ethics embedded well within. It is with this that we can take a spiritual view of society as an organic whole.

In talking about the Hindu moral life, Radhakrishnan depends not only on the spiritual vision by the inward focus of the individual but also affirms that duty and virtue both emanate from the spiritual insight that one seeks. However, he points out that not all are capable of spiritual insight, as they are often clouded by ignorance or caught by desires and proclivities that are based more on the senses or intellect. Interestingly, while intellect is given supreme importance by the Western rationalists,

Radhakrishnan claims that spiritual consciousness is supreme and subsumes aesthetic, ethical and cognitive values within it.

In lay man's language Radhakrishnan presents a view that spiritual growth and upliftment is the key to seeing the Truth in all spheres of life. It is only with this insight that national progress can be true to its nature benefitting all. The soul of man must rest on secure foundations (Radhakrishnan, p399).

For souls to be in harmony, everything must be steady and non-contradictory so that a person can pursue higher goals. This implies that the informed statesmen must act in a manner to ensure such conditions for people that they may be able to pursue the path of spiritual growth and seek insight into Truth.

This is much similar to the capability of approach of Amartya Sen which states that the government must provide such conditions to its people so that they are free to pursue their preferred course of action as well as higher goals. Kautilya, too, in the Arthśāstra asserts the importance of *artha, kāma* and *dharma* as a stepping stone for *mokṣa* (Sinha, 2018, p73).

Radhakrishnan's notion of spiritual insight is similar to that of Plato's Philosopher Ruler who is able to see the sun or the ultimate Good or reality (Plato, 1987, pp245-249). Spiritual insight may even defy conventional morality but it is truth as it comes from the realisation of underlying Reality. Radhakrishnan presents to us how Hinduism and its flexibility based on universal Truth can lead the way for a more harmonious world view and a spiritually conscious nation that works towards unity and dignity of all.

His philosophy is one of metaphysical idealism set in the strong belief that Hinduism is coeval with Advaita Vedānta (Hawley). He believes the real to be the Brahman which is beyond all finitude and change. *Prakṛti* or *māya* for him is subjective misperception of the Real or Absolute. Brahman is *nirguṇa* or without attributes, lacking diversity and distinction. Even though *māya* is a misunderstood modification of the Brahman, it does not affect the integrity of the Brahman.

Intuition

Radhakrishnan claims that the knowledge of the Real is based on intuition and this leads to integral experience (Hawley). Spiritual apprehension or the kind of awareness of real values which are neither objects in space and time nor universals of thought is called intuition (Radhakrishnan, 2018, p267). The objects of intuition are recognized and not created by us. They are not produced by the act of apprehension either.

Hindu systems of thought believe in the power of the human mind to lead us to the Truth. Ordinary mind is not the highest possible order of the mind but can rise to inconceivable levels through the eye of the mind.

Integral experience co-ordinates and synthesises all experience and integrates them into one unified whole. It serves as the basis of all experience. In other words, all experiences of truth are intuitional. The results of this experience are integrated into the life of the individual and finds expression in the world of action or social relations and thereby ethics.

Intuition transcends reason. Logical reflection is only a fraction of the intuitive experience (Radhakrishnan, 2018, p269). Intuition is the response of the whole man including his intellectual, ethical and aesthetic values to Reality. The different energies of the soul are not divided into silos but modify, support and control each other. Radhakrishnan uses the Sanskrit expression *saṃyagdarśana* or integral insight to show its wholesome nature and point out that it is far from a vision, trance or ecstasy (Radhakrishnan, 2018, p270).

The truths of reason are presented by the work of understanding and are also translated into language through reason. However, the Truth is clearly intelligible only to the one who has the intuitive integral experience. Language can capture the Truth only to a limited extent.

Intuition has a mystical and spiritual quality, in his view. He describes it through a menagerie of terms like religious experience, religious consciousness, mystical experience, self-existent spiritual experience. It is the real ground for man's being as well as the creative centre of the individual. It is from the realisation of the Truth does a human shape his or her actions.

Intuition is also self-certifying or *svatasiddha*. It is sufficient and complete in itself. It is ultimate in the sense that it constitutes the fullest and therefore the most authentic realisation of the Brahman. It is the ground for all other experience. It is self-revealing and immediate. It escapes the limit of language and logic and cannot be defined. It is in intuition that thought and reality coalesce and the distinction between subject and object collapses.

Indian thought requires us to abstract from sense life and logical thinking and to surrender to the deepest self where we get the experience and realisation of the Reality or the monistic truth (Radhakrishnan, 2918, p270). Thoughts and feelings must be deeply harmonised in the light of the intuitive knowledge of the One Real entity Brahman and the given that all souls are one and equal. The spiritual growth of the self and the knowledge of reality grow in tandem.

Ethics for Moral Life

Brahman is the one supreme Reality, while individual souls are only modifications of it (Radhakrishnan, 1914, p168). The metaphysics of the Vedanta serves as the sounding board for its ethics because it looks on all thinking beings and objects of thought as one. The spiritual insight into Reality as oneness cultivates a spirit of *abheda* or non-difference leading one naturally to the ethics of love and brotherhood. Thus, treating everyone as one's coequal.

If all souls are equal and a modification of Brahman, then harm or injury through action or speech amounts to defiling the dignity of all humans. Advaita requires man to be treated always as an end and never as a means to fulfil one's own personal desires (Radhakrishnan, 1914, p169).

Even though man is a part of God, he is not wholly divine. His divinity is a potentiality and it is the task of moral life to eliminate the non-divine element. It is through the exercise of reason that humans can devote themselves to the highest ideals like justice, humanity and righteousness. Violation of any one of these ideals amounts to violation of the dignity of all humankind given that all are equal and one. For the Hindu, the values of the human soul are not earth bound but belong to the eternal monism of the ultimate Truth (Radhakrishnan, 2018, p267). One can transcend the physical laws through discipline and disinterested action.

Rationality also controls the fleeting nature of the senses that make humans prone to the diktats of desire, pleasure and instinct. It allows us to develop the capacity to distinguish the Real from the non-real, the permanent from the fleeting. In doing so, it controls inclinations and the mere push and pull of desire. Reason yields calmness for it controls the senses. The senses are not bad in themselves but unbridled by reason and under unlawful conditions they are bad. They need to be disciplined and not crushed (Radhakrishnan, 1914, p171).

The rational life is marked by unity and consistency with the divine, the supreme Brahman. Such a life will make manifest the Supreme ideal. By relying on the command of unbridled senses, one can only lead a life of passing passions and temporary inclinations (Radhakrishnan, 1914, p172). It will be disconnected and scattered. However, a rational life tests every action against the standard of reason and helps to serve the highest end of man which is service to humanity. These goals come from the intuition of man which is even beyond reason. The spiritual intuition is a creative force that can synthesise values -ethical, cognitive and aesthetic- all of which are a part of the Real but not alone itself.

Knowledge or jñāna in Vedanta, is a part of the spiritual good of humanity. It does not refer to technical disciplines or schools of thought but the power that enables man to make the right decisions in life. It may not conform to convention but it relies on the spiritual insight of Truth. Highest knowledge, however, cannot be attained by turning inwards but by conducting activity in a manner that is based on the true spirit of the Real or unity of all. Such an individual/nation will aspire to make the world happier, nobler and better by shedding the cloak of egoism both personal and national.

Central to Radhakrishnan's ethics is intuition (Hawley). This experience resolves dilemmas and harmonizes seemingly contradictory paths of action. A new harmony is glimpsed in the moment of spiritual insight and old habits tend to go. One acts then, according to the diktats of the rational experience through intuition. Ethical experiences are profoundly transformative and are akin to religious growth. It leads to the identification of ethics with religion.

In times of moral crisis the creative force of ethical intuition comes into force and serves as a guide for righteous action. Ethical intuition, thus, constitutes moral consciousness. This creative intuition springs from

Truth and in this sense its moral precepts hold universal value. The impulse to share moral insight provides an opportunity to test the validity of intuition against reason. A moral hero is one who greatly changes through ethical experience. The moral hero is an ideal of self-sacrifice, joy, freedom and bliss. He is beyond the constraints of ego and individuality.

Mere correct or conventional behaviour clearly does not serve as morality (Radhakrishnan, 2018, p273). The moral hero is also not just content with being moral. It is through the ethical intuition that the moral hero purifies himself of worldly passions and appetites. This primarily emerges from being in communion with the universal spirit.

Most humans are slaves of automatic thinking or habitual thought born out of impulse and emotion. This mental habit has to be broken for moral rectitude. Holding a balance between instinctive desires and cravings and social obligations is the task of moral life. The gap between morality of rules and life of spirit is humongous.

For the Vedāntin, the rule relating to the highest end is the ideal of unselfish service of humanity. It serves as a maxim or absolute moral rule which ought never to be broken (Radhakrishnan, 1914, p178). The ultimate imperative is the conformity to the law of reason- ideal of service and sacrifice. With the equality and unity of all things any misdeed is indeed a misdeed to entire humanity.

When rules conflict one must seek resolution from the supreme commandment as to which is the course most conducive to the realization of Reality. The whole moral life must be rational unity. Even though the physical and empirical world is māya, morality is real to the extent that it is a part of the Real. The world of knowledge and life is not an appearance but it is reality partially understood.

Vedānta considers three levels of reality- *paramārthika*, *vyavahārika* and *pratibhāśika.* The paramārthika level is the Absolute Truth or the realization that we are all one with the Brahman. The vyavahārika level consists of the worldly life where in aesthetic, moral and cognitive values operate and the pratibhāśika level refers to dream state, illusion and error. These also correspond to the three aspects of the mind- superconscious, conscious and sub conscious (Hawley).

Avidyā is the cause of the empirical world. It is the principle of finiteness (Radhakrishnan, 1949, p65-68). It produces the dualism of subject and object when in reality all is one. Māya is only an aspect of Brahman from the vyavahārika level of consciousness.

As long as man exercises his cognitive faculties and understands the world as a modification of the Brahman, he is in a position to exercise moral activity. As the spiritual insight advances, man is able to distance himself and act like a Boddhisattva to remove suffering and ignorance of others who understand the empirical world to be the only reality. In this, man is not guided by external or conventional moral codes but relies on the inner rhythm and harmony between the self and Brahman revealed in intuitive experience.

Ethical principles are not determined by moral convention but by the direct insight of the soul into the Real, the unity or metaphysical monism. People who have this insight have the task of rousing divine possibilities in sinners as every soul has the potential to realize higher levels of reality to achieve moral progress. It is in this context that Radhakrishnan insists on the moral awakening of not just individuals but a nation as a whole. Man must enter into the strife of world to do his duty based on the call of reason derived from spiritual insight (Radhakrishnan, 1914, p183). Every man is required to contribute to the national cause through earnest work. "It is by the adoption of this gospel of work that a nation can grow," says Radhakrishnan.

The philosophy that moral action emanates from values based on spiritual insight and administered by reason can be an antidote to political apathy, lack of organisation, absence of civic virtues, egotism and the attitude of being laid back. There is no fatalism or asceticism that is recommended in the Vedānta but a life of action based on duty, just like Arjuna was asked by Krishna to do in the Bhagvadgitā. It is not renunciation of action but renunciation in action that man must work without desires and instincts guided be reason. It is this that Hinduism brings home to the world.

Doctrine of Karma

The theory of Karma, says that karma is a universal cosmic law and does not conflict with the reality of freedom of the will (Radhakrishnan, HVL p71-73). One cannot manipulate the laws of the cosmos. Theory of karma recognizes the rule of law or ṛta not just in nature but also in the case of mind and morals.

Man has the moral freedom to act in accordance with rationality or not. Even though the theory of karma says, that predispositions are predetermined by our past acts, human character is self-created (Radhakrishnan, 1914, p181). The rational self must give consent to these desires in order that they may be motives or self-conscious desires. The will is free but only limited to some extent by certain natural and social conditions that are predetermined on account of previous karma. Reason enables man to transcend these dispositions. Our duty is to stand for what is right irrespective of the fact that we succeed or not.

Karma is not a mechanical principle but a spiritual necessity which is wrought within our natures (Radhakrishnan, 1949, p73). It is a divine law that cannot be evaded. Sin is not a denial of God but a denial of the soul and betrayal of self. Spiritual growth is linked to the recognition of this rule of law. While consequences of past actions are to be borne, the law tells us to act ethically. There is room for repentance and forgiveness by through karma.

The cards are already dealt out due to the law of karma but how we play them depends upon us and in this way the will is free (Radhakrishnan, 1949, pp74–76). Human actions are determined by the decisions the will takes given its conditions and circumstances. Thus, there is a genuine scope for rational freedom and consequently repentance and penance. The law encourages the sinner mend his actions and does not shut the gates of hope.

Many argue that since everything is a consequence of past actions, the theory of karma entails fatalism. On the contrary, the theory allows man the freedom to use the material at hand in the light of jñāna or knowledge (with the latter not just referring to cognitive knowledge). Man controls the uniformities of nature, his mind and the society and consequently there is scope for genuine freedom of the will. There is no fatalism in the theory of karma and the responsibility of man's actions rests squarely on his shoulders.

It is this moral and spiritual growth and consciousness that Radhakrishnan evokes for the true progress of a nation and not just economic, social or political. It is the duty of the wise to rouse the unmindful to spiritual insight and awakening to what is within.

Dharma

Hinduism is a way of life which allows humans the liberty to think and reflect but imposes a strict code of practice (Radhakrishnan, 1949, p77). It insists not only on religious conformity but also on a spiritual and ethical outlook to life. In other words, practice precedes theory.

Dharma is right action. It comes from the root word dhṛ which means to uphold a thing and also maintain its being. Ṛta is universal order. The latter stands for both *satya* or Truth and also *dharma. Dharma* is conformity to the Truth of things. It means action that is born out of realization of the unity with the Supreme. *Adharma,* is opposition to dharma because moral evil is disharmony with the truth which encompasses and controls the world.

Ethical actions have an overarching unity because man is a part of the one Supreme soul (Radhakrishnan, 1949, p78). It is through contemplation and insight that he recognizes four supreme ends- artha, kāma, dharma and mokṣa. Radhakrishnan treats these four *puruśārthas* or goals of human life as a part of the fundamental human nature. Unless the constitution of the human mind is changed, we cannot eradicate these four goals. This is similar to the notion of the categories of understanding as espoused by German philosopher Immanuel Kant.

Artha refers to the pursuit of wealth and happiness which must be gained through desire or kāma in a righteous manner or through the principles of dharma, if it is to lead to mokṣa (Radhakrishnan,1949, pp80-82). Each one of these requires a code of discipline because to secure our spiritual freedom we have to bind ourselves in certain ways. It is on account of this that even the minutest aspect of life was examined and rules formulated for them in the Dharmaśāstras.

Though various customs and conventions are set, they are renounced when they conflict with reason (Radhakrishnan, 1949, pp 81-82). These codes are not cast in in iron but change with time and culture. However, the conduct of good people or righteous souls is universal and common to all countries, families and societies.

The *śāstras* are scriptures or records of experience of seers who grappled with the problem of reality (Radhakrishnan, 2008, p179). Their claims are not based on the logical validity of statements about God or historical validity of reports of the activity of God. These are based on the true intuitive experience of seers and what they can convey through language. For, the true experience of unity is so profound that it even transcends language.

According to Hindu dharma, man must live by the spirit and not by materialistic aspirations and desires. All activities must be ordained towards mokṣa or complete emancipation of the soul with the realisation of Brahman. The path to this end is the simultaneous employment of *jñāna*, *bhakti* and *karma*. *Jñāna* is not intellectual acumen or dialectical power, as mentioned afore, but realised experience. It is the union with God (at the *vyavahārika* level) and Brahman (at the *parmārthika* level). It is in the light of Truth whatever action that we commit is right action. Truth is synonymous with right action.

Radhakrishnan argues that the essence of all religions is one integral experience based on intuition (Hawley). The various religions derive out of multiple interpretations of this integral experience. The difference is that intuitions abide while interpretations change. Religious intuition is a confluence of cognitive, aesthetic and ethical facets of life. These are parts of it but the experience is full and immediate.

This intuition validates all other spheres of life as it is the realisation of the Truth or Brahman or one universal soul. Ethics, values, beauty and goodness are not known to senses or reason but are immediate in intuition. Religious intuition is identity of the self with ultimate reality expressed in the declaration of absolute monism -'*tat tvam asi*'. It is the realisation of the unity of *ātman* and Brahman. Such a person has the knowledge that there is harmony or oneness underlying all conflict.

Intuition or integral experience co-ordinates and synthesizes life's experiences. It gives the individual awareness and appreciation of unity. It is serves as the basis of all experience and creative ingenuity whether it may be philosophical, scientific, moral, artistic or religious.

The words of the *śruti* and *smṛti* are considered as valid for they are the records of personal intuitions that have autonomous or universal character. Truths of the *ṛsis* are not products of logical reasoning or systematic philosophy but are the result of spiritual intuition, *dṛsti* or vision. *Ṛsis* are not authors but seers who were able to discern the eternal truths by raising their life-spirit to the plane of universal spirit.

The Intuition Behind Vasudhaiva Kutumbakam

The world demands an intuitive approach to international cooperation and understanding (Radhakrishnan, 2008, p173). No political understanding can be met without understanding at the cultural level. The idea is to overcome facile generalisations, which are misleading and it is only through true human experience that peace can become a permanent affair.

Radhakrishnan points out that India may have gone through various phases through the course of its long history- detachment, anger, shame, excitement, adventure etc. and yet all through this runs an idea which attempts at realizing an equilibrium- a wholeness of human nature. The country may be mobile in events and vicissitudes but constant in depth.

The Indian understanding of reality and religion has withstood the tests of time. The deep underlying thread that has bound it through centuries comes from the approach to realisation of reality. Radhakrishnan says that four *sūtras* or aphorisms from Brahma-sūtra explain the Indian approach to religion and ethics. According to them, firstly there is a need for knowledge of the ultimate reality along with a rational approach to it. Thirdly, we must experience reality and lastly reconcile seemingly conflicting aspects of the nature of ultimate reality. This is because even though intuitive experience may be same, the interpretations vary.

Indian philosophy is essentially an enquiry into the nature of man (Radhakrishnan, 2018, p257). To the Indian mind, philosophy hold importance in practically dealing with the problems of suffering and anxiety of the human race. The attempt is to consider and find a solution by not contemplating the world externally but from within. The interpenetration of God and the world, ideas and facts, is the central tenet of Hinduism. The religious soul after contemplation of the ultimate reality turns to the world of practical life.

It is essential to liberate not only bodies from starvation but also minds from slavery (Radhakrishnan, 2018, p259). The moral hero is one who works for peace with humility and love towards entire mankind. The fact that he has the true knowledge based on intuition or integral experience allows him to defy social norms and customs that go against rationality. Religion, which for Radhakrishnan, is akin to intuitive insight brings courage and adventure. In other words it impels one to act ethically for the future of all out of fortitude and there is no room for asceticism or fatalism of any kind.

Such humans look at tradition as something fluid and mobile while having a clear vision of the transforming age. Political crises emerge when there is loss of faith and weakening of the moral fibre. It is essential to reign in the senses and overcome passions of greed and avarice.

Chaos in the world is rooted in the chaos of our mind. It is only the path of spiritual renewal that can bring unity in spirit, thought and action. The problem with the current public policy is that it is based solely on scientific or rational models on the assumption that man's soul is divided into two - moral and intellectual.

The modern intellectual is moulded by methods and concepts of modern science and is highly dependent for his decisions on verifiable facts and tangible results. In such a framework whatever cannot be measured or calculated is unreal. Social groups comprising of such minds have no other purpose except forwarding material wealth. Economic welfare is the end of all existence.

The denial of the divine by the preachers of secular humanism has resulted in a complete lack of spiritual growth of the soul and suspended the freedom of the rational will. Man can never be at rest, even if his physical needs are amply met. Peace of mind is remote and the conditions that need to be created for human excellence are impossible under such a framework.

The chaos in the world can be countered by developing a sense of belonging to one whole, like the Vedāntin does (Radhakrishnan, 1983, pp10-11). Community ideals must be the backbone of citizen actions. Moreover, every kind of injustice must be removed and people must have a sense of contentment. The people should be so well endowed with the basic conditions of life that they can work towards consecration by embarking on a path towards the realisation of reality. Thirdly, people must feel that they have common purposes whatever, their caste, creed or community.

Mass psychology and mass hysteria are a perfect recipe for rebellion (Radhakrishnan, 1983 p12). As nations grow closer together they must understand the need for a unifying spiritual authority or ideology. This ideology must assert a sense of belonging to the whole. Different cultures must try and understand this unifying philosophy for world peace and progress.

Applying his ethical and spiritual ideals to the world, Radhakrishnan attempts to create a framework on the basis of which we bring a human community together as a world community by removing injustice and surrendering a part of our sovereignty for greater world peace.

With India having held the G20 presidency for 2022-23, Radhakrishnan's thought holds contemporary relevance and offers a modern view of the dictum '*Vasudhaiva Kutumbakam*', which was the motto for the year. These two words mean that 'the world is one family'. This is serves as an all-embracing outlook that encourages us to progress as one universal family transcending borders, languages, and ideologies (Modi, 2023).

As Radhakrishnan points out that there should be no justice and frustration among people in their attempt to pursue their higher goals, similarly the G20 through this ancient Indian dictum similarly proposes a human centric approach for progress.

"As one Earth, we are coming together to nurture our planet. As one Family, we support each other in the pursuit of growth. And we move together towards a shared future - one Future - which is an undeniable truth in these interconnected times," -Narendra Modi. The very notion of a shared future entails that we must all consider ourselves as parts of one whole as envisaged by Radhakrishnan who insists on a human community with the strong belief in oneness of all reality.

The pandemic has created a new world outlook. At the time when Radhakrishnan espoused his philosophical sea changes were also rocking the world, with imperialism being brought down to its knees by the force of a simple philosophical outlook of millions of Indians.

With the new post-pandemic world order there are three important changes, among others (Modi, 2023). The first is a realisation to make a paradigm shift from a GDP-centric view of the world to a human-centric one. The second is to focus on resilience and reliability in global supply chains to prevent any kind of inequities and injustices. Thirdly, there is a collective call for boosting multilateralism through the reform of global institutions.

The first and third as needs of a growing global community have been suggested by Radhakrishnan as well derived out of Vedāntin ideals. As far as the second is concerned, while there is no direct reference, Radhakrishnan points out that basic needs should be met to the extent that suffering is not perpetrated on any section of the human community.

In India, living in harmony with nature has been a norm since ancient times and the country has been contributing towards climate action even in modern times (Modi, 2023). When we consider ourselves as part of the one spiritual universal soul all material and non-material beings become one. Radhakrishnan's thought, thus, extends to the pressing needs of environment and climate change as subsumed in under the concept of *vasudhaiva kutumbakam.* It is only when we realize through intuitive experience the oneness of all, that policies for climate action matched with actions on climate finance and transfer of technology gain momentum.

G20 has become a people-driven movement in modern times much as Radhakrishnan focused on human capacities to bring a change in humanity as a whole. With over 200 meetings organised in 60 Indian cities across the length and breadth of our nation, hosting nearly 100,000 delegates from 125 countries by the end of our term, India has made real effort towards bringing a change through the realisation of the philosophy of *vasudhaiva kutumbakam.* The clear attempt is to lend an ear to every local voice for a human community that surpasses geographical boundaries.

Conclusion

There is no difference between the East and West for religion and science are only two aspects of the same reality (Radhakrishnan, 1983, pp38-39). The rational and spiritual are inextricably bound together. One of these aspects may be more prominent in different periods but that does not imply that one half of mankind is more scientific or progressive than the other. Human beings are fundamentally the same and hold the same deep values.

Isolated existence of human groups has become outdated. The world economy is drawn together by technology. However, modernisation is not just akin to industrialisation. As communication techniques change by the second, new values emerge every now and then. Humans have become bound to each other through a relationship of interdependence which is essential for their very existence. The world has become a unit and it is time that we see the Unity or Reality that is proposed by the very structure of Indian philosophical thought. It is such dictums as v*asudhaiva kutumbakam* that bear within the reality seeking the world to be treated as one unit.

Nations can last long, only if they adhere to the moral law (Radhakrishnan, 1983, p42). The moral law emanates for all mankind from the inner voice, conscience, the divine law which is not written by hand but is available to our intuition. It binds the members of the human family together and entails a sense of duty for the safety and happiness of the whole human family. The interdependence of nations is so close that no one nation can be hurt without injury to the rest.

The new order that we seek through v*asudhaiva kutumbakam* requires a strong belief in co-existence, which is one way of ridding the world of intolerance and misunderstanding. The new order is neither national or continental, eastern or western but universal. India with its huge spiritual heritage can contribute truly to the richness and variety of the world.

It is through the intuition of a metaphysical unity that most confrontational issues between humans and nations can be resolved. Radhakrishnan's vision of the application of his philosophy to create a unified world has special relevance today. Hunger and despair are not nationality specific and the spiritual force of human kind is essential to overcome these hurdles across nations. Today, countries have joined hands to address and solve socio-economic problems transcending borders, races, groups and ethnicity and the moral-spiritual approach can only be the course to the success of this endeavour.

References

1. Secular humanism is a philosophy that embraces human reason, logic, secular ethics, and philosophical naturalism, while specifically rejecting religious dogma, supernaturalism, and superstition as the basis of morality and decision making.
2. Plato (1987). The Philosopher Ruler. The Republic. Penguin. London.
3. Radhakrishnan, S. (1949). The Hindu View of Life. Upton Lectures. George Allen and Unwin. London.
4. Radhakrishnan, S. (2008). The Indian Approach to the Religious Problem. The Indian Mind. Ed Moore, Charles, A. Motilal Benrasidas. Delhi.
5. Radhakrishnan, S. (1969) The World's Unborn Soul. Radhakrishnan Reader- An Anthology. Bhartiya Vidya Bhavan. Mumbai. Ed K.M. Munshi & R.R. Diwakar.

6. Radhakrishnan, S. (2018). The Spirit in Man. Contemporary Indian Philosophy-Essentials of Indian Philosophy and Culture. Routledge Revivals. Routledge. New York. Ed Radhakrishnan, S. & Muirhead, J.H.
7. Sinha, Pradhan Gunjan (2018). Ethical Perspectives on Kautilya's Arthaśāstra. Dharma in Governance- Towards a Welfare State. Aditya Prakashan. Delhi.
8. Hawley, Michael. Sarvepalli Radhakrishnan. Internet Encyclopaedia of Philosophy. https://iep.utm.edu/radhakri/
9. Modi, Narendra. (2023). Human-Centric Globalisation: Taking G20 to the Last Mile, Leaving None Behind. Press Information Bureau. Government of India.
10. https://pib.gov.in/PressReleasePage.aspx?PRID=1955326#:~:text='Vasudhaiva%20Kutumbakam'%20%E2%80%93%20these%20two,borders%2C%20languages%2C%20and%20ideologies.
11. Radhakrishnan, S. (1914). Ethics of the Vedanta. International Journal of Ethics. https://ia803207.us.archive.org/35/items/jstor-2376505/2376505.pdf.

Applying Radhakrishnan's philosophical ideas to Today's Challenges: Climate Change as a Case Study

Manish Kumar

Introduction

This paper explores the relevance of Dr. S. Radhakrishnan philosophical teachings. It addresses one of the most pressing issues of our time: climate change. He was a prominent 20th-century Indian philosopher. He emphasised the synthesis of Eastern and Western thought. He advocated for a harmonious relationship between humanity and nature. The paper seeks to offer new perspectives and solutions to the current climate crisis. It does this by analysing his three key ideas namely synthesis of Eastern and Western philosophy, practical Vedanta and spiritual realism. It demonstrates how Radhakrishnan's philosophy could inspire effective environmental stewardship. It could also foster global unity in the face of environmental challenges.

As we grapple with the complexities of contemporary global challenges, particularly the multifaceted issue of climate change, it becomes imperative to seek guidance from philosophical thought leaders who have traversed the intricate intersection of ethics, spirituality, and rationality. One such luminary is Dr. Sarvepalli Radhakrishnan, whose profound synthesis of Eastern and Western thought provides a compelling framework for addressing today's environmental crises. This article embarks on exploring the application of Radhakrishnan's holistic worldview, particularly his advocacy for integrating Eastern spirituality with Western rationality, as a beacon for formulating effective strategies for climate change mitigation and adaptation.

Radhakrishnan's philosophy is deeply rooted in the idea of a harmonious universe. He believes in the interconnectedness of all life. This idea echoes through his extensive body of work. Radhakrishnan explains the deep wisdom in Eastern spiritual traditions. He does so in influential writings like "Eastern Religions and Western Thought" (1939) and "The Hindu

View of Life" (1927). He also calls for a dialogue with the Western scientific and rational approach. His perspective is not merely a confluence of thought. It is a vibrant tapestry of holistic living, ethical responsibility, and intellectual curiosity. All of these are critical in the context of contemporary environmental concerns.

As we delve into Radhakrishnan's philosophical contributions, it is essential to highlight the relevance of his thought in the current discourse on climate change. He advocates a balanced approach. It incorporates the ethical and spiritual insights of the East. It also includes the technological and empirical advancements of the West. Radhakrishnan's vision encourages the development of sustainable technologies and policies. It also promotes a transformation in individual and collective consciousness. This emphasises moral responsibility towards the environment and future generations (Radhakrishnan, 1948).

In the following sections, we will further examine Radhakrishnan's philosophy. We will look at how his integrative approaches can be used in policy-making. We will also explore their potential in technological innovation and grassroots movements. They can effectively combat climate change. These approaches include Synthesis of Eastern and Western Philosophies, Practical Vedanta, and Spiritual Realism. The paper aims to contribute to the ongoing dialogue on sustainable and ethical environmental practices. It draws inspiration from Radhakrishnan's timeless wisdom.

Synthesis of Eastern and Western thought

Radhakrishnan's intellectual journey was marked by his deep study and understanding of both Eastern and Western philosophies. He recognized that both traditions, despite their apparent differences, essentially seek to understand the same ultimate truth. However, they do so through different paths. In his influential works, "Eastern Religions and Western Thought" (Radhakrishnan, 1939) and "The Hindu View of Life" (Radhakrishnan, 1927), he emphasised the importance of a harmonious relationship between the spiritual insights of the East and the rational, scientific approaches of the West. Bilimoria (2018) writes, "Sir Sarvepalli Radhakrishnan was one of the early modern leaders of Indian Philosophy. He was very fond of Western thought." He took the ancient classical tradition as his model. Radhakrishnan spent a good part of his speculative life attempting to reconfigure Indian thought to fit the vesture, maybe the toga, of his Greek heroes, namely Plato and Plotinus. To an extent, he was influenced by Hegelianism, which came across via F. H. Bradley: Occidental in form, and Indian in content".

In fact Radhakrishnan was one of the rare modern philosophers who was able to synthesise Eastern and Western philosophy because reconciling diverse world views have its own challenges and considerations as Malkani (1963) notes "The PROBLEM of philosophical synthesis may be considered in a general way or in a specific form. In the former case, one would like to put different philosophical views together and reconstruct a whole view, which would reconcile all partial views. This is a process which is difficult to accomplish. It is open to question whether there can be any such thing as a whole or complete view which can accommodate all so-called partial views."

The broader context within which thinkers like Radhakrishnan operated was not simple. It was not an easy task. They sought to bridge Eastern and Western thought. However, Radhakrishnan believed these two worlds could have a dialogue. He thought this could lead to a more complete understanding of reality. In the preface of Eastern Religions and Western Thought, he wrote, "It is not quite proper for me to write a book where I have to depend, at least in part, on translation." But, I thought it was no use waiting for a scholar who had proper and critical knowledge of Sanskrit, Hebrew, Greek, Latin, French, and German. Such a scholar has not yet been born." Even translations could be used with care and judgement, so I felt it was that someone with some knowledge got together the main points in order"

In "Eastern Religions and Western Thought," Radhakrishnan explores how Eastern spiritual traditions intersect with Western philosophical thought. He delves into the similarities and differences between these traditions, emphasising how Eastern religions, with their focus on spiritual and introspective insights, can complement the more rational and empirical approaches of Western philosophy. In this work, Radhakrishnan traces the likely impact of Indian mysticism on Greek philosophy and the development of Christian thought. He highlights connections through Alexandrian Judaism, Christian Gnosticism, and Neo-Platonism. He suggests that Christianity has origins in the East. It became intimately connected with Graeco-Latin culture. He also suggests that a revived

Christianity could emerge. This could happen by renewing engagement with Eastern spiritual heritage. This synthesis is presented as a way of bridging the philosophical and spiritual traditions of the East and West. It offers a unique perspective on their interconnections and mutual influences . He writes " In their wide environment religions are assisting each other to find their own souls and grow to their full stature. Cross-fertilization of ideas and insights is unifying men's thoughts. This process is influenced by centuries of racial and cultural traditions and earnest endeavour. Perhaps unconsciously, respect for others' viewpoints and appreciation of other cultures' treasures are growing. Confidence in each other's unselfish motives is also growing. We are slowly realizing that different opinions and convictions are necessary for each other. They work together to create a larger synthesis. This alone can give a spiritual basis to a world brought together into intimate oneness by man's mechanical ingenuity.

Radhakrishnan often highlights the potential for a harmonious relationship. He sees it between the intuitive, inner-focused wisdom of Eastern traditions. He also sees it between the outward-looking, scientifically inclined Western thought. He argues that both approaches aim to understand deeper truths about existence and the human condition. Despite their differences, they share this goal.

Practical Vedanta

Vedanta, one of the six orthodox schools of Hindu philosophy, has evolved significantly over centuries. Its roots can be traced back to the Upanishads, ancient Indian texts that form the philosophical basis of Hinduism. Radhakrishnan's interpretation of Vedanta in the early 20th century marked a significant departure from traditional views. He recontextualized Vedanta, making it relevant to contemporary societal challenges and global philosophical discourse.

"The heart of the Vedanta's message is this: The deepest Reality is one undivided Spirit, Brahman, which is the ground of all existence (Radhakrishnan, 1929). This eternal Consciousness manifests itself in the phenomenal world of multiplicity, appearing as the myriad forms of nature and the countless individual selves. But these differences are superficial, like the waves on the ocean. In essence, all is Brahman. The individual self, Atman, is not apart from Brahman; it is Brahman itself, limited by the veil of ignorance. The purpose of human life is to remove this veil of ignorance and realize the identity of Atman with Brahman. This realization is moksha, or liberation, the supreme good, the end of all suffering (Radhakrishnan, 1927).

"Now, this philosophy of Vedanta is no mere academic abstraction. It has the most profound practical implications for our daily lives. It tells us that at the bottom of our hearts, we are not separate individuals, battling for existence in a hostile world. We are one with the ultimate Reality, one with all beings. This realisation should transform our attitude towards life. It should foster a deep sense of love, compassion, and unity with all creatures. It should inspire us to live lives of righteousness and service, motivated by the pure joy of self-realisation, not by selfish desires (Radhakrishnan, 1948).

"The teachings of Vedanta can guide us in every aspect of our lives. In our personal relationships, it teaches us to see the divine spark in everyone and to treat each other with respect and understanding. In our professional lives, it teaches us to work with integrity and dedication, not for personal gain, but for the good of all (Radhakrishnan, 1929). In our social and political lives, it teaches us to work for justice and equality and to strive for a world where everyone can live in peace and harmony (Radhakrishnan, 1948).

He interpreted Practical Vedanta as applying Vedanta's philosophical principles to everyday life and social issues. This approach emphasises the relevance of Vedantic teachings. It addresses contemporary problems and guides moral and ethical conduct. Radhakrishnan viewed Vedanta not just as a metaphysical doctrine. He saw it as a practical guide for living a meaningful and ethical life. He advocated for harmoniously integrating spiritual wisdom with daily actions and responsibilities. Radhakrishnan's interpretation of Vedanta posits that all existence is essentially one. He especially focuses on the non-dualism (Advaita) aspect. The apparent differences are due to ignorance. This worldview encourages seeing the self in others and the environment. It fosters a sense of unity and interconnectedness with all forms of life (Radhakrishnan, 1929). Radhakrishnan highlights the rational, ethical, and spiritual dimensions of Vedanta. This makes a compelling case for its application in addressing contemporary issues. He viewed the Vedantic way of life with a strong emphasis on fulfilling social responsibilities through a moral compass guided by Dharma (righteous duty) and Karma (selfless action). This path leads to self-realization and liberation (Muthuswamy, 2018).

Radhakrishnan argued that Vedanta is not contrary to reason. It complements reason by providing a deeper understanding of existence beyond empirical observation. This philosophical tradition encourages a questioning attitude and critical thinking. It also encourages a search for truth, all of which are essential for understanding and solving complex problems like climate change.

The ethical teachings of Vedanta emphasize harmony, self-restraint, and respect for all life forms. It advocates for righteousness and non-violence. These principles can guide ethical environmental policies and sustainable practices (Radhakrishnan, 1948). In his 1908 work, The Ethics of Vedanta and its Metaphysical Suppositions, he highlights the ethical implications of Vedanta philosophy. He focuses on rebirth and karma, debated in colonial India.

Vedanta's spiritual insights foster a profound sense of connectedness with the world. This is the spiritual dimension of Vedanta. This perspective can inspire individuals and communities to act with greater responsibility toward the environment. They recognize that harming nature ultimately harms oneself. He writes "The world is not a chaos, but a cosmos, a divine manifestation. Everything is interconnected, everything is an expression of the one infinite reality. When we realise this, we experience a profound sense of peace and joy." (Radhakrishnan,1927)

Radhakrishnan emphasised the role of intuition in human experience. He considered it a distinct and self-sufficient form of experience. He believed that intuition is self-certifying, self-established, and self-evident. It brings a sense of calm, confidence, joy, and strength. He argued that this experience is the fullest realization of the Real (Brahman). It also serves as the ground for all other experiences. For Radhakrishnan, intuition is both truth-filled and truth-bearing. It escapes the limits of language and logic, transcending expression. Yet, it also provokes expression. He saw intuition as a creative force in various spheres of life, indicating progress and creativity as its inevitable results.

Furthermore, Radhakrishnan recognized the interplay between various forms of cognitive experience. These include sense experience, discursive reasoning, and intuitive apprehension. He suggested that sensory knowledge is closest to intuition. It helps us know the outer characteristics of the external world. Discursive reasoning, which follows sensory experience, synthesizes known facts and incorporates intuition. He believes intuition clarifies relationships between facts. It also aids in discovering new knowledge. This new knowledge becomes a subject for logical analysis. Radhakrishnan argued that intuition and logic are not separate entities. Instead, they are interconnected aspects of understanding reality.

Radhakrishnan believed religious and philosophical beliefs involved doubt. He thought questioning, not belief, strengthens religiousness. He also emphasized the dignity of being rational beings. He argued that we should respect this dignity and diminish the power of deception. Radhakrishnan believes reason is essential for scrutinizing religious beliefs. He also uses it to reject false teachings about God and religious concepts.

Radhakrishnan's views offer a nuanced understanding of Vedanta. They highlight the symbiosis of rationality and intuition in our quest for knowledge and truth. This perspective can be particularly relevant in addressing complex global issues. For example, it's key for addressing climate change. Both empirical understanding and deeper, intuitive insights are crucial.

Spiritual Realism

Radhakrishnan conceptualised Spiritual Realism. It is a philosophical framework. It asserts the primacy of the spiritual dimension. It helps us understand the ultimate nature of reality. This view is not just a theoretical construct. It has profound implications for how we perceive and interact with the world. The ultimate reality is inherently spiritual. The physical world is merely an expression of that deeper essence. It's as if the physical realm is a grand tapestry woven with spiritual threads. Each element, from the soaring mountains to the delicate petals of a flower, whispers of the divine.

Furthermore, Dr. Radhakrishnan emphasises the integral connection between these two dimensions:

The material and the spiritual are not two independent realities. They are two aspects of the same ultimate reality. The spiritual is the deeper and more fundamental aspect, but it manifests itself in the material. The true beauty emerges when they come together to form a harmonious composition. In Spiritual Realism, the physical world and its elements gain their true meaning and purpose when understood within the context of the underlying spiritual reality. Similarly, the physical world and its elements gain their true meaning and purpose when understood within the context of the underlying spiritual reality.

To understand this deeper reality, Radhakrishnan encourages us to move beyond the limits of reason and logic.

"Ultimate reality is spiritual experience. The world can be understood only in the light of the spirit. The spirit can be realized only in and through the world."(Radhakrishnan 1953)

The implications of these insights extend far beyond mere philosophical contemplation. Spiritual Realism fosters a profound sense of unity and interconnectedness. We recognize the divine spark that shines within both ourselves and all other beings. This understanding leads to a more ethical and compassionate approach to life. It encourages us to act with respect for all creation and strive for the betterment of the whole.

Radhakrishnan's concept of Spiritual Realism offers a powerful lens. It helps us reimagine our relationship with the world. By recognizing the primacy of the spiritual and the interconnectedness of all things, we pave the way for a more harmonious and meaningful existence. We are guided by compassion, purpose, and a deep connection to the divine essence that pervades all.

Radhakrishnan posits that the ultimate reality is fundamentally spiritual. This perspective does not deny the existence or importance of the physical world. Instead, it views the physical as a manifestation or expression of the underlying spiritual reality. In this view, the material world is interwoven with the spiritual. Understanding the latter is essential for a true and complete understanding of existence.

Some philosophical views might dismiss the material world as illusionary or insignificant. However, Radhakrishnan's Spiritual Realism recognizes the physical world's reality and value. However, it posits that this physical existence gains its full meaning and purpose only in the context of the spiritual. Thus, there is an integrative approach. It sees both the material and spiritual realms as interconnected and interdependent.

Radhakrishnan emphasizes that rational thought and empirical evidence are important. However, they are not enough to fully understand reality. This is especially true for its spiritual aspect. He advocates for the role of intuition in perceiving and understanding spiritual truths. In this context, intuition is seen as a type of direct knowledge. It goes beyond the limits of rationality and sensory experience.

Spiritual Realism carries significant ethical and moral implications. Recognizing a deeper spiritual reality fosters a sense of unity and interconnectedness among all beings. This perspective encourages a moral and ethical approach to life. It emphasises values like compassion. It emphasises reverence for life. It emphasises a sense of responsibility towards the broader universe.

His spiritual realism respects the diversity of religious and spiritual experiences. It acknowledges there are many ways to understand and experience the spiritual dimension. This reflects a pluralistic and inclusive approach to spirituality. Spiritual Realism is a philosophical stance. It elevates the spiritual dimension as central to understanding the nature of reality. It integrates the material and spiritual, emphasising the importance of intuitive knowledge, and carries ethical implications that encourage a holistic, compassionate, and inclusive worldview.

Implementing Radhakrishnan's Philosophical Insights in Contemporary Climate Change Mitigation

Climate change isn't just a scientific or technological hurdle. It's a complex issue with profound ethical, spiritual, and societal dimensions. Tackling it effectively requires a transformative shift in how we view our relationship with the environment, demanding a concerted global effort from all sectors of society.

In recent years, moral and spiritual perspectives on environmentalism have gained significant traction, particularly regarding climate change (Father Francis 2015). It emphasises the need for a holistic approach integrating moral values and spirituality into environmental discourse and action. The profound connection between Indian spirituality and sustainable development goals offers a valuable framework for understanding and achieving sustainability, emphasising ecological awareness, interconnectedness with the environment, and a lifestyle that respects and preserves nature (Giri & Kumar, 2020).

Ethical considerations play a crucial role in shaping sustainable futures within environmental psychology. Integrating ethical and cultural values in addressing climate change highlights the importance of personal identity, cultural and spiritual values, and ethical decision-making in promoting sustainable ecological development (Benz et al., 2022).

The integration of ethical, moral, and religious perspectives into sustainability actions is increasingly recognized as vital. It explores the ethical, moral, and philosophical aspects of religion in relation to sustainability. They emphasize the importance of integrating religious and moral values into approaches for addressing climate change (Prianto et al., 2021).

The perception of climate change as a moral issue among young adults. A significant portion of students recognize climate change as an ethical concern, influencing their willingness to engage in pro-environmental actions (Markowitz, 2012). This demonstrates the potential impact of framing climate change as a moral issue on public engagement and policy responses.

Recognizing the limitations and potential contributions of both science and religion is crucial in addressing climate change's critical challenges. Tucker (2015) argues for the need for broader environmental ethics in dialogue with the science of climate change. He recognizes that both science and religion offer valuable insights and perspectives for addressing this complex issue.

Climate change isn't just a scientific or technological challenge, but a deeply ethical and spiritual issue demanding a transformative shift in our values and attitudes towards the environment. This transformation necessitates a holistic approach that integrates moral, ethical, and spiritual dimensions with scientific understanding and technological solutions. Only through a collaborative and global effort encompassing all sectors of society can we effectively address this multifaceted challenge and build a sustainable future.

In the context presented earlier in this article, Radhakrishnan's three pivotal philosophical insights—namely, the synthesis of Eastern and Western philosophical thoughts, practical Vedanta, and spiritual realism—emerge as a significant framework to confront the complex challenges posed by climate change. Although Radhakrishnan himself did not directly address climate change, as the term and its related issues were not part of the public discourse during his time, his philosophies hold profound relevance today. Scientific advancements and technological solutions play a crucial role in mitigating and adapting to climate change. However, they alone are not enough. The crisis requires a deeper shift in our values and attitudes. It calls for transforming how we see ourselves and our connection to all life. Radhakrishnan's philosophy provides invaluable insights into ethics and spirituality.

Bridging East and West: A Unified Philosophical Approach to Climate Change Policy Making

Radhakrishnan's integrated approach can inform the creation of nuanced, culturally sensitive environmental policies. Combining Western technology with Eastern harmony with nature can lead to more sustainable environmental regulations. It can also make them more broadly accepted. Sarvepalli Radhakrishnan's integrated approach offers a profound and innovative perspective in environmental policy formulation. This approach suggests that a combination of Western technology and Eastern philosophies can greatly improve environmental regulations. Especially those who value harmony with nature. This fusion aims to ensure sustainability and broader acceptance, addressing environmental challenges in a holistic and culturally sensitive manner.

Let me illustrate with the example of recent philosophical and moral dilemmas surrounding the Paris Climate Accord that revolve around equity, ethics, and practicality in global environmental policy. The philosophical and moral dilemmas of the Paris Climate Accord, when viewed through the lens of Radhakrishnan's philosophical insights, present a nuanced framework for addressing these complex challenges.

Equity and Responsibility Distribution: The first dilemma of the Paris Agreement involves the equitable distribution of climate change mitigation responsibilities among nations. Developed countries, with a history of higher emissions, face pressure to assume greater responsibility while developing countries emphasize their need for growth and seek more lenient targets. Radhakrishnan's synthesis of Eastern and Western philosophies can aid in addressing this dilemma by advocating for policies that blend technological advancement with a communal sense of ethical responsibility, thereby ensuring fair contributions from both developed and developing nations.

Anthropocentrism vs. Ecocentrism: The second dilemma revolves around the philosophical debate of anthropocentrism versus ecocentrism. The former views nature primarily as a resource for human use, while the latter argues for the intrinsic value of all ecosystems and species. Radhakrishnan's insights, particularly in Practical Vedanta, align with ecocentrism by emphasising ethical stewardship and the interconnectedness of all life. This philosophical stance can help policymakers reconcile development with ecological preservation.

Moral Responsibility and Global Justice: The third dilemma involves the moral responsibility and global justice aspects, where industrially advanced countries are scrutinized for their historical emissions and their role in protecting vulnerable populations affected by climate change. Radhakrishnan's philosophy, especially his emphasis on spiritual realism, can inform a perspective where nature is valued beyond its utility, advocating for a globally just approach to climate change mitigation and adaptation.

Pragmatic vs. Idealistic Approaches: Lastly, the Paris Agreement faces a dilemma between pragmatic and idealistic approaches. The voluntary nature of national commitments raises concerns about their sufficiency to meet global climate goals. Radhakrishnan's approach could offer a balanced perspective, advocating for sustainable development that harmonizes economic needs with environmental integrity.

Radhakrishnan's integrated approach offers an innovative and essential framework for environmental policy formulation in the contemporary world. By blending Western technological prowess with Eastern ecological wisdom, policymakers can develop regulations that are not only effective in addressing environmental challenges. They can also create regulations that are respectful of diverse cultural values and traditions. This holistic approach ensures that environmental policies are sustainable, equitable, and broadly accepted, leading to a more harmonious coexistence with the natural world.

Blending the power of practical Vedanta and spiritual realism into the life of a common person's environmental journey

Incorporating Radhakrishnan's teachings of Practical Vedanta and Spiritual Realism into the everyday life of an ordinary individual can profoundly impact their environmental awareness and actions. These principles advocate for an ethical and mindful way of living, deeply rooted in respect and care for the environment. This lifestyle goes beyond mere awareness, embedding environmentally conscious decisions into daily routines, such as reducing waste, conserving energy, and choosing sustainable products. More significantly, it cultivates a mindset of compassion and empathy, not only towards fellow human beings but towards all forms of life, thereby fostering kindness and consideration in all interactions.

Community engagement and collaboration form another critical aspect of implementing Radhakrishnan's philosophy in daily life. By participating in local environmental projects, community gardens, or supporting eco-friendly businesses, individuals embody a commitment to collective environmental stewardship. This active involvement not only contributes to sustainable practices but also influences others through personal example, spreading awareness about environmental issues within one's social circle. It's about creating a ripple effect of sustainability that starts with individual actions and extends into the community, facilitating a broader collective impact.

Radhakrishnan's perspective also imbues a sacred view of nature, encouraging individuals to see the natural world as a vital, revered entity. This reverence for nature can significantly deepen one's commitment to environmental stewardship. Practices that help cultivate a spiritual connection with the environment, such as spending time outdoors, engaging in meditation, or participating in nature-centric rituals, can foster a sense of unity and harmony with the natural world. This spiritual bond with nature not only enhances personal well-being but also reinforces the commitment to preserving and appreciating the beauty and significance of the natural environment.

Finally, the moral imperative for environmental protection is a crucial element of Radhakrishnan's teachings. It calls for recognizing a deeper, ethical responsibility to protect the environment, transcending beyond practicality or convenience. This philosophy advocates for acknowledging the intrinsic worth of nature, valuing it beyond its material utility to humans. By embracing this approach, individuals are encouraged to advocate for the preservation and respect of the natural world, recognizing its inherent value and our ethical duty to protect it for future generations. In summary, Radhakrishnan's philosophies offer a comprehensive and spiritually enriched framework for environmental engagement, blending ethical action with a profound respect for the natural world.

Conclusion and Future Perspective

The philosophy of Sarvepalli Radhakrishnan offers a nuanced approach to addressing environmental issues, blending the precision of Western technological advancements with the depth of Eastern spiritual values. This synthesis ensures that technological progress is pursued not just for its own sake but in a manner that is ethically grounded and in harmony with nature. By integrating spiritual values into the development and application of technology, we can ensure that our advancements contribute positively to the environment, embracing a path of sustainable development that respects both our planet's resources and its inherent spiritual significance.

Furthering this integrated approach, Radhakrishnan's philosophy emphasizes the importance of holistic education. By infusing education systems with a blend of scientific knowledge and ethical, and spiritual awareness, we can foster a generation equipped to make informed and responsible environmental decisions. This form of education empowers individuals to understand and address environmental challenges not just through scientific lenses but also with a sense of ethical and spiritual responsibility. Such a comprehensive educational framework is crucial for cultivating a deep-seated respect for nature and a commitment to sustainable living practices.

Finally, Radhakrishnan's vision promotes global dialogue and collective action. In facing environmental challenges like climate change, it is essential to foster collaborative efforts that cross-cultural and disciplinary boundaries. This global approach facilitates a coordinated response to environmental issues, ensuring that solutions are not developed in isolation but in a manner that respects and integrates diverse perspectives. This collective action, grounded in Radhakrishnan's philosophy, encourages us to transform our worldview, embracing a holistic perspective that intertwines ethical responsibility with a spiritual connection to our environment. This transformative approach not only addresses immediate environmental concerns but also fosters global unity and cultural integration, paving the way for a sustainable and harmonious future.

References

1. Benz, A., Formuli, A., Jeong, G., Mu, N., & Rizvanović, N. (2022). Environmental psychology: Challenges and opportunities for a sustainable future. *PsyCh Journal.*
2. Bilimoria, P. (2018). S. Radhakrishnan: 'Saving the Appearances' in East-West Academy. *Sophia.* https://doi.org/10.1007/S11841-018-0691-4.
3. Carroll, J. (2016). The Environment is a Moral and Spiritual Issue. In *The Palgrave Handbook of Sustainability* (pp. 49-71). Springer.
4. Carson, R. (1962). *Silent Spring.* Boston: Houghton Mifflin.
5. Gupta, A., & Ferguson, J. (Eds.). (1997). *Culture, Power, Place: Explorations in Critical Anthropology.* Durham: Duke University Press.
6. Father Francis,Encyclical Letter Laudato si' on care for our common home (24 May 2015) Retrieved from https://www.vatican.va/content/francesco/en/encyclicals/documents/papa-francesco_20150524_enciclica-laudato-si.html
7. Markowitz, E. (2012). Is climate change an ethical issue? Examining young adults' beliefs about climate and morality. *Climatic Change,* 114(3-4), 479-495.
8. Næss, A. (1989). *Ecology, Community and Lifestyle: Outline of an Ecosophy.* Cambridge: Cambridge University Press.
9. Prianto, A., Nurmandi, A., Qodir, Z., & Jubba, H. (2021). Climate change and religion: from ethics to sustainability action. *E3S Web of Conferences.*
10. Radhakrishnan, S. (1927). *The Hindu View of Life.* George Allen & Unwin.
11. Radhakrishnan, S. (1929). *Indian Philosophy, Vol. 2.* George Allen & Unwin.
12. Radhakrishnan, S. (1932). *An Idealist View of Life.* George Allen & Unwin.
13. Radhakrishnan, S. (1937). *Religion and Society.* George Allen & Unwin.
14. Radhakrishnan, S. (1939). *Eastern Religions and Western Thought.* Oxford University Press.
15. Radhakrishnan, S. (1948). The Ethics of the Vedanta. *Philosophy East and West,* 1(1), 3-17.
16. Radhakrishnan, S. (1951). *The Principal Upanishads.* Harper & Brothers.
17. Radhakrishnan, S. (1952). *The Philosophy of Rabindranath Tagore.* London: George Allen & Unwin Ltd.
18. Radhakrishnan, S. (1962). *Recovery of Faith.* Harper & Brothers.
19. Sen, A. (1999). *Development as Freedom.* New York: Oxford University Press.
20. Tucker, M. E. (2015). Can science and religion respond to climate change. *Zygon,* 50(4), 949-961.
21. Vivekananda, S. (1903). *Jnana-yoga (Vol. 4).* Advaita Ashrama.

Dr. Sarvepalli Radha Krishnan: A Philosopher Par Excellence

Nishant Kumar

Introduction

Dr. S Radhakrishnan was a philosopher par excellence. He advocated for Indian social values, religion and wisdom stock. The 'teacher-taught', 'science religion', 'individual-collectivity' and affection and love are some of the binaries that he was interested in. The paper traces his foundation as to why he became so precise as a master, philosopher and Vice-President.

Dr. Sarvepalli Radha Krishnan became the first Vice President and second President of India. Dr. Krishnan was born on 5 September 1888 in a Telugu-speaking Brahmin family at Tirutani village in Chittoor district of the then Madras Presidency. The village is located about 84 km from Chennai, formerly a part of Andhra Pradesh and is currently in Thiruvallur district of Tamil Nadu. The birthplace of Dr. Krishnan is as famous as a pilgrimage. Dr. Krishnan's forefathers once lived in Sarvepalli village and settled in Tirutani village in the middle of the 18th century. Dr. Krishnan was a boy from a poor but learned family. His father's name was Sarvepalli Virasmiah and his mother's name was Sitamma. His father worked in the Revenue Department. Dr. Krishnan had four brothers and one sister. Radhakrishnan was the second child. The responsibilities of such a large family were handled by his father with great difficulty and care. For this reason, Dr. Krishnan's childhood also passed through a lot of trials and tribulations.

Student Life

Krishnanan's childhood was spent in religious places like Tirutani and Tirupati. The initial eight years of Dr. Krishnan's life was spent in Tirutani. Despite his father's religious restrictions, Krishnanan was admitted to a Christian Missionary school i.e. Luther Missionary School in Tirupati (1896). His father understood the importance of education. The next four years of his education were in Vellore. After this, he was enrolled at the Madras Christian College, Madras. In fact, Krishnan was a brilliant student since childhood. Dr.Radhakrishnan aptly memorized the Bible during his college studies. For this, he was awarded the distinction of merit. Along with college studies, he studied Swami Vivekananda and other philosophers. In 1902, he passed the matriculation examination and he started getting scholarships. In 1905, he brought the first position in the Faculty of Arts examination. He was well-versed in psychology, history and mathematics. After taking a master's degree in philosophy in 1918, he was appointed assistant professor of philosophy at the Mysore College. Later he became a professor in the same college. Dr. Krishnan became very popular at the international level due to his philosophical articles and research ideas. He was a great scholar of philosophy. His thoughts are important even today. His brilliance was recognised and he continued to get scholarship in college. In fact, he remained a brilliant student and ideal teacher throughout his student and teacher life.

At that time, early marriage was prevalent in the Brahmin families of Madras. To continue with existing practices and keep compatibility with the existing system, Radhakrishnan was married to Sivakamu on 8 May 1903 at the age of 14. Sivakamu's age was only 10 years. After three years of marriage, his wife started living with him. Although his wife was not very educated, she knew Telugu well and could also write in English. In 1907, Sivakamu enrolled in art and graduated with first class, she too had an intrinsic interest in philosophy. In 1908, Radhakrishnan received a daughter, who was named Sumitra. Radhakrishnan received his master's degree in arts in 1909. He obtained a degree in philosophy. During his post-graduation, he continued teaching tuition to earn his livelihood. He wrote some articles on philosophy which remained unpublished. He was also well-versed in Sanskrit and Hindi. His interest in Vedas, Upanishads and religious texts made him a successful and diligent student, researcher and above all an inclusive individual.

Though the influence of education creates a widespread impact on society, education becomes problematic when it is not well integrated with ethics and morality. At that time there were a lot of Christian institutions, especially better educational institutions that shaped the Indian intellectuals. However, the hidden part of the agenda is education does not trickle down alone but also includes the philosophy of the West. The philosophy then shapes the way of life. The result of this was that the importance of Indian culture and deities received reduced space and conservatism. As such, the heterogenetic and orthogenetic features do not provide adequate space for becoming. This particularity created the faintest seismic ramble for India's cultural tradition. Radhakrishnan became uncomfortable with such a wind of ideas and advocated for the Indian culture, history and faith as meaningful as life itself. Radhakrishnan started thinking, rethinking and cogitating on these ideas. Radhakrishnan knew that there was consciousness in the thoughts of any culture. Radhakrishnan showed interest in knowing the ancient truth, along with introspection, studied the relevant subjects and understood the practicality involved in it. He believed that it is true that Indian culture is completely unshakable and infinite. He concluded that Indian culture is based on religion, knowledge and truth which gives the true message to living beings.

Radhakrishnan understood that life was very short, and happiness and sorrow were surrounded the human beings. It was detrimental that everyone had to go through it. Death is an unchanging truth that does not understand the difference between poor and rich, high and low, and so on. He believed that true knowledge is that which ends the ignorance inside us. He believed that a life of simple contentment is better than the arrogant life of the rich, in which dissatisfaction prevails. A calm mind is better than those parliaments and Darbaris where there is a noise of thunderous applause. Dr. Krishnan was successful in understanding the moral values of Indian culture. He wanted to test the criticisms of Indian culture. That is why it has been said that criticisms are the reasons for refinement. The families of Indian society teach the lesson of development of their children, keeping them away from sin, avoiding troubles, and helping the needy. Radhakrishnan understood that equality towards all religions is the distinctive identity of Indian culture, morality, discipline, humanity, equality, faith and patriotism are the goals of Indian culture.

Radhakrishnan considered the whole world just as a school. The fact is that the lesson that formal institutions fail to give, one finds in day-to-day operations in the global world. The global world is continually changing, evolving and experimenting with itself. He believed that education is the only option by which the human mind can fully be utilized. That's why education should be managed in a way that can provide robust impetus to all. In his address at AD Nabra University, UK, he said that human beings are born equal. The whole goal of human history is the salvation of mankind is possible only when the basis of the policies of the countries establish peace in the whole world. Radhakrishnan used to influence youth, students and intellectuals with his expression, effective address, and use of tickling words. He used to urge the students to adopt high moral values in their lives. He used to teach a subject only after studying it deeply. He used to make a subject like philosophy which he elucidated simple, interesting and enjoyable. He used to deal with the students as a teacher in the form of a skilled student, empathetic guardian and close relative to them. He wanted students to be given special treatment by the teacher. If the student was not catching up, more focused attention was to be given to him.

When Radhakrishnan came to India after returning from Europe and America, many renowned universities conferred honorary degrees on him. His distinguished scholarship always became the subject of reverence. Radhakrishnan's first meeting with Pandit Jawaharlal Nehru at the Calcutta Congress session in 1928 informed about his socialistic and egalitarian vision for mankind. Although Radhakrishnan, being a member of the India Educational Service, could not participate in the activities of any political organization, he did not flow from it and here he gave wonderful speeches. In 1929, Manchester University invited Radhakrishnan to give a speech here and here he gave a serious introduction to his intellectualism. Radhakrishnan was the Vice Chancellor of Andhra University from 1931 to 1936, Professor at Oxford University from 1936 to 1952, and Professor at George V College (Kolkata University) from 1937 to 1941. After being Vice-Chancellor of Kashi Hindu University from 1939 to 1948, he joined UNESCO in 1946 as India's representative.

There is no doubt that the whole nation was convinced by Radhakrishnan's intellectualism. After the independence of the country, he was made a member of the constitution-making committee. As a member of the constitution-making committee from 1947 to 1949, Radhakrishnan was also the chairman of various universities. Radhakrishnan's personality was so strong that the then senior freedom fighters wanted him to play a role in the making of the constitution, while Pandit Nehru wished that Radhakrishnan's speech should be held at the time when the historic session of the Constituent Assembly was held. The addresses ended at midnight in the night and after that, the Constitutional Parliament was sworn in under the leadership of Nehru.

Radhakrishnan's role in the context of diplomatic work after independence was commendable and better in the interest of the nation. On the insistence of the senior people, he moved forward with diplomatic relations with the Soviet Union. Then after this, Vijay Lakshmi Pandit was chosen as his new successor. The selection of Radhakrishnan as a diplomat by Pt. Nehru was considered to be surprising. Many people estimated that he was not to be put into the arms of diplomacy as his basic nature was philosophical. But Radhakrishnan proved that he was able to make responsible decisions in the Nahru's regime. Radhakrishnan proved to be better than all the diplomats appointed in Russia. Radhakrishnan remained disciplined, committed and unconventional even in daily life. For example, diplomatic meetings used to go on for a long time at night, but they would participate only till 10 o'clock in the night and then go to sleep. Even as a teacher, he did not give long lectures or hours for accurate knowledge dissemination. He taught his students with all compassion of mental attraction.

In 1952, Dr. S. Radhakrishnan was elected Vice President after coming from the Soviet Union. The new post of Vice President was created under the constitution. Nehruji again surprised the general public by selecting Radhakrishnan for this role set. People wanted to know the reason why no politician was elected to the post of vice president. He got through it. Radhakrishnan completed the very earnest and ardent job of the Vice-President and Speaker of the Sansad. Every MP was pleased with his behaviour. His role as a Vice President and also as a Speaker of the Parliament brings him into the mainstream to learn a multiplicity of goalposts. All the senior leaders were happy with his behaviour. He was always ready to follow the democratic norms.

The birthday of Dr.Radhakrishnan i.e. 5th September is celebrated as Teachers' Day across the nation. His contributions to the world of ideas are awesome. His own thoughts and his principles are the symbols of today's society and today's educational system.

It must be noted that Dr.Radhakrishnan was given the title of *Sir* by the British Government in 1931 immaterial of the fact that whether they were respectful. When he became the Vice-President, Dr.Rajendra Prasad, the first President of independent India, awarded him the country's highest award i.e. Bharat Ratna in 1954 for his great philosophical and educational achievements.

Radhakrishnan emphasized the knowledge of the otherworldly rather than the information and technical ability of this world. Knowledge - does not accept duality as an end, but considers it as a means to achieve a higher life and outlook, they accept that in modern society Knowledge and technical skills are important, but they should act as a means to build a higher vision. He considered science to be helpful in the knowledge of the spiritual world. The way life develops from matter, intelligence from life and consciousness of values from intelligence. In the same way, divine experience developed from the consciousness of values. Human life developed from semi-human. Similarly, divine life developed from human life. This is the higher life or the highest spiritual ideal. This is the main purpose of education.

According to Radhakrishnan, self-knowledge helps bring a person in contact with the entire humanity. Also, it is helpful in the fulfilment of human aspirations and hopes. Self-knowledge is achieved in an environment of freedom. Therefore, education encourages a person to think, brainstorm and understand and give a better chance. He considered spiritual freedom as the real freedom. He said that the person is the centre of the world. The expression of life is the true self-rule of the human soul. Radhakrishnan had unwavering faith in the spiritual power of man. He placed science, reason and tradition above spiritual power. He believed that the periphery of world science looked at the external shape of objects, and the diversity and polymorphism of the universe. But the centre of existence, from where all things come and go, can be realized only by solitary contemplation.

Dr. Radhakrishnan considered education as a life-long process, in which human learns from the teacher, learn by themselves, learn from life and its experience, and learn at every step at every moment, in his home, communities, letter learns through magazines and electronic techniques. Thus he learns continuously throughout his life. In other words, according to Radhakrishnan, 'whole life is experience', the reason for this is education. The thoughts and theories of Radhakrishnan present a holistic vision of humanity where science, religion and tradition are in amicable interaction.

Reference

1. Anand, V. (2011).Dr RadhaKrishnan's contribution to contemporary thought, mainstream, Vol. L, December 24, retrieved on 6 Feb 2015.
2. Dr Santosh Kumar Behera (2015) Educational thought of SarwpalliRadha Krishnan international research journal of interdisciplinary & multidisciplinary studies (IRJIMS) ISSN:2394-7969(online)vol-1,issue-1.
3. International journal of creative research thoughts, ISSN:2320-2882, vol- 11, issue 3 March 23.
4. The Hindu view of life: Dr SarwpalliRadha Krishnan
5. Search for truth: Dr SarwpalliRadha Krishnan

Dr. S. Radhakrishnan Educational Ideology with New Education Policy (2020) Perspective

Arnav Keyur Anjaria
Priyanka Chugh

Introduction

The paper seeks to explore the contributions of Shri S Radhakrishnan as a Philosopher and as India's Stalwart Academician. Dr. S. Radhakrishnan was a contemporary idealistic philosopher and an ardent preacher of Indic philosophy. An original thinker, spiritualist, philosopher, professor, the Bharat Ratan awardee, the first vice-president of independent India, and a great philosopher who contributed immensely to the field of education.

The paper presents a philosophical account of Dr.Radhakrishnan's idea of Holistic Development, and it further highlights the adaptation of these ideas in the National Education Policy 2020, which unarguably is a tipping point in the history of the Indian education system. He not only theorised educational concepts, but also put them into practice in his teaching. As a result, in his philosophy of education, he synthesised idealism and realism, mysticism and pragmatism. Dr.Sarvepalli Radhakrishnan is considered a visionary primarily, as the paper argues that he laid down the key framework of an Indic Education system suited to the Modern Era yet deeply grounded by the ethos and the exuberance of India's ancient traditions highlighting a historical trajectory of ideas of Dr. S Radhakrishnan that have had a transformative resonance, especially in the context of the National Education policy 2020. Hence this paper moves beyond being merely a glossary of ideas but rather through a discursive analysis, presents the nature of Indian Philosophy as an action-oriented entity unlike its other counterparts. Drawing parallels from different contexts, the authors argue to highlight Dr. S. Radhakrishnan's contribution as a Philosopher of the Indic perspective.

The spectrum of philosophical discourse in India is diverse, distinct and multi-dimensional. The innate nature of Indian philosophy exemplifies the glory and the paramount richness of India's ancient past. The development of different or many different philosophical traditions evokes a reverence for a literate society that brought to the fore a unique discursive entity that made a novel epistemological intervention with unmatched and impeccable precision. This philosophical legacy that emerged from different centres ranging from Nalanda, Takshila, and Vikramshila amongst many others highlighted the democratic, multi-vocal and value-oriented nature of India's ancient education system. The spirit of inquiry and debate has long been enriched through scholarly debates similar to the Greek Dialogics. An example of this is today found in the Monastic debates between the students of Philosophy in Tibetan monasteries. Various philosophical traditions have long adopted the framework even before it was deemed as Hegelian Dialectic. In this context, it is of relevance to understand that S. Radhakrishnan was not only one of India's finest statesmen and diplomat but also an erudite philosopher. He was trained and influenced not merely by Western Philosophical ideas but also by a scholar whose methodological roots lay deeply grounded in Indic philosophy.

As he rightly once asserted "Education should be men making and society making" Originally a teacher by profession, Dr. S. Radhakrishnan highlighted the nuances of Holistic learning and teaching through his philosophical commentaries.

Just as has been the nature of Indian Philosophical schools, the approach has been to deal with complex issues of life and universe and the objective has been to offer and search for a solution. The constant search for complex and cumbersome problems of life and its purpose has made the domain of Indian philosophy an enclave enriched by constant interventions and innovations since late antiquity. This has also deemed Indian philosophy as a Philosophy not confined to the source, but rather it has through the ages acquired the fluidity of being a Philosophy in practice. Several different Indian societies, societal traditions and perspectives, in a newer or not so newer form draw their roots in a certain branch of Indian philosophy. In this context, as a stalwart Indian philosopher, S. Radhakrishnan exemplified the tradition and his approach to putting ideas into practice.

Dr. Radhakrishnan's account of Epistemology is a modern interpretation that carefully enquired about knowledge's source, nature, and validity. He was of the view that knowledge is inextricable from self-realisation. One cannot exist without the other it is knowledge that develops our differentiation between different objects. He states that "knowledge is concealed in ignorance and when the latter is removed the former manifests itself." (Radhakrishnan S., An Idealistic View of Life, 1929). The process of understanding divides knowledge into two sub-categories first, direct knowledge derived as sensual knowledge and second, indirect knowledge as intellectual knowledge.

His conception of the study of Epistemology is based on possible sources of knowledge and refers to three probable sources the *first*-sense *experience* which develops an impression of the physical qualities of an object for instance, an apple is red and is developed through the sensory organs of the eyes. The *second source of knowledge is intellectual knowledge* which is indirect and representative as the data supplied by our senses is analysed by the intellect. The knower and known are two different aspects here. Both the first and second sources of knowledge are limited in scope. The *third source of knowledge is Intuitive Apprehension,* Intuition (samyakjñāna) is the absolute and highest form of knowledge based on the direct realisation of the object. Here the known and knower are both the same. Radhakrishnan acclaims that the innermost realisation of the soul is intuition and the absolute can be attained via the third source of knowledge. Intuition is comprehended whole where the mind is cultivated well and attainment of perfect knowledge which is actual, real and above reasoning. He states that "Intuition is self-established (Svathsiddha), Self-evidencing (Svatahsamvedya), self-luminous (Svayamprakāsh)." (Radhakrishnan S., An Idealistic View of Life, 1929).

Dr. S. Radhakrishnan as a Philosopher

Dr. S. Radhakrishnan was a contemporary idealistic philosopher and an ardent preacher of Indic philosophy. An original thinker, spiritualist, philosopher, professor, the first Bharat Ratan awardee, the first vice-president of independent India, and a great philosopher who contributed immensely to the field of education. In the following section ideas of Radhakrishnan concerning Metaphysical idealism theory as propounded by Radhakrishnan followed by his Analysis of Indic and Western Tradition.

Metaphysical Idealism Theory as Propounded by Dr. S. Radhakrishnan

His metaphysical idealistic philosophical roots are a synthesis of 'Advaita Vedanta' and absolute idealism. The monistic character of Vedantic tradition talks about the existence of one supreme being combined with absolute reality. According to him, the Indian philosophy provides an in-depth understanding of life. Advaita refers to non-dual and Vedanta refers to Sampradaya. Therefore, Advaita Vedanta refers to the non-dual existence of one supreme being in the religion.

The conceptual interpretation of metaphysics as propounded by Dr. S. Radhakrishnan is constituted of the Brahman, Jīva, World and Māyā as the ultimate reality. In the metaphysical idealism embraced by Dr. S. Radhakrishnan as an Advaitin, he advocated for an idealism that recognised reality and variety of experience (Prakṛti) in the world while retaining the concept of a completely transcending Absolute (Brahman), an Absolute that is equal to the self (Atman). While the world of experience is not ultimate reality since it is susceptible to change and is marked by finitude and plurality, it does have its genesis and sustenance in the Absolute (Brahman), which is devoid of all bounds, variety, and differences (Nirguna). Brahman is the source of the world and its manifestations, yet these modes do not affect Brahman's integrity. An absolute of reality (Sat), Consciousness (Cit) and Freedom (Ānanda). Reality as a whole has four sides the absolute Braham, the creative spirit, Iśvara, the world spirit Hiranyagarbha and the world, the Virat-Svarūpa. (Thawani)

Jīva translates as *Life* which according to Dr. S Radhakrishnan should be a rational life not merely confined to existentialism. A rational life based on reason, and unselfish devotion to ideals of humanism like righteousness, ethics, morality, justice and virtue. Jīva is a vital component in Dr. S. Radhakrishnan's account of metaphysics while accepting the Vedantic view of jīva, presenting as not a static entity and quintessentially part of Atman. The self (Jīvatman) is limited and finite and is thriving constantly in a process of self-realisation with the ultimate goal directed towards the universal self (Atman), the true empirical self which includes all. The true topic, according to Dr. S. Radhakrishnan, is the basic, self-sustaining, universal spirit. It cannot be provided directly as the object. Plato,

Aristotle, and Kant are all remembered here. According to Plato, the human mind is the offspring of the everlasting world mind. Aristotle talks of a divine and creative active reason at the summit of the soul. Kant differentiates between the synthetic principle and the merely empirical self. All of their points of view refer to the self as a subject.

The world according to Dr. S. Radhakrishnan is dynamic, and resolute. He offers an Evolutionary theory of the world with a teleological basis advocating a case as influenced by Hegel's view of the word process affected by continuity and change, nature is ever evolving itself.

Māyā, placed in between absolute being and non-being by Shri S. Radhakrishnan is neither idealism nor realism and not a theory. The concept of Māyā is not limited to illusion but a declaration of philosophical facts answering questions like what are we and the world that surrounds us. Subjectively it is known as Avidyā and objectively known as Māyā.

Religion and metaphysics are not mutually exclusive in Dr. S Radhakrishnan's opinion. He claims that metaphysical endeavours provide religious thinking with dignity and vigour. Radhakrishnan metaphysics is not anti-faith. It is the only thing that can restore man's spiritual completeness. "No culture can persist unless it supports this endeavour and inspires trust that man is capable of insight into the nature of the process in which he participates," (Radhakrishnan S., Religion and Culture, 1932) says Shri Radhakrishnan.

A Comparative Analysis of Indic and Western Tradition by Dr. S. Radhakrishnan

Dr. S. Radhakrishnan is known for his constructive criticism of Western philosophy.

He is known for his contribution not only to the field of education, and philosophy but also to disseminating at large the Indian philosophy in the Western World. A major point of distinction as raised by Western philosophers like John Mackenzie and Schweitzer is that Indian philosophy talks about not just the ongoing life but the *life after* death or Moksha the freedom from the cycle of life and death. One of the major questions in the domain of philosophy is 'what is the aim of human life? How to discover the aim or achieve it?' Even Buddha talked about the sorrows of human life.

In his comparison of Western philosophy with Indian philosophy he expiated the latter against the former as uniformed Western criticism. In his work, *The Hindu View of Life* proclaims that philosophy does not deal with facts which is the work of science but about understanding the purpose of life. Provides a simplistic rational understanding of the Hindu Way of life (Philosophically) to the Western world. A pious but not rigid follower of Sankara Vedanta (Founder of Advait Vedanta), Dr. S. Radhakrishnan like Sankara firmly believes that philosophy is only a way to understand the world we live in and the apogee reality is absolute. To give a cogent sensible and acceptable expounding concept of the world, the absolute and the soul he employs Māyā as a tool. He says that the "*Doctrine of Māyā* is supposed to repudiate the reality of the world and thus make all ethical relations meaningless. The world of nature is said to be unreal and human history illusory. There is no meaning in time and no significance in life". (Radhakrishnan, 1948) Presenting a realistic view of the world he says that Māyā is not hallucination or imaginary, similarly, the world is a derived being and Māyā is as real as the world. Therefore, he believed in absolute reality as one.

In his further development of the East and West philosophical distinction, he highlights that the West is inclined towards dogmatism related to the outer world and its exploration limited to second-hand knowledge. The East on the other hand is based on spiritual awakening and spiritual experience. While the West is rational and logical, and the East is religious and mystical predominantly.

He further, rigorously developed upon the distinction between matter and spirit. The Western tradition of philosophy talks about mind as matter while the Indian tradition as advocated by the traditional admirers of the school of thought has shed light upon spirit. The material or physical world is distinguished by two characteristics: continuity and change. Dr. S. Radhakrishnan includes the scientific understanding of matter and calls our attention to two key contributions to it, discarding the old notion of matter as an atomic, inert, and indivisible entity. First, matter is an energy system; it is dynamic, variable, and not an immobile reality. Second, nature is a linked system made up of cosmic waves of energy. As a result, Dr. S. Radhakrishnan creates a vibrant and energising picture of the cosmos.

Like other contemporaries of his time who believed in Indian absolutism which is Self-realisation as the highest goal of human life, Dr. S.

Radhakrishnan held the same view. Absolutism as advocated by Sankara can be reached positively and not necessarily make a case of negative ultimatum, therefore, asserting that spirituality the spirit as its goal of human life can be achieved even by being a part of this worldly world. He is of the perception that the amalgamation is spirit which is common everywhere irrespective of Indic or Western ideological thought.

Dr. S. Radhakrishnan's views on Education

Knowledge is a cogent apparatus that unlocks human potential to its maximum capacity. Philosophers and educationists in India have emphasised enough on the indispensable role of education and knowledge. One such educationist is Dr. S. Radhakrishnan who did outstanding work in the field. An idealistic philosopher but his ideas on education are pragmatic and based on universality, humanity and cooperation. (Choudhary) He believes that in a diverse nation like India education is a tool to uplift the society socially, economically, and culturally. He believed everyone should be educated. For education, the right type potentially solves numerous problems. It provides unlocks the potential of humans to view things beyond time and space.

Aim and Function of Education

The University Education Commission (1948) was chaired by Dr. S. Radhakrishnan he developed the ideas on education with great enthusiasm. He wanted to create a classless society with equality as a characteristic feature of such a society. He gave eight aims of education.

Firstly, Personality Development, the aim of education is man-making with a balanced individual personality with knowledge attainment, character development, social, moral, cultural and spiritual values and wisdom generation.

Second, Character Development, a principal goal of education is all-round character development with values of honesty, goodness and righteous ethics.

Third, Spiritual Development, Dr. S. Radhakrishnan gave immense importance to spiritual education. The all-round development of man is not limited to intellect or mechanical skill attainment but also should inculcate spirituality.

Fourth, Economic self-sufficiency development, since education aims to ensure the overall development of man with economic independence irrespective of gender. Therefore, Dr. S. Radhakrishnan was of the view that schools should offer vocational skills to the children so that upon learning the child as a grown-up will contribute to national income by working as a skilled technician in factories or companies.

Fifth, Scientific Attitude Development, The goals of education should be to help children develop their abilities to create, discover, and invent something new, original, and valuable. Science is to be put to practical use. In the pursuit of research and study, we must cultivate an inquisitive and dedicated attitude.

Sixth, Cultural values Transmission, a culture-rich country has evolved in several aspects. Education must play a vital role in preserving, enriching, transmitting, and changing a country's culture. Education makes culture fruitful.

Seventh, International Understanding development. International Understanding was an essential goal of education for Radhakrishnan. He campaigned for the establishment of a new international order, the expansion of the global community, and global citizenship. He stressed education as a tool for fostering international understanding and mutual cohesiveness among border residents.

Eighth, National Integration, is a major goal of education. It is also one of India's fundamental wants. For the promotion of nationalism, religious education, mass education programmes such as social services, communal life, and the study of social services were prioritised.

Curriculum in Education

Dr. S. Radhakrishnan agreed with R. Tagore on the medium of instruction in our schools. As a result, Dr. S. Radhakrishnan advocated for the use of the regional language as the medium of education. He believes that making the regional language the method of spreading knowledge is the actual approach to touching the hearts of the people. This is the only method to spread the news throughout India. If we do not maintain India's sacred Sanskrit and beautiful languages and help them flourish through usage and exercise, the very springs of Indian higher life may be extinguished.

In his University Commission Report published in 1949, Dr. S. Radhakrishnan lays the outline of a curriculum that according to him wholesome and aims at the overall development of the human personality The curriculum should have subjects like literature, languages; and social studies subjects (economics, geography, history); philosophy, (theology, morality, civics); Maths; Arts/Music; Vocational Subjects; Sports; Science; Yoga and religion. He further, suggested the three-language formula i.e., the study of regional language, mother tongue and federal language. He even emphasised the learning of Sanskrit as a part of the curriculum.

Dr. S. Radhakrishnan argued that a loss of self-control leads to a decline in academic, character, and integrity standards. Discipline is required for yoga and spiritual practises. He felt that discipline would only lead to self-realization. He emphasises that pupils should be taught to tackle life's issues with the fortitude, self-control, and sense of balance that the current circumstances necessitate. Games and other corporate activities should be well-funded.

Men and women are equally competent in academics. Women constitute half of the world's population and with the same view, Dr. S. Radhakrishnan laid immense emphasis on women's education. A society cannot progress if women are not academically taught. Women's education should be viewed as a humanistic endeavour rather than a physiological one. Investing in women's education will lead to the teaching of two families one of her own (maternal side) and the other of her in-law's family.

Teaching Methods

Although he did not fixate on any particular method of teaching but stressed two aspects first what to teach? and second how to teach? The first aspect refers to the methodology of teaching for which Dr. S. Radhakrishnan mentioned a plethora of options that can be used by a teacher in the class to teach effectively. These methods are seminars, text-book learning, observation, experiments, and tutorials amongst others,

Role of Teachers

"Teacher is the cornerstone of the arch of education". A great teacher, according to Radhakrishnan, constantly helps us think for ourselves in new conditions. They attempt to broaden our knowledge and assist us in seeing correctly. The Indian school system hasn't altered much since he warned against it 66 years ago. Without qualified and competent instructors, educational institutions, curriculums, instructional tools, educational planning, and so on are all useless. Dr. Radhakrishnan's ideas about the "ideal teacher" go counter to many current teaching methods. He advised against idolising instructors as gurus and becoming a religious congregation without an open mind. He urged the kids to challenge and critique their professors. The most important job for educators is to improve their students' moral and ethical behaviour. As previously said, Dr. S. Radhakrishnan is not content with simply presenting information. The goals of life should be the growth of the soul and the attainment of liberty. The goals of education and the role of the teacher cannot be very dissimilar.

New Education Policy 2020

Society is dynamic and the needs of the education system of the country must be comprehensive and provide wholesome development to the children, and the upcoming future generations of the nation. India adopted the Sustainable Development Goals (2015) of which Goal 4 asserts that inclusive equitable and quality education for all. With such a promising commitment there was a need to reframe the education policy, after a gap of 34 long-awaited years the New Education Policy, 2020 was announced by the government of India. A comprehensive policy with a vision to suit the needs of the 21st century. A policy aiming to suit all sections of students from primary to higher senior secondary education, the underlying goal to provide equitable, inclusive, quality education to students irrespective of the differences and begetting responsible citizens for tomorrow. Indeed, with the rapidly changing work environment, it is increasingly essential that children not only study but also learn how to learn. Thus, education must shift away from content and toward teaching students how to think critically and solve issues, to be creative and interdisciplinary, and to innovate, adapt, and absorb new material in unique and changing sectors. To make education more immersive, comprehensive, integrated, inquiry-driven, discovery-oriented, learner-centred, discussion-based, adaptable, and, of course, pleasant, pedagogy must develop. In addition to science and mathematics, the curriculum should include basic arts and crafts, humanities, games, sports and fitness, languages, literature, culture, and values to develop all aspects and capabilities of learners and make education more well-rounded, useful, and fulfilling. Education must develop character, preparing students to be ethical, rational, compassionate, and caring while also preparing them for profitable, meaningful jobs.

The gap between the current state of learning outcomes and what is required must be bridged through undertaking major reforms that bring the highest quality, equity, and integrity into the system, from early childhood care and education to higher education.

The goal must be for India to develop a world-class education system by 2040, with equitable access to high-quality education for all students regardless of social or economic background.

Vision and Objectives

The NEP aims to transform the overall education system of the country. The main objectives of the policy are:

i. The NEP aims to promote universal access to education.
ii. It proposes to promote multi-disciplinary education.
iii. Vocational education strengthening
iv. Encouraging innovation and research
v. Improving Educational Quality
vi. Promoting inclusion and equity
vii. Maintaining global competitiveness

NEP Major Features

The features of the New Education Policy:

i. **5+3+3+4 Design**: The earlier 10+2 pattern of education in India has been shifted with NEP 2020. The learning framework will be separated into four sections based on the age of the pupils., foundational (Ages 3 to 8 years), preparatory (age 8 to 11 years), middle school (ages 11 to 14 years), and secondary school (age 14 to 18 ears). In addition, the new education policy states that kids shall be taught in their mother tongue until the fifth grade.

ii. **Restructure Board Exam**: The framework of the board examination will be modified to make it simpler for students to perform during the exam. The major goal of the test will be to focus on the student's essential talents rather than memory. Along with this, the government has instituted the option of two board examinations so that students may assess their performance and make necessary adjustments.

iii. **Four-Year Undergraduate Program**: The undergraduate programme has been for four years. If the student is pursuing their undergraduate programme while conducting research, they will be allowed to apply immediately for a PhD programme.

iv. **Multiple Exit Option**: With multiple exit options Students may withdraw from their courses at any time. They will obtain a certificate after finishing one year of the course, a diploma degree after completing two years, and a degree in the course itself after completing three years.

v. **Multidisciplinary Higher Education**: Students can drop out of their courses at any time. They will obtain a certificate after one year of the course, a diploma after two years, and a degree after three years.

vi. **Single Regulatory Authority**: Regulators who have been in charge of the education system will no longer be in charge. UGC, AICTE, and NCTE will be phased out and replaced with a single rule.

The New Education Policy and Thoughts of Dr. S Radhakrishnan

Dr. Krishnan defines education as the stimulation of everything good in man and the eradication of all that is wrong or worthless. He prioritised the growth of intellectual freedom and the capacity for responsible criticism. He advocated for teaching men and women the 'art of life,' which included understanding human interactions and cooperating with others. He also intended to include a variety of arts and other extracurricular activities so that children are trained to be skilled. In today's technologically advanced culture, encouraging creativity should play a significant role in the educational process. Considering all of these factors, studying Radhakrishnan's educational philosophy appears to be quite important. Dr. S. Radhakrishnan was a staunch supporter of free and compulsory education for all children, regardless of gender, caste, creed, or socioeconomic background, as envisioned in the National Education Policy 2020.

From the perspective of society, India's existing education system is more or less incapable of achieving the aim of healthy character development and the formation of moral values in pupils. The National Education Policy-2020 text stressed the same point. The aims of economic, industrial, and technical progress, as well as intellectual development, cannot be met unless pupils are instilled with spiritual values, democratic values, constitutional values, moral values, and excellent character. He provided a proper road map for accomplishing these aims in the draught of the University Education Commission (1948-49). The concept of long-term goals is covered in the NEP-2020. In this context, Dr. S. Radhakrishnan stated in a draught of the University Education Commission that the religious, spiritual, and moral aspects of progress should not be overlooked while technology advances. Without these, education is incomplete.

Dr. S. Radhakrishnan's educational ideas have enormous importance in current times. Dr. S. Radhakrishnan began by stating that only the appropriate sort of education could cure many social problems in the country. Radhakrishna's educational thinking combines idealistic realistic aspects with existential philosophy. It will achieve the modern educational goal of all-round growth of the students. It should encourage human pleasure and well-being.

Dr. Radhakrishnan was a visionary man although his philosophical ideas were ideological, his education philosophy was expedient. Equivalent to Indian philosophy it is not just purely a work of Vedas or Upanishad theoretical in form but provides a practical approach to life. Interestingly, Bhagwat Gita one of the most celebrated texts in mythology is a source of how to deal with life as a discourse between Shri Krishna and his great friend Arjun. Dr. S. Radhakrishnan was a key figure in nascent India's educational landscape. He not only theorised educational concepts, but also put them into practice in his teaching. As a result, in his philosophy of education, he synthesised idealism and realism, mysticism and pragmatism. Dr. Krishnan had two contacts with education, which provided him with a unique perspective on the Indian educational system and its difficulties. On the practical side, he was a renowned philosopher who taught in colleges and universities in India and abroad; he served as

Vice-Chancellor of several universities and was a member or head of numerous important committees and commissions. On the theoretical side, he used his broad understanding of philosophy to the debate over the objectives and purposes of education. Union Home Minister Mr Amit Shah said after launching the A. M. Naik Charitable Trust School in Powai, Mumbai, that if one reads the compilation of Dr. Radhakrishnan's speeches, it is clear what Dr. Radhakrishna had envisioned for primary, secondary, and higher education, and this is reflected in the National Education Policy, 2020. (India Education Diary Bureau Admin, 2022).

Conclusion

The Indian context has had two heroes of emancipation, the social emancipator Dr. B.R. Ambedkar and the Indian education emancipator Dr. S. Radhakrishnan. His ubiquitous effect as an educator is still felt today. He was a multidimensional creative genius who produced innovative contributions in a wide range of subjects. When we think of Indian philosophy or religion, or when we seek a modern interpretation of Indic philosophy, we automatically think of his name. For him, education was not just about imparting education, but more about the social-moral-personality development of a student. He was a visionary with an ideological philosophical basis but his ideas on education are pragmatic, following a practical approach to the implementation of education in the country. The visionary envisaged an education policy in the British Era as contradictory to Lord Macaulay's education policy of 1858. His educational theory was founded on solid social and psychological grounds. He envisaged an education system that was action-oriented, the relevance of his educational philosophy was relevant back then, it was relevant in the 21st century as seen in the case of the drafting of the New Education policy, 2020 and will be relevant in future policy drafts.

Bibliography

1. Radhakrishnan. (1948). *The Hindu View of Life.* (G. Allen, & Unwin, Eds.) London.
2. Radhakrishnan, S. (n.d.). *The Principle Upanishads.*
3. Hawley, M. (n.d.). Retrieved September 2023, from Internet Encyclopedia of Philosophy : https://iep.utm.edu/radhakri/#H2
4. Radhakrishnan, S. (1929). *An Idealistic View of Life.* London, United Kingdom: George Allena & Urwan Ltd. .
5. Radhakrishnan, S. (1932). *Religion and Culture.* Delhi: Hind Pocket Books (P.) Ltd.

6. Thawani, P. (n.d.). RADHAKRISHNAN: HIS PHILOSOPHICAL STANDPOINT.
7. Choudhary, S. (2006). *Educational Philosophy of Dr. Sarvepalli Radhakrishnan.* New Delhi, India: Deep and Deep Publications Pvt. Ltd.
8. Radhakrishnan, S. (n.d.). The Ethics of The Vedanta. *International Journal of Ethics,* 168-183.
9. Anita Rampal, S. (2022, Septmeber 05). *NEP: Revisiting a Legacy of Policy Visions on Teachers' Day.* Retrieved August 31, 2023, from The Wire: https://thewire.in/education/nep-revisiting-a-legacy-of-policy-visions-on-teachers-day
10. Resource, M. o. (n.d.). *National Education Policy 2020.* Retrieved August 2023, from Ministry of Human Resource Development Government of India: https://www.education.gov.in/sites/upload_files/mhrd/files/NEP_Final_English_0.pdf
11. PIB. (2023, August 01). *Salient Features of NEP, 2020.* Retrieved August 31, 2023, from PIB: https://pib.gov.in/PressReleaseIframePage.aspx?PRID=1847066
12. Yadav, R. (2023, April). National Education Policy, 2020: A Way Ahead.
13. Gnanakumaran, S. P. (n.d.). A view on Radhakrishnan's ideas on World. 152-160.
14. Dar, R. A. (2018, Septmeber). Educational Thought of Dr. Radha Krishnan. *International Journal of Advanced Multidisciplinary Scientific Research (IJAMSR), 1*(7), 41-56.
15. Subramony, D. R. (April, 2017). Dr Radhakrishnan as a Philosopher. *International Journal Online of Humanities (IJOHMN)*, *3*(2).
16. Perumal, D. M. (2019, August). DR. S. RADHAKRISHNAN'S AND HIS PERCEPTION OF HUMANISM. *8*(7), 54-55.
17. Kesherwani, R. M., & Srivastava, D. (2014, July - September). Educational Outlooks of the Philosophy of Radhakrishnan. *5*(7), 49-54.
18. Mishra, A., & Shresth, S. (2022, November). A Study of Philosophical and Educational Views of Dr. Sarvepalli Radhakrishnan with Reference to National Education Policy-2020. *International Journal of Research in Humanities & Soc. Sciences, 10*(11), 33-37.
19. Dey, K. (n.d.). Thoughts and Ideas of Dr Sarvepalli Radhakrishnan and their Impact on the Modern Trends of Indian Higher Education. *International Journal of Research Publication and Reviews, 2*(2), 125-128.
20. Radhakrishnan, S. (n.d.). The Vedanta Philosophy and The Doctrine of Maya. 431-451.
21. Debnath, D. P. (2019). A Peep into the Philosophy of Dr. Sarvepalli Radhakrishnan Relating to Education. *Pramana Research Journal, 9*(6), 1235-1241.
22. Subba, D. D. (2018, january). Radhakrishnan's Moral Education and Peace in the Contemporary World. *International Educational Applied Scientific Research Journal (IEASRJ), 3*(1), 5—7.
23. Behura, D. K. (2010, Septmeber). The Great Indian Philosopher : Dr. Radhakrishnan. *Orrisa Review, LXVII*(2), 1-4.
24. Radhakrishnan, S., & Moore, C. A. (Eds.). (1987). *A Source Book in Indian Philosophy* (Sixth ed.). New Jersey, United States America: Princeton University Press.

25. India Education Diary Bureau Admin. (2022, September 05). *NEP 2020 Is Reflective Of What Was Envisaged By Former President Dr. Sarvepalli Radhakrishnan: HM Amit Shah.* Retrieved September 01, 2023, from India Educationary.com: https://indiaeducationdiary.in/nep-2020-is-reflective-of-what-was-envisaged-by-former-president-dr-sarvepalli-radhakrishnan-hm-amit-shah/
26. Vyas, P. (n.d.). Radhakrishnan on Religious Harmony And Social Ethocs. 194-203.
27. Pal, B. C. (n.d.). The Value of Life in Radhakrishnan's Philosophy. 71-76.
28. Radhakrishnan, S. (1959). *Eastern Religion and Western Thought.*

Sarvepalli Radhakrishnan: His Role in Education

K.N. Mishra

Introduction

Many Saints, Rishis, erudite individuals, educators, and philosophers were born in our wonderful land. These great individuals transmitted the light of their knowledge and wisdom throughout the world, not just in India. Dr. Sarvepalli Radhakrishnan, a prominent Indian philosopher, scholar, and statesman, was born on September 5, 1888, in Tiruvallur district of Tamil Nadu, India. A few characteristics of this personality include being a philosopher, an exceptional teacher, a scholar of the highest calibre, a creative genius, a great humanist, a spiritualist, a man of vision, a man of mission, a man of principles, an idealist, an orator with the gift of expressiveness, an original thinker, an eminent author, and ultimately holding the title of Executive Head of India. He was one of India's greatest educators. He illuminated not only India but the entire world, with his exceptional personality and intelligence. In the galaxy of intellectuals, he shines like a bright star. He was a great Indian son. In India, his birthday is observed as Teacher's Day. He carried the flame for Indian education. During the twentieth century, he played a vital role in defining India's intellectual and political landscape. Radhakrishnan's contributions to Indian civilization as a philosopher, teacher, and leader have left an everlasting impression. His contribution to education, philosophy, religion, culture, science, and other fields was reprehensible. Dr. Radhakrishnan defines education as a tool for social, economic, and cultural transformation. Education should be used effectively for social and national integration, as well as to increase productivity. Education is important not only for information and talent but also for helping us live with others. According to him, education should not only teach us how to live successful lives but also help us uncover "enduring values." His initial interest was teaching, and those who studied under him remember him fondly for his excellent teaching abilities.

Understanding of Duty

Radhakrishnan understood the essential duty and significance of a teacher. He was both highly thoughtful and a man of good moral character, dedicated to the teaching profession. He served India gratefully since she needed him in her manner. Radhakrishnan showed his versatility as a teacher, administrator of the education system, and administrator to the people of the country. It is impossible to find a teacher who can compare to Radhakrishnan in terms of the talents and virtues he showed during his lifetime.

Early in life, Radhakrishnan had modest beginnings. His father was a subordinate tax official, and the family was middle-class Brahmin. Even with little resources, Radhakrishnan's insatiable curiosity helped him achieve academic success. He attended the Lutheran Mission School in Tirupati after receiving his early schooling in Tiruttani. Radhakrishnan was given a scholarship to study at Madras Christian College because of his academic excellence. He devoted all of his time to studying philosophy and literature there, eventually earning an honours degree in 1906. His scholastic prowess and insatiable curiosity led him to seek postgraduate studies in philosophy at the University of Madras and subsequently the University of Calcutta.

Academic Development

Radhakrishnan started an extraordinary academic career that lasted for a number of years. He started his academic career as a philosophy professor at the University of Mysore. He then became an instructor at a number of famous universities, such as the University of Oxford and Calcutta. Radhakrishnan was acknowledged as a brilliant scholar because of his lectures, which were noted for their depth, clarity, and intellectual rigour. He gained international recognition for his profound understanding of Indian philosophy, particularly Vedanta, and his capacity to reconcile Eastern and Western intellectual ideas. When Radhakrishnan received an invitation to give the esteemed Gifford Lectures at the University of Edinburgh in 1936, his standing as a significant philosopher around the world was cemented.

Radhakrishnan's influence extended beyond academia as he was instrumental in moulding India's political system. He began serving as the vice chancellor of Andhra University in 1931 and then took over the position at Banaras Hindu University. When he was proposed to the League of Nations Committee for Intellectual Cooperation in 1936, he made his political debut. Later, from 1949 to 1952, he represented India as ambassador to the Soviet Union, demonstrating his abilities as a statesman and diplomat. When Radhakrishnan was appointed Vice President of India in 1952, his political career achieved its pinnacle. Throughout his reign, he made a strong commitment to international relations, culture, and education. He became the first Indian President in 1962 and was the first to be awarded the country's highest civilian honour, the Bharat Ratna, during his tenure.

As President, Radhakrishnan's job was not only ceremonial; he actively engaged in tackling socio-political issues. He was a voice of reason who worked to close the divide between various societal groups. His great sense of duty, humility, and dedication to the welfare of the country were hallmarks of his leadership.

The philosophical and educational views of Dr. Sarvepalli Radhakrishnan are highly significant and pertinent in the current educational environment, where concerns about the quality of education are the reason why the problem of unemployment is getting worse every day, the number of universities and other higher education institutions is growing daily, but youth moral values and character are declining, and the outlook on national integration is shifting.

Radhakrishnan was a kind of idealistic philosopher whose thought was based on the Adwait Vedant. He made a comparison between Western philosophical traditions and Indian philosophy. He exalted Hinduism and Indian thought in opposition to ignorant criticism from the West. He described the relationship between matter and spirit, stating that while matter demonstrates the supremacy of the human brain, humans also possess a non-natural factor called the spirit of man, which governs matter and surpasses both the quality and potential of matter. He underlined that while he truly believed in the benefits of religion, science and religion are not mutually exclusive in their pursuit of truth and the welfare of humanity. Indian philosophy's ethical precepts are vital to children's whole development.

Views on Education

In 1956, Dr. Sarvepalli Radhakrishnan said, "Education must be humane in order to be complete; it must encompass not only intellectual training but also heart refinement and spirit discipline." Since it ignores the heart and soul, no education can be considered comprehensive. Education must aim to achieve wisdom and truth in addition to facts and information. "Education should be how men and societies are made," he declared (Radhakrishnan 1960).

When we investigate our nation's current educational system, we find a lot of ambiguous information. India's current educational system is beset by a moral values crisis and a crisis of character. In this sense, the educational philosophy of Radhakrishnan aims to build moral values and character of humanity. Dr. Radhakrishnan fervently argued in favour of free and compulsory education for all children in the nation, regardless of socioeconomic background, gender, caste, or creed. India's comedies and commissions have all embraced this national vision for education. Dr. Radhakrishnan's educational thought has enormous value in modern times. Dr. Radhakrishnan stated that only the appropriate kind of education could alleviate many societal problems that threaten the country's survival. Dr. Radhakrishna's educational philosophy was based on a combination of idealistic, realistic humanity and existential philosophy. It helps achieve modern goal of education, namely the all-round development of the kid. It should enhance human well-being and enjoyment. The success of democracy is dependent on its leader, it solely depends on education.

Dr. Radhakrishnan made a comparison between Western philosophical traditions and Indian philosophy. He exalted Hinduism and Indian thought in opposition to ignorant criticism from the West. He described the relationship between matter and spirit, stating that while matter demonstrates the supremacy of the human brain, humans also possess a non-natural factor called the spirit of man, which governs matter and surpasses both the quality and potential of matter. He underlined that while he truly believed in the benefits of religion, science and religion are not mutually exclusive in their pursuit of truth and the welfare of humanity. Indian philosophy's ethical precepts are vital to children's whole development. In 1956, Dr. Sarvepalli Radhakrishnan said, "Education must be humane in order to be complete; it must encompass not only intellectual training but also heart refinement and spirit discipline." Since it ignores the heart and soul, no education can be considered comprehensive. Education must aim to achieve wisdom and truth in addition to facts and information. "Education should be the means by which men and societies are made," he declared (Radhakrishnan 1960). The primary goal of education, according to Dr. Sarvepalli Radhakrishnan's idealistic Adwait Vedant philosophy, was the elevation of the soul in harmony with the material world in search of the ultimate truth. His emphasis was placed on how education may help children develop holistically. Education's main goal should also be character development.

Dr. Radhakrishnan's influence as an educator extended beyond the classroom, into educational policy and reform. He understood the significance of democratizing access to education while improving its quality and relevance to meet society's changing requirements. Dr. Radhakrishnan established the University Grants Commission (UGC) in 1953, which was a significant contribution to educational reform. As the first Chairman of the UGC, Dr. Radhakrishnan was instrumental in coordinating and maintaining higher education standards throughout India. The UGC's responsibility to promote quality in higher education through grants, scholarships, and academic initiatives underscores Dr. Radhakrishnan's dedication to developing a culture of excellence and innovation in the field. Dr. Radhakrishnan also underlined the value of teacher education and professional development as a foundation for educational change. He thought that teachers were the agents of change in the educational system and campaigned for their empowerment through training programs, better working conditions, and recognition of their services to society.

Dr. Sarvepalli Radhakrishnan's legacy as an educator lives on today, influencing pedagogical methods, educational policies, and institutional frameworks in India and beyond. His emphasis on holistic education, ethical principles, and teacher empowerment remains relevant in educational debate and practice, influencing educators, politicians, and students alike. The establishment of Teacher's Day in India observed annually on September 5th in honour of Radhakrishnan's birthday, serves as a poignant reminder of teachers' vital contributions to society and emphasizes the significance of investing in their professional development and well-being.

Dr. Sarvepalli Radhakrishnan's educational ideas are still very relevant in today's India, Radhakrishnan's approach to education was heavily impacted by his philosophical worldview, which emphasized the individual's overall development. He thought that education should not only impart knowledge, but also promote moral, intellectual, and spiritual development. For Dr. Radhakrishnan, education was a transforming process that enabled people to reach their greatest potential and make important contributions to society.

Radhakrishnan's pedagogical philosophy revolved around the concept of "spiritual humanism," which emphasized humanity's interconnectedness and the universal pursuit of truth and enlightenment. He contended that education should create in students a sense of empathy, compassion, and ethical responsibility for others, building a culture of mutual respect and understanding. Radhakrishnan highlighted the importance of values, ethics, and intellect in education. This is consistent with the present requirement for a comprehensive approach to learning, as articulated in India's National Education Policy (NEP 2020). The policy is consistent with Radhakrishnan's vision, emphasizing holistic development, which includes cognitive, emotional, and ethical components of schooling. The NEP 2020's emphasis on curricular flexibility and trans-disciplinary learning aligns with Radhakrishnan's conviction in education's ability to adapt to society's changing requirements. His plea to bridge the gap between traditional Indian knowledge systems and modern education is echoed by the policy's emphasis on incorporating local knowledge and cultural practices into the curriculum. Radhakrishnan's dedication to character development and ethical principles is still relevant in a world fraught with moral quandaries. The NEP 2020 acknowledges the need of instilling values such as empathy, respect, and integrity in order to generate responsible citizens. This is consistent with Radhakrishnan's view of education as a transforming process that transforms people into morally upright and socially responsible citizens.

Radhakrishnan's educational philosophy centred on cultural integration. The NEP 2020 recognizes and celebrates India's unique cultural fabric. The policy emphasizes the incorporation of Indian knowledge systems, languages, and cultural practices within the educational framework, which is consistent with Radhakrishnan's vision of education that is firmly embedded in the country's cultural ethos. Radhakrishnan's emphasis on teacher empowerment and professional development resonates with the

NEP 2020, which considers teachers as fundamental to the educational system. The policy advocates for a teacher-friendly environment that includes training and professional development opportunities.

Dr. Sarvepalli Radhakrishnan's educational ideas are relevant to today's India, particularly in light of the national education policy 2020. According to society, India's existing education system fails to foster character development and moral ideals in kids. The National Education Policy-2020 text stressed the same point. Achieving economic, industrial, technological, and intellectual progress requires instilling spiritual, democratic, constitutional, moral, and character qualities in students. In the proposal of the University Education Commission (1948-49), he provided a clear roadmap for achieving these aims. The concept of long-term goals is covered in the NEP-2020. In the proposal of the University Education Commission, Dr. Sarvepalli Radhakrishnan emphasized the importance of religious, spiritual, and moral development alongside technological advancements. Education is not complete without these. Dr. Sarvepalli Radhakrishnan consistently pushed for free and compulsory education for all children, regardless of gender, caste, creed, or socio-economic class, as outlined in the National Education Policy 2020.

Dr. Sarvepalli Radhakrishnan's educational concepts, based on a blend of tradition and modernity, are still relevant in contemporary India. The National Education Policy 2020, which emphasizes holistic development, ethical values, cultural integration, teacher empowerment, and the use of technology, is strongly aligned with Radhakrishnan's educational philosophy. Radhakrishnan's beliefs guide India's efforts to develop an inclusive, adaptable, and transformative education system. By acknowledging the interconnection of information, values, and culture, the NEP 2020 establishes the groundwork for an education system that not only teaches skills but also develops individuals into responsible, empathetic, and culturally aware citizens. In this sense, Dr. Sarvepalli Radhakrishnan's legacy continues to inspire and shape India's educational landscape in the twenty-first century.

Conclusion

Dr. Sarvepalli Radhakrishnan's legacy as an educator spans time and space, representing the ageless ideals of enlightenment, empowerment, and social justice. His visionary leadership, pedagogical insight, and unrelenting dedication to quality continue to inspire a new generation of educators and students, underlining education's transformational ability as a catalyst for personal and societal change. Radhakrishnan's legacy as an educator demonstrates the long-term relevance of his life and work, acting as a beacon for future generations.

References

1. Anurag Mishra et al. (2022). A Study of Philosophical and Educational Views of Dr. Sarvepalli Radhakrishanan with Reference to National Education Policy-2020. International Journal of Research in Humanities & Soc. Sciences. Vol. 10, Issue: 11, November: 2022
2. Dar, Rayees. (2018). Educational Thought Of Dr. Radha Krishnan. International Journal of Advanced Multidisciplinary Scientific Research. 1. 41-56.
3. https://en.wikipedia.org/wiki/Sarvepalli_Radhakrishnan
4. Kakuli Dey (2021). Thoughts and Ideas of Dr Sarvepalli Radhakrishnan and their Impact on the Modern Trends of Indian Higher Education. International Journal of Research Publication and Reviews Vol (2) Issue (2) (2021) Page 125-128.
5. National Education Policy – 2020. https://www.education.gov.in/nep
6. Porai, sumit & Saha, Birbal. (2013). Call To Rise Above One-self: Dr. Sarvapalli Radhakrishnan as A Role Model for the Indian Teachers In 21st Century. 3. 1-3.
7. R. Subramony (2017). Dr. Radhakrishnan as a Philosopher. International Journal Online of Humanities (IJOHMN). Volume 3, Issue 2, April 2017.

Reflection of Dr Sarvepalli Radhakrishnan's Philosophical and Educational Thought in the Present Education System

Nibedita Priyadarshani

Introduction

Many Saints, Rishis, intelligent people, educators, and philosophers were born in our land. These great individuals illuminated the entire world with their knowledge and wisdom in India. One of India's greatest philosophers and educators was Dr. Sarvepalli Radhakrishnan. The paper describes Dr. Sarvepalli Radhakrishnan's philosophical and educational perspectives in relation to the National Education Policy 2020. In this study, a descriptive library survey methodology was used. Primary information was gathered from well-known books written by Dr. Sarvepalli Radhakrishnan. A comprehensive review of the University Education Commission was carried out in order to obtain information about the philosophical and pedagogical viewpoints of Dr. Sarvepalli Radhakrishnan. Various publications and academic works of well-known authors were also evaluated. We looked at his educational and philosophical stances in relation to the NEP-2020 recommendations. Conclusions were drawn from the meticulously conducted literature research. Dr. Sarvepalli Radhakrishnan's important contribution to education is more relevant now, especially in light of NEP-2020.

In fact, a nation climbs to the heights of influence and achievements with proper education, which is the most important tool for the development of the individual and the enrichment of the social life. We should train our young people in the necessary skills and give them a new direction, a new goal, a new vision of society. With the right education, we become efficient, professional and civilized citizens. Knowledge is a great tool that can be used to maximize human potential. Dr. S. Radhakrishnan is one of the Indian philosophers and educationists who made significant contributions to the spread of knowledge and education. He was an eminent philosopher, educator, thinker, humanitarian and spiritualist, a man of values, a famous writer and an advocate of education. He was also the first Vice-President and the second President of the Republic of India. He received the Bharat Ratna, India's highest honour. He had clear, simple and visionary ideas. The contribution of Dr. Sarvepalli Radhakrishnan greatly benefited the fields of philosophy and education. He was particularly known for his thoughtful, rational and constructive criticism of the philosophical views of Western philosophers. He brought the sacred light of Indian culture and philosophy to the Western hemisphere. Dr. Sarvepalli Radhakrishnan devoted his entire life to modern philosophy. He influenced the intellectual development of a civilization by comparing different philosophical schools.

He made a remarkable and important contribution to modern philosophy. He influenced the intellectual development of a civilization by comparing different philosophical schools. With his unique way of thinking, he visualizes the ideas of knowledge, mission, awareness and development. He placed great emphasis on people and spiritual growth so that they could fully express their inner self. According to him, human personalities can't grow properly on all fronts without spirituality. Spirituality can strengthen a person's optimistic and constructive outlook and their inherent divinity. In his unique explanation, Radhakrishnan argued that religion, philosophy and science are all interconnected. Science tried to solve the problems.

Life sketch of Dr Sarvepalli Radhakrishnan

Dr. Sarvepalli Radhakrisnan was born on September 5, 1885, in Tirutari, a very small temple town in northwestern Madras. He was the second child of two poor Brahmins, Sarvepalli Veeraswami and Sitamma. He completed his primary education in Tirutari. Dr. Radhakrishnan, a resident of Vellore, graduated from Madras University in 1902 and received a scholarship at Voohe College. He received a scholarship in 1904 to study for the B.A. at the Christian College, Madras. He began his M.A. course in philosophy in 1906. "The Ethics of Vedanta and its Metaphysical presupposition" was the title of his dissertation. He began his teaching career in 1909 as a lecturer in philosophy at the Presidency College of Madras. He completed his License to Teach (L.T.) from the Teachers Training Institute in 1910 to become an Assistant Professor. He was promoted as Professor in 1916 at Rajahmundry's Govt. Arts College (A.P). In 1936, he was appointed Professor at Oxford University, London. In 1936, he was appointed Vice-Chancellor of the Banaras Hindu University.

He was ambassador to the Soviet Union on July 12, 1949. He was elected as the first President and Vice-President of Rajya Sabha in 1952. In 1962, he became the second President of India. He took his breath in the year 1975.

Philosophy of Dr. Sarvepalli Radhakrishnan

It becomes evident from his writings that Dr. Radhakrishnan was an idealist philosopher based on Advait Vedanta. Dr. Sarvepalli Radhakrishnan asserted that spirit is the ultimate reality. There are three names for the Universal spirit: God, Ishwar, and Brahman. The ultimate power, which appears in the universe in various forms, is the ultimate reality. The world's expressions of spirit are matter, life, and mind. He provided insights into the actual world and real living. He said that knowing the truth was not enough; what was needed was applying it to real-world issues. He disclosed that the word "absolute" means "infinite," meaning that God is whole in and of himself. Plants and animals are manifestations of ultimate reality. Spirit unity travels from part to the whole. In the context of the universe, it might be an illusion or the creation of an extraterrestrial cosmic God. Dr. Radhakrishnan clarified that knowledge can be gained through integral experience rather than only through the senses alone. Intuition, cognitive experience, and psychic experience are all parts of integral experience. Dr. Radhakrishnan stated 'Truth, beauty and Goodness' are ultimate values. Non-violence is the great mental quality one can acquire that is filled with love and good wishes for others.

Educational Philosophy of Dr Radhakrishnan

In addition to giving us a second chance at life, education enables us to see our own potential. Emancipation of the individual is the aim of education. As a result, we need an education that addresses the mind, body, intellect, and spirit with a holistic approach. Education should mould students' minds to respect deep reflection, stick to the truth, and have the fortitude to disagree with the masses. According to Radhakrishnan, for education to be comprehensive and compassionate, it must include not only academic instruction but also the cultivation of a refined heart and a disciplined spirit. An education cannot be considered complete if the heart and the soul are disregarded (Occasional Speeches and Writings, 1956, p.142). "Education to be complete must be humane; it must include not only training of the intellect but refinement of the heart and spirit," explained Dr. Sarvepalli Radhakrishnan in 1956. Education must aim to achieve wisdom and truth in addition to facts and information. According to him, education should be the domain of men and society (1960, Radhakrishnan).

He declared that the goal of education is to uplift humanity's best qualities and drive out its worse or undeserving ones. He places a lot of emphasis on the growth of critical thinking skills and intellectual independence. He supported teaching both sexes the "art of living," or the study of interpersonal relationships. He said that no nation in the world can continue to rule for an extended period of time. What counts is the moral contribution we make to the well-being of humankind. So let's endeavour to develop the qualities of compassion for the afflicted and charity in judgement. If we adopt this position, tensions around the world will rapidly decrease (Occasional Speeches and Writings, 1956, p. 142). Democratic thinking needs to be encouraged in education. Students should be prepared for democracy and freedom rather than authoritarianism and localism through their education. Science ought to be used in practical endeavours. We should foster a spirit of curiosity and dedication in our pursuit of research and study. Despite the abundance of technical and intellectual aptitude, moral and spiritual vitality is at an all-time low. Man is made whole via the pursuit of truth and its application to improve human lives. The goal of education is to transform us into morally and socially responsible, civilised humans. We need to understand the physical, organic, and social environment in which we exist. We need to have a basic understanding of both the universe's overall design and the pursuit of truth. Our problems become easier to handle and our responsibilities get lighter as we reach the truth. The glow of joy illuminates our route (Occasional Speeches and Writings, Third Series, 1963, p.87). The goal of education is to develop the capacity for discernment in addition to the acquisition of knowledge. Intelligence is not as crucial as judgment. There are a lot of smart men in our country these days, but not enough honourable men. We ought to foster an appreciation for integration. In daily life and administration, purity is crucial. Education ought to foster an inquiring spirit as well as a commitment to the study of science and scholarship. Our undergraduate years are wasted on meaningless and insignificant things. We require character education.

The aims of education highlighted by Radhakrishnan are as under:

Character Building

A nation's citizens have high moral standards and a great nation can be established. According to Radhakrishnan, one of the main objectives of education is character development. He has made the case for character-building instruction. He believed that a man's character is the result of his mental habits or the sum of the impressions he leaves on others through his words and deeds. Rather than a great performance, a man's actual character can be found in his everyday actions. According to Radhakrishnan, character determines fate, and having integrity of character is necessary in all facets of life (Choudhury, S., 2006, p. 80). Education will not be sufficient if it does not teach pupils the values of love, truth, goodness, and beauty. He believed that character development was crucial.

Education for man-making

Education is essential to the creation of humans; culture is indispensable. According to Radhakrishnan, culture is the process of changing oneself in order to produce power of spirit, sanity of mind, and sweetness of temper. He placed a strong emphasis on the cultural aspect of education. Man has put a great deal of effort and time into creating his culture. A country with a vibrant culture advances in a variety of ways. Education is essential to the preservation, enhancement, transmission, and modification of a nation's culture. Education fosters the growth of culture. Choudhury (2006), pp. 81–821.

Development of spiritual values

Radhakrishnan has given education for the growth of spiritual values in people the right amount of room. Radhakrishnan places great importance on spiritual education. If education does not foster a feeling of spirituality in students, then in his opinion, it is false. Without a spiritual perspective, a person's development is hindered both physically and intellectually. This state is detrimental to the progress of humanity. According to Radhakrishnan, human growth should not be confused with the accumulation of academic or technical information. It is the spiritual development of man. Education should promote a manly spirit and human mentality by instilling moral values and excellent habits.

Vocational Development

Students' vocation efficiency should be developed through education. Craft-centered education was stressed by Radhakrishnan. He suggested that rural schools start teaching about agriculture. The purpose of education is to provide children with the knowledge and abilities necessary to sustain themselves economically. The goal of education should be to prepare students for the workforce so they can support themselves. According to him, an individual can increase the wealth of the nation by increasing their own income by involvement in national farms and businesses (Choudhury, S., 2006, p. 84).

Curriculum

According to Radhakrishnan, education ought to be oriented towards life. He outlined his idea of curriculum in the 1949 report he prepared for the university committee. Languages, literature, social studies (geography, history, economics, etc.), philosophy, ethics, theology, morals, politics, civics, mathematics, science (natural, human, etc.), yoga, and religion are among the subjects he supported students taking classes in. Additionally, he supports requiring science and math classes for students. In addition to Hindi and English, he has argued that students should also study their mother tongue or other regional language. He argued that studying Sanskrit is essential to comprehending both the lofty ideals found in the Vedas and Upanishads, the Bhagavad Gita, and other ancient literature, as well as indigenous culture. In addition to Hindi and English, he has argued that students should also study their mother tongue or other regional language. He argued that studying Sanskrit is essential to comprehending both the lofty ideals found in the Vedas, Upanishads, Bhagavad Gita, and other religious works, as well as native culture. He placed a strong focus on using his mother tongue as the major medium of instruction at lower levels and eventually replacing English in higher grades with his mother tongue (Choudhury, S., 2006, p. 90). In order to accelerate intellectual development, Radhakrishnan has suggested taking classes in history, geography, economics, philosophy, etc. To apply it to the growth of society and the human race, students need to be knowledgeable about the previously listed subjects (Choudhury, S., 2006, p. 91). Furthermore, Radhakrishnan suggested that the curriculum includes instruction in women's education, religious and spiritual education, mass education, and vocational training. He aims to incorporate a few subjects in the curriculum for women's education that would be particularly helpful for their unique responsibilities in life. He suggested subjects for women's education that teach ideal character traits, such as literature, history, science, religion, ethics, the Puranas, housekeeping, arts, sewing, domestic work, home science, childrearing, worship, and meditation. Through education, she should learn about the problems related to family administration and acquire the skills needed to solve them. He contends that as long as women remain in the back, no society can progress sufficiently (Choudhury, S., 2006, p. 113). Dr. Radhakrishnan has idealistic beliefs. His educational philosophy is utopian. Mathematics must be taught along with the intellectual and moral pursuits that Dr. Radhakrishnan emphasised curriculum, including poetry and art.

Methods of Teaching

Methods like lecture method, learning by discussion, questionnaire method, seminar method, etc. were suggested by Radhakrishnan. Intuition is the best source of knowledge. For attaining knowledge all senses should be involved. Mass media can be used for the better learning. Teachers must be aware of teaching aids and media to make classroom teaching lively and interesting. The teacher serves as the student's role model. A teacher should therefore possess knowledge, moral integrity, and an idealistic disposition. Students' minds are influenced by the personalities of their teachers. The teacher is society's reflection. The men and women who are hired as teachers have a significant influence on the type of education that our youngsters receive from society. He asserts that self-control is a prerequisite for discipline. Since it is a private concern, it cannot be enforced. It needs to originate from the spirit within. Students could develop self-discipline through yoga and other spiritual pursuits. He contends that excellent discipline follows from having a strong character. Developing one's personality is more significant than acquiring knowledge. He also raised his concern about women's education. "No society can progress satisfactorily with women's backwardness; if women are illiterate, then society will remain illiterate," declared the University Education Commission in 1948–1949. He therefore focused on women's education. He placed a strong emphasis on women's education and correctly stated that women make up the majority of society.

National Education Policy-2020

The Indian government developed the National Education Policy 2020, which is regarded as the country's first educational policy for the twenty-first century. Examining the NEP-2020 policy paper demonstrates that the goal of the project was to realise each person's potential in order to build a just and equitable society. The National Education Policy's four main pillars are accountability, access, equity, quality, and affordability. The philosophical aim of education, according to NEP-2020, is to better prepare people for the world by fostering in them qualities like logical thinking, empathy, courage, resilience, scientific temper, creative imagination, and ethically pure foundations and values.

The National Education Policy-2020 (NEP-2020) was intended to create engaged, productive, and contributing citizens for constructing an equitable, inclusive and plural society as envisaged by the Indian Constitution. Philosophically, the NEP-2020 envisioned that the purpose of education is to nurture human beings so they can be enriched with rational thinking, empathy, courage, resilience, scientific temper and creative imagination with sound ethical moorings and values. He very strongly advocated for free and compulsory education for all children irrespective of gender, caste, creed and socio-economic status which is envisaged in the National Education Policy 2020.

The community claims that the existing Indian educational system does a poor job of assisting students in developing high moral standards and exceptional character. The National Education Policy-2020 document also addressed a related topic. Without improving students' backgrounds with spiritual, democratic, constitutional, moral, and character qualities, it is difficult to meet the goals of economic, industrial, technological, and intellectual development. He offered a workable plan for accomplishing these objectives in the University Education Commission's draft (1948–1949). The topic of sustainable goals is covered in the NEP-2020. Dr. Sarvepalli Radhakrishnan stated in the University Education Commission's draft that it is crucial to remember the moral, religious, and spiritual dimensions of progress as technology develops. Without these, learning is insufficient. For all children, free and compulsory education is mandated under the National Education Policy 2020, irrespective of gender, caste, creed, or socioeconomic status. Dr Sarvepalli Radhakrishnan accepted this notion. He wanted the inclusion of various arts and other extra-curricular activities so that children's hands might be trained to skilful use. In a technologically advanced society, fostering creativity should have an important place in the educational process. The same is given paramount emphasis in the present education system.

Conclusion

The above explanation makes it rather evident that the educational value-based goals in the NEP-2020 document are extremely relevant to the current status of education. The educational philosophy of Dr. Sarvepalli Radhakrishnan serves as the foundation for these goals. Thus, in light of the contemporary state of education, Dr. Sarvepalli Radhakrishnan's philosophical and pedagogical views are quite relevant. He thought that self-discipline and democratic governance are very relevant in the current context. His philosophical and pedagogical theories should be integrated into the current educational system. Stakeholders in the existing educational system must abide by these in order to improve its value-based quality. When implementing National Education Policy 2020, the Dr. Sarvepalli Radhakrishnan school of thought should be realistically integrated throughout the entire educational system. Dr. Sarvepalli is respected and admired by all.

References

1. Adinarayan, P. (2016). Educational thought of Sarvepalli Radhakrishnan, International Journal of Advance Research and Innovative Ideas in Education, ISSN (O) 2395-4396, pp. 4202-4207, www.ijariie.om
2. Aggarwal, J.C. (2002). Theory and Principles of Education, 12th Revised Edition, New Delhi: Vikas Publishing House Pvt. Ltd.
3. Bala, R. & Seth, V. (2016) Educational implications of the philosophy of Dr Sarvepalli Radhakrishnan in the present context, RTE Academy for international journals of Multidisciplinary Research, www.raijmr.om
4. Basu (1982). Essay in the History of Indian Education, Concept publishing company, ISBN: 8170-221595,9788170221593.
5. Chaudhary, S. (2006). Educational Philosophy of Dr. Sarvepalli Radhakrishnan, New Delhi: Deep and Deep Publications Pvt. Ltd.
6. Dey, K. (2021). Thoughts and Ideas of Dr. Sarvepalli Rdhakrishnan and Their Impact on the ModernTrends of Indian Higher Education. International Journal of Research Publication and ReviewsISSN2582-7421.
7. Lal, R.B. & Sharma, K.K. (2015). History, Development and Problem of Indian Education.
8. R.L.B.D. Meerut, ISBN 978-81-910554-8-1 p. 178.

9. Mc Dermolt, R.A. (1970). Radhakrishnan: Selected Writings On Philosophy Religion and Culture E.P. Dulton and Company, INC New York.
10. Mishra,A. & Suman, S. (2022) A Study of philosophical and educational views of Dr Sarvepalli Radhakrishnan with reference to National Educational policy-2020, International Journal of Research in Humanities & Social science, ISSN-2347-5404, vol.10 (II)
11. National Education Policy-2020, Ministry of Education, Government of India.
12. Radhakrishnan, S. (1924). The Philosophy of Upanishads George Allen & Unwin Ltd. London.
    Radhakrishnan, S. (1930). Indian Philosophy Vol II. The Macmillan Company London: George Allen & Unwin Ltd. NewYork.
13. Radhakrishnan, S. (1956). Recovery of Faith, George Allen & Unwin London
14. Radhakrishnan, S. (1960). The Concept of Man, George Allen & Unwin London
15. Sundaram, K.M. (2020). National Education Policy-1986 v/s National Education Policy-2020: A Comparative Study: IRJAS, Volume 02 Issue 10S October 2020, e-ISSN 25824376.
16. TOI, (August 17, 2022). NEP: IIT-M Launches Centre for Indian Knowledge Systems. New Delhi/Agra,p.18.
17. https://www.sanskritimagazine.com/india/traditional/knowledge-systems-of-india/
18. https://en.m.wikipedia.org/wiki/Sarvepalli_Radhakrishnan
19. https://deb.ugc.ac.in/Uploads/SelfLearning/HEI-P-U-0543/HEI-P-U0543_SelfLearning_20210723102951.pdf.

Dr. Sarvepalli Radhakrishnan's Philosophical Legacy: Metaphysics, Ethics, Aesthetics and their Relevance to Public Administration

Nidhi Katoch

Introduction

The philosopher, the second President of India and most importantly the great teacher, Dr. S Radhakrishnan doesn't need any introduction. He was an eminent scholar and one of the prominent philosophers of the 20th century. Sarvepalli's bachelor's degree thesis was titled "The Ethics of Vedanta and its Metaphysical Presuppositions". It was published at the age of 20 and he received tremendous accolades for it. He made a great contribution to the field of philosophy and bridged the gap between Eastern and Western ideologies. Other than that, his contribution to education, religion, and ethics and his integrated approach to these subjects continue to have an impact and inspire people who work to promote moral and spiritual values in society. The philosophical contents in his visualisation were very much embedded since his childhood and blossomed over the period of time. He chose metaphysics and religious philosophy for research purposes. He critically examined Indian philosophy and religion to determine what was live and dormant. Advaita Vedanta and the oneness of Atman and Brahman were focal points of his ideas on metaphysics. He emphasised the significance of moral principles that have a spiritual foundation in ethics. He praised Indian art and culture's spiritual and philosophical facets on an aesthetic level. The paper focuses on his contributions to metaphysics, ethics and aesthetics and their relevance in the field of Public Administration.

"It is the intense spirituality of India and not any great political structure or social organisation that it has developed that has enabled it to resist the ravages of time and the accidents of history."- Dr. S Radhakrishnan.

Dr. S. Radhakrishanan was an internationally renowned philosopher and academician. A true believer in idealistic values, he represented Indian values and thoughts all over the world. Despite the one-sided ideology of

Western philosophy, Dr. S. Radhakrishnan believed in integrating both Eastern and Western ideologies. It shows a congruency in bridging the gap between not only the east and west but also the rest. His books, such as "Indian Philosophy" and "The Philosophy of the Upanishads," presented straightforward explanations of complicated Indian philosophical principles, making them more understandable to a global readership. His works and ideas are still relevant and inspiring today's philosophers, politicians, administrators and researchers. The paper provides insight into the philosophy of metaphysics, ethics and aesthetics of Dr S. Radhakrishnan and how these ideas are useful in modern-day Public Administration.

Philosophy of Dr. Sarvepalli Radhakrishnan

Radhakrishnan's philosophy was deeply influenced by Mahabharata, Bhagwat Gita, Upanishads and also thinkers like Sankara and Ramanuja. He believed that his idea of Hinduism was universal and defended it against Western criticism. He reinterprets the Upanishads and Vedas and provides the world with a new wisdom of Hinduism both as a religion and a way of life.

Metaphysics

He regarded Hinduism as a scientific religion founded on facts rather than intuition or religious experiences. He explained that intuition is of the Savatassiddha (self-certifying) and Svasamvedya (self-evidencing) types, as well as the Swayam Prakash (self-luminous) type. He was a renowned Vedanta advocate who redefined Advaita Vedanta for a modern audience. Idealism underpins his philosophy (Kishore, 2021). Radhakrishnan was a devout Advaita Vedanta adherent. His works easily demonstrate the impact of Advaita philosophy. He not only reinterpreted but also reconstructed, Sankara's Advaita Vedanta philosophical theories through the lens of developing modern science and technology, as well as through the lens of Western ideology (Sharma, 2020). To Radhakrishnan, intuition is the pinnacle of experience. Intuition is the broadest and, consequently, most genuine realisation of the Real (Brahman), making it the ultimate realisation. Radhakrishnan explains intuition serves as the foundation for all other types of experiences.

Radhakrishnan's idealism acknowledged the actuality and diversity of the world of experience (prakti) while retaining the concept of a completely transcendent Absolute (Brahman), an Absolute that is equal to the self (Atman). While the world of experience and everyday things is not ultimate reality because it is subject to change and is marked by finitude and multiplicity, it does have its origin and support in the Absolute (Brahman), which is free of all limits, diversity, and distinctions (nirgua). Brahman is the source of the world and its manifestations, but these modes do not affect Brahman's integrity (Internet Encyclopedia of Philosophy (IEP, n.d.).

Radhakrishnan revised what he believed to be Sankara's view of Maya as solely an illusion. According to Radhakrishnan, Maya should not be interpreted to mean a rigid objective idealism, one in which the world is thought to be fundamentally separate from Brahman, but rather Maya denotes, among other things, a subjective misconception of the world as ultimately accurate (Braue, 1985).

Ethics

Character, the habit of will, is self-created rather than predetermined. "An action is good, not because of its external consequences, but on account of its inner will. Virtue is a mode of being and not of doing. It is not something to be found, but a function or an exercise of the will" (Radhakrishnan S., 1914). He rejected the concept of Dharma as in the West but interpreted it as a way of life. Radhakrishnan contends that there is a close connection between religion and ethics. Dharma is the culmination of religious and moral law. Dharma is simply a synthesis of ethics and religion (Naravane, 1964). Experiences with ethics had a profoundly transformational effect on Radhakrishnan. The experience helps to solve problems and bring seemingly opposing lines of action into harmony.

"Every form of life, every group of men has its "dharma, which is the law of its being. Dharma or virtue is conformity with the truth of things, and dharma is opposition to it. Moral evil is disharmony with the truth which encompasses and controls the world" (Radhakrishnan S., 1927).

His reformation of Hindu idealism is based on the ethics of action, which he derived from the Bhagwad Gita, Sikh philosophy, and Mahayana Buddhism. He pointed to the enduring spiritual principles promoted by

Hinduism to attack the West's one-sided advancement in scientific and technological endeavours as well as its emphasis on pursuing comforts and pleasures. He did not believe that achieving the Western way of life was the pinnacle of human potential. Thus, for him, "the religion of the spirit" serves as the pivot around which all of his intellectual commitments revolve (Singh, 1988). Thus, he holds that ethics are extremely important in a man's life. It trains the human spirit and transforms him towards perfection.

Aesthetics

According to Radhakrishnan, aesthetics has profound philosophical and spiritual implications, especially in the context of Indian art and culture. Radhakrishnan states that "all art is the expression of experience in some medium" (Radhakrishnan D. S., An Idealistic View of Life, 1932).

Art becomes mechanical and a repetition of previous themes without the intuitive feeling. Instead of communicating the artist's intuitive encounter with reality, such "art" is an exercise in (re)production (Internet Encyclopedia of Philosophy (IEP), n.d.).

To Radhakrishanan, aesthetics is a synthesis of both arts and science. But still, there is some difference between them. He stated; "Poetry is the language of the soul, while prose is the language of science. The former is the language of mystery, of devotion, of religion. Prose lays bare its whole meaning to the intelligence, while poetry plunges us in the *mysterium tremendum* of life and suggests the truths cannot be stated" (Radhakrishnan D. S., An Idealistic View of Life, 1932).

Relevance to Public Administration

Dr. Radhakrishnan's philosophical views are directly related to the administration and ideal system of governance.

1. Impersonal motive: Selfishness should never be the driving force behind any action. No action should be taken out of self-interest or to fulfil one's desires. Reason teaches us that serving others is the highest goal, and reason must be used to determine what is right in every given situation. If our conscience leads us to believe something is right, we must do it while being well-equipped to handle fortune in all

of its guises. We must behave impartially (Radhakrishnan D. S., Ethics of Vedanta, 1914).

2. Change orientation: Radha Krishna stated, "If the new harmony glimpsed in the moments of insight is to be achieved, the old order of habits must be renounced" (Radhakrishnan D. S., An Idealistic View of Life, 1932). Similarly, for growth and development administration should be adaptive to change.

3. Decision making: Dr. S. Radhakrishnan talked about the importance of decision-making based on intuition as well as codes.

4. Rules: Public Administration is governed by laws and codes code. Radhakrishnan freely acknowledges that established moral rules are the source of the vast majority of moral judgements.

5. Coordination: "Here we find the essence of religion, which is a synthetic realization of life. The religious man knows that everything is significant, the feeling that there is harmony underneath the conflicts and the power to realize the significance and the harmony" (Radhakrishnan D. S., An Idealistic View of Life, 1932). Similarly in Public administration harmony and coordination is important for smooth functioning.

6. Division of work: According to Dr S Radhakrishnan, knowledge acquisition is the obligation of the Brahman; protecting the weak is the duty of the Kshatriya; business and agriculture are the responsibilities of the Vaishya; and serving others is the duty of the Shudra (Radhakrishnan D. S., Bhartiya Darshan-I, 2004). This ancient principle of division of work is still relevant.

7. Science and Arts: The way Dr. Radhakrishanan viewed aesthetics as science and arts, "What the scientist does when he discovers a new law is to give a new ordering to observed facts. The artist is engaged in a similar task. He gives new meaning to our experience and organizes it differently due to his perception of subtler qualities in reality" (Radhakrishnan D. S., An Idealistic View of Life, 1932). Similarly, public administration holds art and science views. According to D. Waldo, Public Administration is art as well as science. Public administration is art because it is related to getting things done. Public administration is science as it observes, conducts research and uses data analysis for functioning.

8. The integrity of thoughts: Dr. S. Radhakrishnan emphasised on integration of both Western and Eastern ideology. Similarly in Comparative Public Administration, we compare two or more administrations and integrate the working of machinery for efficiency and effectiveness.

9. Importance of experience: Dr. S Radhakrishnan stated "Religion is a kind of life or experience. It is an insight into the nature of reality (*darsana*), or experience of reality (*anubhava*)" (Radhakrishnan S., 1927). Similarly, Personnel Administration emphasised experienced members at top-level management. Experience is necessary for the personal growth of any employee and it helps the organisation in the long term.

10. Logical knowledge: The philosophy of Dr. S. Radhakrishnan is that logical reasoning is obtained by the process of analysis and synthesis. He gave importance to logical knowledge for the working of rational systems. In the same way, public administration believes in logical reasoning and rationality.

Conclusion

It is not an unknown fact that Dr. S. Radhakrishnan has contributed immensely to the field of philosophy. His contribution in representing Indian ideology and thoughts can't be ignored. His ideas are relevant in every other field of social sciences. When Indian ideology was considered outdated and of no relevance, his reinterpretation of the Upanishads, Bhagavad Gita, Vedas and many ancient scriptures provided a modernised view of Indian ideology. Despite the criticism from Western ideologies, he emphasized on integration of thoughts. He reinterpreted Dharma as the way of life and mode of behaving. His works in ethics emphasised making man moral through logical reasoning, intuition, experience and following codes. This shows that his work still holds relevance despite being written in the 20th century. As such, the philosophy of Radhakrishnan unfolds many responses to unsolved problems of the day. His thoughts on education facilitate policymakers to design inclusive social policies on the one hand and embrace Hinduism as a religion turns out to be the guardian of gratitude and custodian of culture.

References

1. Braue, D. A. (1985). Māyā in Radhakrishnan's thought: six meanings other than illusion. Delhi: Shri Jainendra Press.

2. Internet Encyclopedia of Philosophy (IEP). (n.d.). Sarvepalli Radhakrishnan (1888—1975). Retrieved from Internet Encyclopedia of Philosophy (IEP) A Peer Reviewed Academic Resource: https://iep.utm.edu/radhakri/#SH2a

3. Kishore, P. (2021, 09 05). Dr Radhakrishnan: Messenger of Indian philosophy. The Sentinel. Retrieved from https://www.sentinelassam.com/life/dr-radhakrishnan-messenger-of-indian-philosophy-553455

4. Naravane, V. S. (1964). Modern Indian thought. New Delhi: Asia Publishing House.

5. Radhakrishnan, D. S. (1914). Ethics of Vedanta. International Journal of Ethics, 24, 174. Retrieved from https://archive.org/details/jstor-2376505/page/n15/mode/2up

6. Radhakrishnan, D. S. (1932). An Idealistic View of Life. London: George Allen & Urwin Ltd. Retrieved from https://archive.org/details/Sarvepalli.Radhakrishnan-An.Idealist.View.of.Life.1932/page/n3/mode/2up

7. Radhakrishnan, D. S. (2004). Bhartiya Darshan-I (Vol. 1). New Delhi: Rajpal & Sons.

8. Radhakrishnan, S. (1914). The Ethics of the Vedanta. The International Journal of Ethics, 24(2), 168-183. doi:https://doi.org/10.1086/intejethi.24.2.2376505

9. Radhakrishnan, S. (1927). The Hindu View of Life. London: Urwin Books.

10. Sharma, S. (2020, July). Radhakrishnan's Perennial Philosophy of Religion. International Journal of Research in Humanities & Soc. Sciences, 8(7), 12-22.

11. Singh, D. G. (1988). Radhakrishnan as a Philosopher. In Dr. Sarvepalli Radhakrishnan A Commemorative Volume 1888-1988 (pp. 1-3). New Delhi: Princeton Hall of India Private Ltd. Retrieved from http://rsintranet.nic.in/intrars/Sarvapall.pdf

Chronology (1888-1975)

1888	Sarvepalli Radhakishnan born at Tiruttani (Madras Presidency) September 5.
1893 -97	Early education at Tiruttani.
1897 05	Secondary education at Tiruttani and Vellore.
1905- 09	College Education at Voorhees College, Vellore and Madras Christian College, Madras.
1909- 16	Assistant Professor, Presidency College, Madras.
1915	Met Gandhiji for the first time. Wrote articles supporting national movement.
1917- 18	Professor of Philosophy, Presidency College, Madras.
1918	Met Rabindranath Tagore.
1918– 21	Professor of Philosophy, Mysore University.
1921– 31	George V Professor of Philosophy at Calcutta University.
1925– 37	Chairman, Executive Council, Indian Philosophical Congress.
1926	Upton Lecturer at Manchester College, Oxford.
	Haskel Lecturer in Comparative Religion, University of Chicago.
1927	Gen. President, Third Session, Indian Philosophical Congress, Bombay.
1928	Met Jawaharlal Nehru at the Annual Session of the Congress at Calcutta.
1929	Hibbert Lecturer at the University of London and Manchester.
1929– 30	Upton Lecturer at Manchester College, Oxford.
1930	Jowett Lecturer, Marry Ward Settlement, London.
1931– 36	Vice – Chancellor, Andhra University, Waltair.
1931– 39	Member, International Committee on Intellectual Co-operation, League of Nations, Geneva.
1936– 52	Spalding Professor of Eastern Religion and Ethics at Oxford

University.

1937– 41 George V Professor of Philosophy at Calcutta University.

1938 Lewis Fry Memorial Lecturer at Bristol.

1939 Elected Fellow of the British Academy.

1939 -48 Vice-Chancellor, Banaras Hindu University.

1940 Represented Oxford University at Santiniketan for conferring Honorary Degree on Rabindranath Tagore.

1946– 52 Leader, Indian Delegation, UNESCO.

1947– 49 Member, Constituent Assembly of India.

1948 Chairman, Universities Commission.

1948– 49 Chairman, Executive Board, UNESCO.

1949 Hon. Fellow, Royal Asiatic Society of Bengal.

1949– 52 Ambassador of India in U.S.S.R.

1951 Fellow of Royal Society of Literature.

1952 Elected as Vice President of India

1952– 62 Hon. Fellow, All Souls College, Oxford .

1952– 54 President, General Conference, UNESCO.

1953– 62 Chancellor , University of Delhi

1954 Awarded Bharat Ratna. German Order Pour Le Merite.

Hon. Member, Rumania Academy of Sciences.

1956 Goodwill Mission to Belgium, Poland, Czecho-slovakia , the Soviet Union Hungary , Bulgaria and East and Central Africa , Singapore , Indonesia , Japan and China.

Hon. Professor, Moscow University.

1957 Re-elected Vice-President of India.

Goodwill Mission to Indo-China States, China and Mongolia.

Master of Wisdom (Mongolia).

1958 President , General Conference of UNESCO.

Inaugurated the UNESCO Headquarters at Paris.

1959	Goethe Plaquette (Germany)
1960	Goodwill Mission to Scandinavian countries.
1961	German Booksellers' Peace Prize.
1962	Elected President of India. Elected Hon. Fellow of the British Academy.
1963	State visit to Afghanistan and Iran in May: U.S.A. and U.K. in June.
	Hon. Member 'Order of Merit '.
	State Visit to Nepal in November.
1964	President Sahitya Akademi (National Academy of Letters).
	State visits to U.S.S.R. and Ireland in September.
1965	State visits to Yugoslavia, Czechoslovakia, Rumania and Ethiopia in October. Elected Member of the Serbian Academy of Sciences and Arts, Belgrade.
1975	Passed away, April 17, 1975.

Source: The information has been documented from various authentic sources available in the public domain. One of the major sources bing "Sarvepalli Radhakrishnan: A Study of President of India" General Editor K. Ishwara Dutt, Popular Book Services, New Delhi, 1966.

Selected Speeches of Dr. S. Radha Krishnan

Disclaimer: The speeches of Dr. S. Radhakrishnan have been retrieved from various online and offline sources. Most speeches have been taken from 'President Radhakrishnan's Speech and Writings (May 1962-May 1964)' published from Publication Division (1965), Ministry of Information and Broadcasting, Government of India.

One World Nations as Friendly Partners, New Delhi, May 14, 1962

Mr. Officiating Dean, the Acting Dean is not well and does not happen to be here : I thank you and the members of the Diplomatic Corps for the very kind words that you have spoken about me. I hope that your Acting Dean will recover his health soon and will be with us.

I shall be very glad to convey to Dr. Rajendra Prasad the generous and friendly words which you have just said. We all appreciate his great presidentship for about 12 years and the services he rendered not only to our country but to human fellowship. I shall be happy to pass on your message to him. You just said that you were not mere official Heads of Missions but friends. That is a happy idea. What the world needs today is not a juxtaposition of competing States but friendly partners working for the one supreme cause of making the world a happy home for humanity. We should look upon ourselves not as rivals but as friends with a common purpose in view. The years ahead of us are crucial, crucial because of the spectacular achievements which we have won in the realms of science and technology. They may be used for good purposes or for evil purposes: it depends on us and it is our hope that all these things will be utilized for the service of man and not the destruction of humanity. We in our narrow mindedness sometimes crave not so much for our own happiness as for the unhappiness of other people. We should be large-minded enough to know that the happiness of other people contributes to our own happiness. What makes other people happy should make us also happy. Man is a mixture of elements, so much of nobility in him, yet so much of wretchedness; so much of magnanimity, yet so much of meanness; so much of greatness, and yet so much of litdeness. We are all mixtures of these elements. Once Tolstoy was asked, "Have you seen the devil ?" Tolstoy replied, "I have not." the interlocutor said, "Look into the mirror, you will find one !" That is what Tolstoy was told. In other words, each one of us has in him certain elements of a diabolic character as also certain elements of a divine nature. We must strengthen the higher elements of our nature and weaken because we cannot cure them altogether, the other elements which we also share. It is this dual character of human beings that is responsible for much that is happening in the world. We have co-operated a good deal. Take sixteenth century science.

Address to the Anti-Nuclear Arms Convention, New Delhi, June 16, 1962

Copernicus was a Pole, Galileo was an Italian, Kepler was a German, Newton was an Englishman — all of them contributed to the development of science. Today in the twentieth century, our modern science owes a great deal to the contributions made by persons of different nationalities. It has become one international world, economically we are becoming interdependent; In several cultural matters we are also interdependent; scientifically, too, we are interdependent. With regard to human rights, we want to bring about the achievement of human rights for all people and freedom from disabilities — political, social and economic — from which many of us happen to suffer.

The world is meant to be a partnership. It is meant to be a friendly universe. We are born to love, not to hate. We are born to help one another, not to destroy one another. But by propaganda and indoctrination we begin to think that we are superiors and that others are not our equals. That kind of thing is due not for the natural impulses of the human being. The human being naturally loves another. It is by indoctrination that we seduce man from his natural generosity of spirit, sympathy and fellowship into devious methods. That is what we do. Our one aim in this world should be that we should not exaggerate, should not misrepresent, should not indulge in propaganda, but listen to the voice of truth, obey the call of compassion. If we are able to do it, this world will become one and we will all be proud of what we have achieved. Just as we are all friends here, our nations should all become friends. If that happens, that is the kind of consummation which we sincerely desire. Let us therefore, raise our glasses to the world as a partnership and nations as friendly partners in that one world. The testing of nuclear weapons, as going on today, has not only immediate but long-term effects. It causes untold damage to unborn generations. Our invitation letter stresses this aspect : "Give our children a chance to grow up as we did." This is possible only if there is complete nuclear disarmament. The world is full of tensions arising from the growth of new nations, from the passion for independence of non-self-governing peoples, from the demand of less advanced people for a larger share in the world's goods, from the racial policies adopted by certain States and from the inequalities between the rich and the poor nations. The most acute and urgent problem is the cold war between the two blocs which acts as piling up vast destructive nuclear power. In this explosive condition of international deterioration any miscalculation may lead to a catastrophe.

The Convention is not only against the testing of nuclear weapons but against their use in any war. Even if we ban the testing of nuclear weapons, destroy the nuclear armaments, stop their production, we cannot erase the knowledge of nuclear know-how from men's minds. As soon as hostilities break out, nuclear weapons will be produced and used. Military researchers are planning deadlier weapons at lower cost. A time will come when almost all nations will have the knowledge and the power to make nuclear weapons. We must, therefore, assume that in another war on a large scale, if the present conditions continue, nuclear weapons will be used, resulting in the obliteration of our enemies as well as of ourselves. So long as we retain war as a method of settling international disputes and include nuclear weapons in our armoury, they will be used at some stage. There is now no alternative to a peaceful settlement of even the most intricate international problems. If we wish to abolish the use of nuclear weapons, we must work for the abolition of war itself as an instrument for settling international disputes. The resources, natural and human, which we now have, if uncontrolled, may lead to disaster; if controlled and properly directed, they may lead to a better world than we had ever before. The future is in our hands. The passions, the illusions and the tensions which provoked wars in the past cannot be allowed to persist in the future. We will survive or perish together by the choice we now make. History must take a new direction if man's deepest desire for peace is to endure and prevail.

It is unfortunate that man is losing faith in himself. We suffer from a feeling of utter helplessness. We seem to have lost our initiative and judgment. We live in an age which seems to be purposeless, which is greatly concerned but unconvinced, which hesitates between the past and the future. The human mind is at conflict with itself. We do not choose evil and accept it but it chooses us, enters us slowly and consumes us. This is because man has ceased to be a creative person. He is reduced to the status of an object shaped by impersonal forces. This is man's self-defeat.

Our excuse is that other people are doing the same thing. Living in this world we have to behave like others, *sastram sastrenaiamyati,* arms are overcome by arms. We should realize that the progress hitherto achieved is due to the free spirit of man which fights all closed societies and rebels against the rigidity of the past. The inspiration of the infinitely improbable has been the impetus to all progress. In any society a small minority overcomes spiritual inertia and asserts the force of spirit which is unconquerable. It resists the status quo. If we care for the sick, the weak, the old, the decrepit; if we have abandoned the beliefs that the gods would be pleased by the burning alive of children, witches, and our enemies; if we have abolished duelling and slavery; if the rack, the stake and the Inquisition are relics of the past, it is because of the force of spirit. The absence of any preconceived pattern in history, the contingency, the unforeseeability, the haphazardness of history point to the intervention of the free spirit of man. The future of mankind is wide open. There is nothing inevitable about it. It is wrong to assume that human nature is static and unchanging. Man's sensitivity to evil has increased. Many beliefs and practices which we once adopted are now discarded. What we once regarded as right are now discarded as wrong. Human nature has changed in the past and will change in the future. In this world of mortal peril, that is the immortal hope that sustains us.

We should realize that behind the hand that releases the bomb is the heart that sets the hand in motion. If the finer feelings of man are deadened, it is because we have been trained to look upon evil as inevitable — "Evil, be thou my good." Man can grow in mind and heart, and control the physical environment which he has changed a great deal. Human nature has changed a great deal, and by a determined effort we can bring about other changes.

The first change to be effected is in our attitude to the nation-State. A nation as an experiment in social living with its graces and values has a place, but as an instrument of power and exploitation it has been ruinous. Nations should not be causes of irritation to one another. They should be sources of blessing. If we have a proper perspective of history we will realize that many great nations and civilizations have disappeared. Their days are over and their altars smoke no more. We need not assume that our own nation will endure, though others may pass out. A nation will endure only if it conforms to the law of love, of co-operation. Belief in complete unqualified national sovereignty is out of date in the present world. The future sends our minds back into the past, the recent past.

East and West, London, June 21, 1963

Lord Mayor, Your Royal Highness, Distinguished Guests : I am very grateful to you, Sir, for the lavish words which you have used in talking about me and my country, which shows your generosity and affection for us, which I appreciate deeply. You referred to the concept of Commonwealth. Her Majesty the Queen, with great imagination and skill, is doing her utmost to convert that concept into a living reality, and we are all indebted to her for that. You spoke about our taking over parliamentary democracy, your system of law, including minor processes, procedures and practices in our Parliament from your thought and practice. My friend, the Speaker of our Lower House, the Lok Sabha, People's House, is here. He will testify to the fact that every day he has to turn to May's Parliamentary Practice twice or thrice; and we took up parliamentary democracy and we have adopted adult franchise. It is a symbol that we wish to treat all people as equals whatever be the race, sex, class or community and what we are now attempting to do is to make the life of these people somewhat ampler and richer than it used to be. In this task of modernisation, we have been receiving great assistance from this country and others also, this country pre-eminently. We are thankful to you for that. One thing occurred to me — that in one or two matters we may have something to teach you. In our parliament we have about 52 lady members, but I am told that in this Commons, the Court of Aldermen, etc., there is not a single lady. Another thing that I may tell you is Mr Gandhi had a day of silence. He thought we talked too much, and it is better for us to have one day when we shut our mouths and don't waste words. I think, if there is less talk in the world, the world will be a better place. Someone spoke about the pursuit of knowledge and duty which you find is not peculiar to Great Britain, but is also found elsewhere. There is no question that whether you take the pursuit of truth or the pursuit of beauty or the pursuit of sanctity or holiness, these are not the monopolies of any countries or continents. You have sanctity and holiness in the West, as you have scientific achievement in the East. This is a question of distribution of emphasis, in different ages possibly. Once upon a time, in mathematics, grammar, logic, etc., the East had considerable contributions to make. Today, the West is making tremendous progress in science and technology, but that does not show any kind of inaptitude in the one of this or the other. The rational and spiritual sides constitute two essential aspects of human nature, and wherever you find human nature you will find the capacity to reason and the capacity to contemplate. Both these things are to be found all over the world and we need not make distinctions on such things. We had the good fortune during our struggle to have for our guide a man of spirit, a man in whom you saw the hidden fire, the secret kingdom in which the Invisible dwells. He called himself a religious man, and as a religious man he felt that every kind of tyranny has to be opposed, tyranny of nation over nation, class over class, race over race. He worked for the equality of man, and die brotherhood of man, that was the great ideal for which Gandhi lived and died. He asked us to wage war against every kind of injustice, oppression, iniquity, a war in which no lives were lost, no homes were burnt, but the participants came out chastened in spirit. He was the man who told us that eternity is not something distant or in the future. It is there, dwelling in the present in every man, and whatever work we undertake must be undertaken with the perspective of the Eternal. That is the kind of advice which Gandhi gave us, and it is because we had such a man for our guide that the relations between our two countries have been smoothly broadened out into one of friendship and partnership in the pursuit of the great task of humanity. He made this statement : "I do not wish to live in this world if it is not united. I do not wish to live in this world if it is going to be a cockpit of strife among sovereign nations, with national hysteria, with racial bigotry, and organised jealousies." He said such a world is not fit for human beings to be in. He wanted the world to get united. That is what he said. When you look at the way in which we have progressed in our century, how we started it with complete confidence in the stability and security of the world. We thought everything was going to run smoothly, that we would enjoy the fruits of our labours and we would settle down. Came the First World War, which shattered our illusions and smashed our ideals. We found ourselves living in an artificial atmosphere. The war came and we won the war, but the peace was lost. What happened? Unconditional surrender.

The enemy must be squeezed till "the pips squeaked". There is the great saying which the Buddha gave us : "Victory breeds hatred; the conquered live in sorrow." He taught us this 2,500 years ago. Victory breeds hatred; the conquered live in sorrow and wait for an opportunity to wreak their vengeance. Nihilism, disillusionment, despair, overtook the world; and we had the Second World War. We won it. Today, we are still obsessed by the terrific anxieties of what we are going to do with these spectacular techno logical devices and nuclear weapons.

If we do not learn from the past, we have to live it over again. The two World Wars have not taught us to settle down in peace, to live together in peace and amity. What is it that prevents us from adopting the same procedure before passing through a terrific catastrophe ? Is it necessary for us every time to live through bloodshed, to make this world into a shambles, and then get together and say we want to live together as friends and no more as enemies? Here is a golden opportunity for the great leaders of religion, of politics, to express the will of the age, to express the purposes of Providence, the desire of the whole universe that we are intended to live together as friends and not look upon one another as enemies, disguised or in some other way. A union of hearts, a communion of minds, these are the things which we require today. We have all the opportunities.

Science and technology have given us the resources by which we can feed the whole world. They have given us the resources by which ideas could be circulated all over the world. Radio communications, transport, all these things have made it possible for us to believe that the one nationality which we have is the human race and the world is our home. All the things that are necessary for establishing such a kind of functioning reality are available to us. All that is necessary is a shake-up of human nature, a regeneration of human nature. It has to come out of its rut. The status quo is not a way of life. It is something which we have to breakthrough. There have been periods in the history of man, when we broke through the surface of such deadlocks and came to recognise one another as friends. It is such an opportunity that is now awaiting the human race. We live at a very crucial period in human history. It depends on the leaders, the political leaders, the religious leaders, all the leaders who have got the power to influence the minds and motives of men; it is for them today to call out boldly, squarely, without ambiguity or prevarication. The world is intended to be our home. Everyone is our kindred. It is a family that we have to establish on earth. That is the thing that is now open to us. The Commonwealth has brought together a number of races, a number of nations. They all work together as members who acknowledge certain ideals. I do not say acknowledgment of ideals means the implementation of those ideals; it does not follow. We have acknowledged so many things in this world. Yet there is this thing in man's nature. The Good that I would,

I do not; the Evil that I would not, that I do. That has been told us. In our country we have a saying : "I know the right but I cannot adopt it. I know the wrong, I cannot abstain from it." It is there that we have duality in human nature; this human being is a paradox, a contradiction; at once the glory of Creation and the scandal of Creation. That is what he is. What you need is a regeneration of human nature. You must enlarge your vision, increase your understanding, grow in grace. That is what is necessary if we are to get off into a new type. It is my earnest hope and devout prayer that all those who have got the authority, the power, the influence and the leadership will do something to bring to a halt the present piling up of armaments, the present testing of nuclear weapons, and that about these things which are disastrous to humanity, they will have the courage to say, "Stop this thing. This is unworthy of man."

Lord Mayor, you hold an important position. This building has been here for 500 or 600 years and there has been a Lord Mayor for 515 years. Am I right? Something like that the Lord Mayor has a very important position. I do hope that when he has a chance, he will do his utmost to bring about this ideal of one family on earth. It was St Paul who told us, God is above all, through all and in all. If it is so, why should we not practise this in our everyday life ? That is my hope and the Corporation will no doubt do its best.

The Emerging World Society, The Council of Asian Relations and World Affairs, Kathmandu, November 6, 1963

Friends : as your President has reminded you, this is not the first time that I am here, addressing this Council. The very existence of the Council shows that we are in a new age, an age of the emerging world society-one society, that is what is beckoning to us on the horizon. Prophets and seers have spoken to us of one family on earth.

mat a ca parvati dev!
pita devo mahesvarah
bandhavah rnanavah sarve
svadeso bhuvanatrayam

We are children of the same parents and, therefore, we belong to one family. The Buddhists proclaim that they wish to see a brotherhood established on earth. Christianity tells us of one family on earth. So does Islam -one God and one brotherhood on earth. These are ideals which have been put before us by our saints and seers for many long centuries, but the conditions for the implementation of these ideals have not been available till our own time. It is now that science and technology have brought about a physical unification of the world. Now we have races and cultures belonging to different areas mingling, one with another, and trying to understand one another.

Silver Jubilee Meeting of the Tuberculosis Association of India, New Delhi, April 4, 1964

Friends : it gives me very great pleasure to be here and congratulate the workers of the Tuberculosis Association of India on the work that they have already achieved. Twenty-five years of existence of this Association is a sign that it has been doing good work and catering for the real needs of our country.

Tuberculosis, as Dr Sushila Nayar has already told you, is both a national and an international problem. It is national because we have millions in this country who suffer from tuberculosis, and we are trying to help them, dispense comfort and happiness to them. Those who are on the public stage get the applause; but the true workers are those who visit homes and soothe those who suffer from tuberculosis, and dispense real comfort and happiness to them.

We founded this Association at a time when the country was not independent. And it has acquired greater strength after Independence. We have to recognize that in the treatment of tuberculosis, there has been great progress : discovery of anti-bacterial drugs, chest surgery, and several other ways in which patients are looked after much better today than before. But the real problem of tuberculosis is the problem of the general poverty of the country; low standards of living, unhealthy surroundings, malnutrition and bad water-supply are the causes of tuberculosis. If we want to eliminate tuberculosis from the life of the nation, we have to raise the quality of the nation and the standards of living of the ordinary people — that is the radical cure for the removal of tuberculosis. What we are attempting to do in hospitals and in other ways is symptomatic treatment; but we have to extend organic treatment to this particular problem. It is, therefore, interconnected with the general level of our well-being, and all those who work for the raising of the material standards of our country are helping to remove the scourge of tuberculosis from the lives of millions of our young people.

It was said that Rajkumari Amrit Kaur had a great deal to do with the development of this Association. She was our unofficial Ambassador to the world at large. By her great charm, refinement, skill in speech and human qualities, she endeared herself to all those whom she met. Her loss is a really great one and I have no doubt that her example will inspire you all. It is a great thing that Dr Sushila Nayar also comes from a similar background. She was a close associate of Gandhiji. If Gandhiji taught us anything, it was detachment and devotion-detachment from pride, from prejudice, from fixed ideas and obsessions and having an open mind and trying to do our best; and devotion to the public welfare, to the common good of the community which transcends not merely national bounds but every kind of limitation.

Today health is a universal problem. That is why you have passports, health certificates, etc. Everyone is interested in the preservation of the health of everyone else. It is these qualities which we have to develop-detachment and devotion. My friend Dr. Sushila Nayar has these qualities and she will try to apply them to the daily lives of our people. I have great pleasure in inaugurating the Silver Jubilee Session of the Tuberculosis Association of India.

Leprosy Relief, Annual General Meeting of the Hind Kusht Nivaran Sangh, New Delhi, April 16, 1564

Friends : I am very happy to be here and meet you all once again. I had the pleasure of meeting you last year at a similar function. We have listened to the reports of Dr. Chadha and Shri Lakshmanan on the progress made last year. It is a satisfactory account, and I wish to congratulate you on the work that you have done.

Leprosy was once upon a time regarded as incurable, and patients who suffered from leprosy were treated as more or less outcasts from society. It is a great improvement that we have effected in that we do not adopt such attitudes now. We know that leprosy is curable; we know that many drugs have been invented and that there are possibilities of surgical intervention also and that people can be rehabilitated not only physically but psychologically. They may be made to accept their position as members of society where they will be able to make satisfactory contributions to society. To make people, who suffer from leprosy feel that sense of dignity is a great achievement on which all the workers deserve to be congratulated.

I know that many foreign agencies have been helping you. The King of the Belgians was on a tour of this country just to visit the Leprosy Centre in south India; and I corresponded with President Luebke of the Federal Republic of Germany; he sent me a cheque to be forwarded to you and you received it. That means that leprosy is treated not merely as a local problem but as a problem which concerns the health of the whole world community. If you want to remove leprosy from the world, you have to start somewhere, and each country will have to start somewhere. By this kind of treatment and work which you do — it blesses him that gives and him that receives— you not only improve the position of the patients but you also begin to realize that there are resources in human nature — resources of compassion and sympathy for suffering people. These qualities are manifested by the leprosy doctors, the leprosy workers, etc. This dharma, or seva, service as we call it, is something which is very difficult to grasp. Many of us think that we are rendering social service. What we are really doing, each individual will know only if he subjects himself to personal examination and scrutiny. There is a passage which tells us:

sevci dharmah parama gahano ydginamapyagamyah

The essence of dharma or service is most profound, very secret; it is incomprehensible even to the yogis. We think that we are doing social service but all the time our motives may be somewhat different. It is essential that everyone who is engaged in this important work should act with a missionary motive, should have a sense of helping those who happen to be weak and vulnerable. I have no doubt that those workers who are dealing with leprosy do adopt such an attitude. They have sympathy for the suffering patient. You know the great saying : who is my neighbour? Whoever is suffering, whoever is in need of help, is your neighbour. Our neighbours are to be found in all parts of the world. Every neighbour of ours who stands in need of our help is our true neighbour, our true brother.

It is in that spirit that you should work and I think you, Ladies and Gentlemen, who are doing this work, have this great ideal before you. It is not merely a question of rescuing leprosy patients but rescuing yourselves from what is fugitive and fragile and trying to do some work which will bring out the better nature, not the fallen nature of humanity. At a time like this when the explosive forces of the world are at work, it is necessary for most of us to realize that we are friendly to one another. Friendliness, forbearance and help for the suffering should be the ideals which should govern our daily conduct. This may be difficult; but all great things are difficult, and I hope that you workers will act in the spirit indicated by your own religion, indeed all the great religions of the world. I wish you well in your deliberations. You will work out your problems and try to make your organization a much better one than it happens to be. It is a matter of great satisfaction to us that voluntary agencies, governmental agencies and foreign agencies are all working together with the one idea of saving the leprosy patients from their suffering.

Unveiling a Portrait of Dr. Rajendra Prasad, Parliament House, New Delhi, May 5, 1964

Friends: I am delighted to be here and unveil the portrait of Dr. Rajendra Prasad. It is the good fortune of this country that in the formative period of our Republic, immediately after the establishment of the Republic, Dr. Prasad was elected President and that he guided the destinies of our country for over 12 years. He was the embodiment of what is best in Indian culture. The peaks of our achievement are symbolized by service, renunciation and sacrifice. These three qualities were embodied in him. His life, from the time he entered the national struggle down to the last day of his life, was devoted to the service of this country. It was in this Hall that he presided over the Constituent Assembly and drew up the Constitution, which is democratic and progressive in outlook. It is true that he took a leading part in many other activities, too. But here we are concerned with his work for the development of the Constitution and the work which he did for human fellowship. The last address which he gave in this city of Delhi was at the Anti-nuclear

Convention. As a true disciple of Gandhiji, he made out that we should try to avoid every kind of violence, that we should struggle to establish peace and friendship among nations; and he formulated a proposal for unilateral nuclear disarmament. Even though it may have appeared to be utopian when he formulated it, it is an ideal to which the whole world looks forward. It was in his lifetime that nuclear developments arose. There were the methods of the past, battles, violent struggles, etc. But when these had taken place, we could still survive as they affected only parts of the world, not the whole of it. Nuclear armaments and nuclear warfare mean the destruction of all the civilized values for which we stand. The methods of the past cannot be regarded as applicable to the present. So, even though we may consider that what he suggested was utopian, yet that is the only thing that can give the human community stability, poise and balance.

We cannot merely ask for nuclear disarmament. We must remove the causes that cause wars. The causes are mutual fear, distrust, animosities and the feeling of insecurity among nations. If we are to survive in this world as peaceful nations, these causes have to be removed. Men must feel that humanity is one whole, irrespective of caste or community, class or race. They must try to widen the horizon of their understanding, advance in knowledge, grow in grace and feel that when one individual in one part of the country or the world suffers, all others do suffer.

Dr Rajendra Prasad, as a faithful disciple of Gandhiji, argued for human fellowship. It is one of the things inscribed in our Constitution. We stand for political justice and freedom, fraternity and fellowship. This is one of the remarkable objectives of our Constitution. We cannot achieve it unless we advance towards it step by step. Many of the things that we do may appear to be very rash from the practical point of view today but ultimately it is the steps that seem to be impossible and it is the push of the impossible that make the world a place in which we can live with some kind of amity and friendship. Rajen Babu held this ideal and the last address he gave to the Delhi people, to the country and the world at large, was the one on unilateral nuclear disarmament. Not that it is going to be realized tomorrow or the day after, but he knew for certain that if this world was to become a happy home, if people were to live together in amity and friendship, that was the only way. We must cease to hate each other; we must cease to have hostilities; we must live with one another and try to develop understanding of one another. It is this ideal that possessed him and he made the proposal even though he was certain that many in his audience would not accept the rationale of it.

I would like to say that he was a faithful disciple of Gandhiji. He was a believer in democracy; democracy, he thought, was a progressive system. What exists today in the name of democracy cannot be regarded as satisfactory. It is something which is perpetually moving forward; if it does not move forward, it is not democracy. It must go on until it embraces the whole world and makes it a happy human community.

I have great pleasure in unveiling this portrait, and I hope that all those who see it will understand the great ideals for which Rajen Babu stood, for which he lived, and for which he died.

Reception at Manchester University, Manchester, June 17, 1963

I am very happy to meet so many of you who are working in this University and in its neighbourhood. It is a matter of gratification for us that you people are getting the best training possible in the several subjects of your choice. You have greater opportunities than many of your fellow-countrymen who have not got the privilege of coming out and getting trained by very competent men in such parts of England. I hope you are taking full advantage of your opportunities, and when you return to our country, I hope, you will be of great service in the development of our country. As you know after we obtained our Independence, our next problem was to fight poverty, to fight hunger, malnutrition, unemployment and other evils, from which millions of our people suffer. And we can remove those things only by the application of science and technology to agriculture and industry. And you, who have come here, I have no doubt, will be of considerable use to us when you get back to our country and try to help us in rebuilding our economy.

I was gratified here to see so many of you from so many parts of our country and it gave me special satisfaction to see a number of people from Pakistan who are also getting training here. It is a matter of great pleasure for me to see that you are all working together here in a spirit of amity and harmony. It is my hope and desire when you return to our country, you will forget your small differences-differences of province, region, language and districts from which you come and work together as belonging to one great country which has, in spite of all the vicissitudes through which it has passed, a great tradition that has come down from four to five millennia. It gives you a sense of satisfaction that you were able to encounter all the troubles that faced you, able to survive and able to stand up, even today, to be a nation which is able to contribute its might to the development not only of the country but of humanity at large. That is what you should work for. The real obstacles to any kind of progress in the world are due to exploitation of man by man-whether it is political or economic, or racial. Unless we are able to remove this kind of exploitation this world cannot settle down.

We want to see a world that is a family of free nations, co-operating one with another for the purpose of building up a happy home for humanity. The obstacles are generally due to this kind of exploitation. Don't imagine that the differences between the so-called rival ideologies are very vital and great. Only the other day in a radio programme of the Soviet Union the question was raised "What is meant by capitalism?" and the answer was given, "The exploitation of man by man." To "What is communism ?" the answer was "The opposite of it." You needn't imagine that exploitation is the peculiar quality of the capitalist systems and that the Communist systems are free or vice versa. We are all struggling to achieve the same ends. One thing that is happening today is that capitalism is moving away from its own fundamental positions, as they were some years ago, and communism is also moving away from some of the positions it occupied once upon a time.

When you find a man like Khrushchev declaring to you openly, "We have a great deal to learn from capitalism," and Soviet foreign policy has for its fundamental principle, compromise; and when he says that the inevitability of war between the two systems is an outmoded doctrine, whatever may have been its validity at the time it was formulated, today in this nuclear context it has no meaning whatsoever. There will be no justice at all if we should stick to these principles which were enunciated once upon a time. Marx himself said, "I enunciated certain doctrines but there is no such thing as Marxism." He himself at the beginning of his career said, "Religion is the heart of a heartless world." Later on, when he found religious people compromising with iniquities he said, "It is the opiate of the people." There has been a change in his standpoint from the first when he declared that religion was the heart of a heartless world to the position when he said it was the opiate of the common people, lulling them into a sense of false security. In other words there is no such thing as the immutability of social and political institutions. They are all time-changing. There is nothing which is fixed or static in this world. We call the world something which perpetually moves, which is never static which is never stagnant. Our culture has been able to survive all the shocks which it has encountered for the simple reason that it has the quality of self-renewal: it met different cultures— the Aryan and the Dravidian, the

Hindu and the Buddhist, the Christian and the Jew. The Hindu and the Muslim, the British and the Western influences, etc. All these things have been made into part of one common culture, which we call the Indian culture. It is neither Hindu, nor Muslim, nor Jewish, nor Christian. It is Indian in its outlook and in its spirit. And every one of us must try to see the spirit of that culture, which accepted differences, which never looked upon diversity as a source of discord but looked upon diversity as something which contributes to the richness, variety and the majesty and the scope of the world. That is how we look upon the varying things which have taken habitation in our country. There is nothing for us to be ashamed about if you look at the fact that 450 million people, belonging to different religions and speaking different languages, are held together under a single administration, without any coercion, without resort to dictatorship or totalitarianism, but by means of persuasion and consent through the working of parliamentary institutions. Show me another 450 million people who have been held together under democratic institutions by the force of sheer persuasion and consent without exercise of any kind of violence or any kind of dictatorship. You will not be able to find it in this world. All that we should do is to strengthen this unity, this sense of belonging to a whole, a whole that belongs to every one of us and not to any particular province or any particular race or any particular religion. You work together in great harmony here. I do not see any reason why, when you go back from this country, you should not work together with the same spirit of harmony and the same spirit of amity and friendship. That is what is necessary there. You must see to it that national coherence is kept up. You must have the sense that you belong to one whole but that whole also should not be regarded as a whole opposed to the others. Nationalism does not mean hatred of other nations; it means that you have the capacity to make your own contribution to the richness of the world. It is that idea you must harbour in your minds. You must have your nation and feel proud that you belong to it. That does not mean that you should hate other nations or not have common bonds binding you with other nations. When you go back, feel a sense of belonging to one whole. Try to look upon the iniquities, injustices and disabilities from which large numbers of our people are suffering as your own; that you have a call to remedy them and overcome them, to do your best to lift up all those people and remove the disabilities that are shackling them and make them proud to belong to your country where everyone's well-being is the concern of the whole. If one part of your body is injured, if your finger is hurt, it is not the finger that feels the pain, but the whole body that feels the pain. If any part of our people is sub- merged or oppressed or is put under disabilities, it is not only those people that suffer; we all suffer, the whole nation suffers and I want you to regard that as the greatest challenge you can face when you go back to our country. You must work also for the unity of the world. We have come to a stage when our nationality is the human race and where the whole world is our home. We must therefore try to do our utmost to remove the disabilities from which other people are suffering. That is why I said racial bigotry, political exploitation and domination, colonialism as you call it and economic exploitation, these things must be removed as speedily as possible, if the causes which produce conflicts are to be removed. I do hope that in all your training you have a scientific outlook, not merely industrial skill. The way to look upon things is not with obscurantist eyes but with fresh eyes, with modem eyes, thinking that nothing is to be accepted by us unless we are able to see that it commends itself to the spirit of our reason.

Your training here, I hope, has given you not merely scientific power and technical knowledge but also a scientific temper, a temper which looks at the facts dispassionately, disinterestedly and in a disciplined way. You are able to do it as worthy sons of our country and worthy citizens of this world.

British Government Dinner, Lancaster House, London, June 20, 1963

IT is a very great pleasure to me to be in the city of Coventry. I think my visit to Great Britain would have been incomplete if I had not come here, and seen for myself the few things which I have had the opportunity of seeing in the short time I have been here. I have visited several cities and had mayoral receptions, but it is the first time I have visited a city which has a Lord Mayor who is a lady, and I hope there will be more cities like this, with Lady Mayors, although they are called Lord Mayor. That is the inconsistency of the British tradition, she is a lady, but is addressed as Lord Mayor.

When I saw Coventry Cathedral I felt that when your old Cathedral was broken down, shattered in the darkest hours of the war, that you was then near to salvation. Man has to be subjected to degradation and despair, to feel that he is deserted by the Divine and by everyone — the, hour is always darkest before the dawn, and it is at that moment that your hearts must be greatly torn. But you felt that Speech at the luncheon given by the Corporation of Coventry, 19 June, 1963 the sun still shone, the clouds would disperse and you would be able to build a Cathedral addressed to the needs of the modern age.

If this age has any particular problem to face it is the problem of the reconciliation of the peoples of the world. You have had conflict with the Germans, while today those very Germans have helped you to some extent by way of recompense for the evils inflicted upon this great city. The trouble about human nature is it knows what the results of a particular line of conduct will be known to them to be disastrous and yet it has not the power to take itself out of the rut, face problems with courage and compassion and avert the catastrophe which we know is inevitable today. Again, we know these nuclear armaments are going up and the nuclear tests are also going on, and it is possible that by a mistake the world may go up in fragments. These puclear tests are depositing radioactive substances in our bodies which may have their effect on unborn generations. We all want peace but we have not the courage, we have not the, strength, to retrace our steps and say that our problem after a war is going to be exactly the same as it is today. The Germans and British did not enter the last war intending that your great country should be totally devastated; people survived, and if there is now a chance of human survival we have to come together.

Why do you not do it today? Why is human nature so twisted in its character? What we must endeavour is to bring about a shakeup in our nature, a complete reorganization of the nature of man, so that man is able to feel that he belongs to one race. We belong to one family; there are accidents of geography and history; we are, in different administrative units, and each must take the opportunity to contribute out of its mind and spirit to world culture. Art and literature' are potent factors, but politics are put higher. Politics are higher, yet they are the things which divide one from another. We have been taught that the purpose of the universe, the purpose of environment, is the establishment of one family on earth and we have all the necessary facilities. We can feed the world, we can clothe the world and we, can shelter the whole world and give opportunities to every individual for self-expression and self-development. All these resources are available to us if only we would divert a fraction of the resources we now spend on armament. If we would do this there would be no scarcity in the world and everyone would be happy to belong to this world. When God created this world he intended to provide things for human fulfilment and not for human destruction. What is needed is a transformation, a moral transformation, a kind of change, the re-making of human nature. We should feel that though we belong to Britain we should not hate other nations. It follows that even as we love our country other people love their countries, and if we are able to understand that national feeling and the humanity and understanding which is the greatest longing of human nature, if we are able to give it a chance of outward expression, it will be a great day for humanity.

I was very pleased to notice the rehabilitation centre here and your Lord Mayor was good enough to tell me how bonds of friendship have been established between this city of Coventry and other cities of the world, both in the East and the West. These are all small steps, but steps which indicate the direction of history. I believe that if these steps are strengthened we will begin to believe that we belong to one human race and the sorrows and sufferings of others must be regarded as our own sorrows that is, if the spirit of compassion can take over and bring about the change. We can then settle down today; instead of going through catastrophe we can settle down to peaceful ways. There are many signs which indicate that we are aware of impending catastrophe and that we are doing our best to avert it. There are co-operative movements in outer space research and in other ways we are trying to get together; in the organization of the United Nations we are trying to work together. We must strengthen the creative side of man and suppress, or obliterate possibly, the vanity, the jealous side of our nature, the suspicion and the fear. It is these jealousies and suspicions that are responsible for the nightmare world we live in today. Let each one make a revolution in himself and the world will be saved.

Message to the Nation for Independence Day, Delhi, August14, 1962

Friends: on the eve of the fifteenth anniversary of our Independence Day, it is my privilege to speak to our people at home and abroad about our achievements and aspirations as well as the tasks ahead of us. All these years, after we stepped into the world of free nations, we have been trying to win for our people a deeper and nobler freedom than what mere political liberty connotes. Gandhiji once said, "I have travelled from one end of the country to the other and I have seen the miserable specimens of humanity with their lusterless eyes. They are India. In these humble cottages, in the midst of these dung heaps are to be found humble folk in whom you find the concentrated essence of wisdom." Here Gandhiji sums up the material poverty and the spiritual wealth of our people. We should strive to remove the former and strengthen the latter.

The plight of the poor is the symbol of our condition. They suffer from malnutrition and so are easily susceptible to disease. The indigent and the destitute live under subhuman conditions. Food, clothing and shelter are the primary needs of our people. By planned economic development we are striving to increase agricultural production so as to meet the needs of our people as well as the requirements of industry and export, encouraging industries that would give clothing to our population at reasonable prices and implementing housing programmes which would provide accommodation for low-income groups. The implementation of the Plans has been somewhat inadequate as there has been little emotional involvement on the part of the staff, managerial and subordinate, in the great national work that they are engaged in. It is essential that our public servants, whether employed in Government service or public and private industries, should have a sense of pride in their work. They should feel that they are engaged in the bloodless revolution of raising the living standards of 440 millions of people and strengthening their moral fibre. All those who work with the people should be humble, kind and considerate. Economic development and clean administration will help to strengthen national solidarity.

We are mechanizing agriculture and industrializing our country. We have now to develop a new ethos, a new spiritual outlook, if freedom and democracy are to be realized in our lives. The wisdom to which Gandhiji refers is ever-vigilant, ever-creative. Though it does not conform to the world, it does not keep away from it. It helps to reconcile and redeem society. Wisdom requires us to be compassionate, to be forgiving, to forbear judgment. Unfortunately, we are more critical of others than of ourselves. We preach from platforms tolerance and understanding but do not manifest these qualities in our daily lives, in our dealings with others. If we cling to the caste hierarchy, if we do not treat human beings with respect and dignity, if we show ourselves to be lacking in sensibility and human feeling, if we believe that we are pleasing God thereby, we do offence to God and to ourselves.

Nirdosam hi samam brahma : the Supreme is faultless and equal to all. Whatever prevents us from knowing the truth and practising love toall, even those who do not belong to our sect, group or denomination, cannot be religious. We should strive to keep alive in our hearts that little spark of celestial fire, love of truth and goodness.

Faith in democracy is the binding force of our society. Democracy will make for modernity. We cannot live in the twentieth century when we are handicapped by the institutions and machinery of an earlier age.This is the source of our national incoherence. If we adhere to the principles and practices of democracy, we will not compromise with disruptive, reactionary and antisocial forces. The recent elections showed that the system of caste and feeling for groups — linguistic and communal have not loosened their hold on the masses of our people. These have impaired the health of our democratic structure. Even in panchayati raj we should be careful that the spirit of caste panchayat does not vitiate its working.

Ethical sublimity is the mark of the magnanimous man; ethical depravity is the mark of the low man. All other distinctions are irrelevant *na kulam kulamitydhurdcaram kulamucyate.* If we are to be truly democratic in our public life and administration, it is essential that no one should be prejudiced or favoured by reason of sex or parentage, race or language, caste or sub-caste, religious faith or political persuasion. While facilities should be provided for all people to train themselves for self-expression and development,' no encouragement should be given to the perpetuation of divisions and sub-divisions. Economic backwardness, and not the caste or the community to which one happens to belong, should be the test for special concessions. The State should provide opportunities of education for the backward people, to whatever religion or community they may belong. In a competitive world, if we are to survive, our ablest men should be entrusted with high responsibility. While appointments to services should be made on grounds of efficiency, the handicaps from which the backward classes suffer should be removed as speedily as possible.

When we look at the world situation, we find that collective passions make us run the risk of universal destruction. While in theory we are convinced of the oneness of the world and the indivisibility of peace, in practice we adopt a narrow nationalist outlook. The dichotomy in our thought and life requires to be removed. Circumstances are compelling us to act on the assumption of One World. It will be our endeavour in the international world to break down barriers, relax tension and foster world unity.

China and Pakistan are our close neighbours, and it is our earnest desire to maintain the most friendly relations with them. Whatever disputes we have with them, we will strive our utmost to have these settled in a peaceful way. Peaceful negotiations, however, do not mean capitulation or the surrender of our legitimate rights. We have faith in the future of man. His nature has changed so often and will change again. His life is not finished; his present stage is not the final one. Man, as he is, is a sketch of what man has to be. He is always becoming, becoming something different and often better. He has now to take a great leap forward in consciousness. Individuals, nations and civilizations are a part of this tremendous process of becoming, becoming sensitized, becoming refined, becoming noble.

Today, let us rededicate ourselves to the task of evolving a cohesive, purposeful pattern of society on the principles of unity, freedom, justice and co-operation.

Banquet in Honour of the King and Queen of Greece, Rashtrapati Bhavan, New Delhi, February 2, 1963

May I first convey to you our most cordial welcome on behalf of the Government and the people of this country among whom I include myself. I hope that you and members of your party will have a very useful, interesting and enjoyable time here.

You have been working to build up a welfare state in your country based on the great ideals of democracy, freedom and justice, ideals which were first formulated in the West by your spiritual ancestors, the ancient Greeks. Bishop Westcott remarked many decades ago that Greece and India were the most metaphysical nations in the world.

It may be true or not, but it is true so far as Greece is concerned. A metaphysician, very eminent in our own time, passed away a few years ago — Whitehead; he observed that the safest generalization which one could make on the vast European philosophical tradition was to say that it consisted of a series of foot-notes to Plato. Plato remains the guide for all the philosophers of the West. In some way the Vedas, including the Upanisads and the dialogues of the Buddha, have supplied spiritual nutriment to millions in the East. There is an emphasis, therefore, on metaphysics, on finding out whether this universe has a pattern or not. Man is not merely a tool-maker, he is also a pattern-maker. When he is faced by the things of the world, he wishes to know whether there is any meaning, any principle, underlying this whole cosmic panorama.

The spirit of science which has resulted in such great advances, from steam to electricity, from electricity to atomic power, from atomic power to space travel, has brought the world together and made it a world in which nations and cultures are brought into close intimacy. That was started in the West by the Greek thinkers. I recall that an Egyptian priest told the Greeks, ' You Greeks are always young." There are two types of people in the world : those with ancient traditions looking back to the past with nostalgia, lamenting the loss of a golden age, there are also young people with open minds, with virgin outlook, untrammelled by any kind of pride or prejudice, not oppressed by the weight of antiquity, saying that they look to the future and wish to have a brave new world. The Greeks were the people who said that they were always young, that the universe was rational and could be understood and that we could find out what the truth is. That spirit of science is something which the Greek thinkers contributed to the world of thought. You cannot get a better definition of democracy than what Thucydides gave. Our Constitution is not meant for the few but it is meant for the many. Here we do not recognize birth or parentage but the contribution made to the service of the community. That will be the test and we shall try to protect the oppressed and provide equal justice for all. You have the fundamental principles of democracy which we are still not able to implement completely in any part of the world. In our own country we have proclaimed these great ideals but we have not been able to translate them into practice completely We are still far from that goal of a truly democratic society. The spirit of reason and the spirit of democracy are there. This sense of values when we are faced by depression, confusion, fear, and anxiety it enables us to turn to the inward sanctuary. That sanctuary is not a place in space, but a state of mind; it is a spiritual consciousness. When we turn to it, we will be able to see the hopes and aspirations. Democracy cannot function well without the inclusion of spirituality.

These three great things — the spirit of reason, the spirit of democracy and emphasis on values — are the things that had been adumbrated by the ancient Greek thinkers and we are trying our best to adopt all of them and put them into practice.

Your Majesty, you have done so much in your country for permeating these ideals through your society. You are trying to develop your industries. We are also doing so. We have trade relations with you; we have cultural relations with you; and I have no doubt that by your visit these relations will be greatly promoted and considerably strengthened.

I am glad that Your Majesty has celebrated the Silver Jubilee of your wedding on the 9th of January and that you are going to celebrate the centenary of the connection of your family with Greece this year in March. We wish you both a very, very happy future.

Contributors

Dr. Arnav Keyur Anjaria is the Head of the Department of Political Science at R.R. Lalan College (Government of Gujarat), Bhuj. He holds a PhD, and MPhil from the University of Hyderabad. In 2012 he was awarded the University Gold Medal for Master of Arts in Political Science (5 Years Integrated) at the same University. He has also been a senior editor at the Forum of Ethno-Geopolitics, Netherlands since 2013. Currently, he is the Co-Principal Investigator for a Project titled "A Translation of Tibetan Sources" under the auspices of the Institute of Eminence at the University of Hyderabad. He has earlier taught at institutions such as Amity University Noida and CVM University, Vallabh Vidya Nagar.

Shri Atulindra Nath Chaturvedi studied Political Science at Hindu College (Delhi University) and International Studies at Jawaharlal Nehru University, Delhi. A media Consultant and freelance writer, he has worked with The Times of India, The Pioneer, Business Today and Tehelka, and regularly contributed articles and book reviews for Outlook, The Patriot and the Indian Express. Chaturvedi has to his credit several books, which include Sri Aurobindo: Spiritual Revolutionary (2002), APJ Abdul Kalam: Scientist and Humanist (2202), Mystic Fire, A Biography of Sri Aurobindo (2022), Dharma Gurus (forthcoming). He has also annotated and written an introduction to Hind Swaraj by M K Gandhi (forthcoming).

Ms. Gunjan Pradhan Sinha is an author, academician and journalist and has been working in the field of public policy and ethics for the past 20 years. She has taught at Delhi's prestigious St. Stephen's College for about a decade. She is a prolific writer with over 2,000 articles in her kitty and her well-received book, Dharma in Governance. She has been engaged in work with the India Foundation, Vivekananda International Foundation and Bhartiya Vidya Bhavan. She has been conducting workshops and courses in Business Ethics as well. She has recently published her article on the Ethics of Genetic Modification in the Routledge Companion to Indian Ethics-women, justice, bioethics and Ecology.

Dr. Jyoti Atwal is Associate Professor of Modern Indian History at the Centre for Historical Studies, School of Social Sciences, Jawaharlal Nehru University, New Delhi, India & Visiting Professor (2022-2027) at UCD School of History, University College Dublin, Ireland. She was also Adjunct Professor at University of Limerick (2017-2022). She specialises in modern Indian history with a focus on gender and history. Her area of interest includes Irish history with special focus on transnational anti-imperial movements and gender. She has published on themes ranging from the transnational movements and World Wars to widowhood, child marriage, gender-based violence, caste and cinema. In 2021, she co-edited a book on India, Ireland and Anti-Imperial Struggle: Remembering the Connaught Rangers Mutiny, 1920, Delhi: Aakar Books, 2021 (supported by Embassy of Ireland, New Delhi). She also co-edited a volume on Gender and Violence in Historical and Contemporary Perspectives: Situating India (London: Routledge, 2020) and a co-edited volume on Gender and History: Ireland 1852-1922, (London: Routledge, 2022). She is also the author of Real and Imagined Widows: Gender Relations in Colonial North India (New Delhi: Primus Books, 2016). She has been a recipient of a teaching cum research grant from Department of Foreign Affairs and Trade, Government of Ireland and has acted as script supervisor in a documentary produced by the DFA. She serves on the advisory board of several projects at University College Cork, University College Dublin and in the UK and USA. She has delivered several lectures internationally and has been on TV and radio programmes on BBC, NPR, RTE, ARD, France24 and Deutsche Welle across UK, America Ireland, Germany and France.

Prof. (Dr.) K N Mishra completed his Ph.D. in Commerce in 1989, specializing in 'Jila Sahkari Bank- Gorakhpur ka ek Adhyayan', demonstrating his dedication to in-depth research and scholarly pursuits. Prior to this, he earned his Postgraduate Degree in Commerce with a focus on Management Accounting in 1985, and his Undergraduate Degree in Commerce with concentrations in Business Law and Statistics in 1983. Dr. Mishra has been recognized for his outstanding contributions to academia and administration. Dr. Mishra's commitment to quality education is further evidenced by his role as the Convenor of the IQAC Cell at Armapore P G College, Kanpur. In this capacity, he has spearheaded initiatives to enhance institutional quality and performance. His dedication to advancing knowledge in the field of Commerce, coupled with his leadership and administrative capabilities, makes Prof. (Dr.) K N Mishra is a highly respected figure in academic circles. He continues to inspire students and colleagues alike through his profound expertise and commitment to excellence.

Shri Kovuuri G. Reddy is an independent journalist, writer and teacher. He is the author of India, Bharat, Hindustan: Handbook on Media and Journalism published by S. Chand. He was the OSD (Media) to the last Chief Minister of Andhra Pradesh based in New Delhi. He taught journalism and media at The Journalism Centre of Harlow College in Essex, England, Anglia Ruskin University and Acharya Institutes, Bengaluru.

Dr. Mamta Anand is a distinguished scholar and educator, serving as an Assistant Professor in the Department of Humanities and Social Sciences (English) at the esteemed Indian Institute of Information Technology Design and Manufacturing, Jabalpur, Madhya Pradesh. With a rich academic background and a passion for literature and philosophy, Dr. Anand has made significant contributions to the field of English studies. Her academic journey includes a Fulbright Fellowship (2008-2009) at Harvard University, where she conducted groundbreaking doctoral research on the influential thinkers Ralph Waldo Emerson and S. Radhakrishnan. During her fellowship, she resided at Colgate University, New York, further enriching her scholarly experience. Notably, her research on Emerson earned her international recognition, including an esteemed award from the Emerson Society based in Washington D.C. in 2006. In 2011, Dr. Anand was conferred with a doctorate from Banasthali University, Rajasthan, marking a significant milestone in her academic career. Her doctoral thesis and subsequent publications have delved deeply into the lives and works of prominent figures in literature and philosophy, shedding new light on their contributions to intellectual discourse. As an author, Dr. Anand has penned the acclaimed book 'S. Radhakrishnan: His Life and Works, published in 2006 by Atlantic Publishers and Distributors, New Delhi. This seminal work has garnered praise for its comprehensive exploration of the life and philosophy of S. Radhakrishnan, a towering figure in Indian intellectual history. Notably, her book is housed in the prestigious Parliament House Library, underscoring its significance in the scholarly community. Dr. Anand's scholarly pursuits extend beyond academia, as her short story 'The Cost of Living' has been published by Sahitya Akademi, New Delhi. This work has been integrated into the undergraduate curriculum at North Maharashtra University, Jalgaon, India, further cementing her influence in literary circles.

Dr. Manish Kumar has studied and worked in different cities across India, France, Switzerland, Russia and the USA before establishing roots in Delhi. Commencing with a degree in Russian Language and Culture from JNU and pursuing subsequent degrees from TISS, Sciences Po, Columbia University, and Amity University, he embarked on a diverse career in environmental campaigns, rural development, workforce development, and international trade and economic relations. Dr. Kumar has worked at corporations, governments, multilateral institutions, and international nonprofits. Additionally, he mentors startups in edtech, healthtech, and government advisories. While continuing his professional journey, he decided to shake things up by enrolling in a Ph.D. program, which he completed in December 2023. His research interests span international mobility, employment-based welfare policies, international trade, the role of migration, and the impact of technologies on shaping welfare policies. In addition to his academic pursuits, Dr. Kumar is an amateur philosopher, Barista, Traveller, Vipassana and OSHO meditator, proficient in Hindi, Bhojpuri, English and Russian.

Dr. Nibedita Priyadarsini has obtained her M.A. (Education, Geography &Psychology), PhD (Education), from Kurukshetra University, Kurukshetra, Haryana and B.Ed. from Utkal University, Odisha. She has also qualified for the U.G.C (NET) in Education. She worked more than 5 years as a Lecturer, N.A.G.D. College, Amroha, U.P. She has worked as a Senior Lecturer in the Department of Curriculum & Instructional Technology, Faculty of Education, University of Malaya, Kula Lumpur, Malaysia for one year. She has also contributed twenty-four articles to National and International journals and fifteen chapters in edited books. She attended thirty-eight national as well as international conferences in India and abroad. Currently, she is working as an Assistant Professor (Education), at Rani Dharm Kunwar Govt. Degree College, Khanpur, Haridwar, Uttarakhand.

Ms. Nidhi Katoch is an esteemed Assistant Professor at Punjabi University, Patiala, where she imparts her expertise in Public Administration to Bachelor's and PG Diploma students of Human Rights. With a solid foundation in Sciences from her undergraduate studies, she adeptly connects with students across various academic disciplines, providing mentorship in both academic pursuits and personal development. Beyond her teaching responsibilities, Nidhi actively engages in academic conferences and workshops to continuously enhance her pedagogical and research skills. Her passion for literature is evident through her active involvement as a blogger since 2019, garnering readership from diverse corners of the globe. In her role as an Assistant Professor, Nidhi fosters an inclusive and supportive learning environment, where she encourages critical thinking and fosters a love for learning among her students. Her dedication to education, coupled with her commitment to community engagement through volunteering activities, reflects her holistic approach to academic and societal contributions.

Dr. Nishant Kumar is a native of Bada Singhanpura in the Buxar district of Bihar. Having done PhD in Public Administration, he has contributed books and research papers to the existing stream of knowledge. He has also served as a guest lecturer and motivational speaker at many national and international forums. His exploration, and unwavering commitment to unraveling the intricacies of the human experience, particularly within the context of nationalism and democracy in India stands out to be exceptional. Dr. Kumar is a fervent scholar, a curious observer, and a dedicated advocate for understanding the social fabric that binds diverse races of humanity. His academic odyssey began with a fervent curiosity about the forces that shape the social realities and the mechanisms through which power is wielded and contested in society. He embarks on a voyage of intellectual inquiry and collective introspection, guided by a shared commitment to understanding, empathy, and solidarity.

Ms. Priyanka Chugh is a research scholar at the Department of Political Science, Jamia Millia Islamia, New Delhi. Pursued her Post-Graduation from Amity University, Uttar Pradesh and Graduation from the University of Delhi, She qualified for UGC-NET JRF in 2022. She has presented papers at national and international conferences held at Jawaharlal Nehru University and the University of Delhi. Her research interest lies in the South Asian domain with a trivial focus on India-China relations. Along with security studies, the geo-political contours among nations and women's contribution in various fields fascinate and captivate her interest in research pursuits.

Dr. Sunil Shukla is the Director General of the Entrepreneurship Development Institute of India, Ahmedabad. He has been closely working, for more than three decades now, in entrepreneurship education, research, training and institution building. Dr. Shukla is a well-known figure in entrepreneurship education and research. He joined the institute in 1993 and since then he has contributed relentlessly to the development of the institute in different capacities. Dr.Shukla plays a primary role in crafting policies and impact-making, developmental interventions in the country. He is the current Editor of 'The Journal of Entrepreneurship', a leading journal in the field of Entrepreneurship. Dr. Shukla is the principal author of Global Entrepreneurship Monitor (GEM) India National Reports (2014 onwards). He is the national team leader of the GEM India Chapter which conducts the largest annual study of entrepreneurial dynamics.

Shri Uttam Prakash is a distinguished public servant with over two decades of experience in shaping accountable, transparent, and responsive public governance in India and Afghanistan. His expertise encompasses a wide range of domains, including public policy, digital governance, social security, programme management, capacity building, and democracy deepening. Currently serving in the Government of India, Shri Prakash holds the position of Regional Provident Fund Commissioner (EPFO Head Quarters), where he focuses on social security administration, compliance management, customer services, and social media outreach. Prior to his current role, he held several key positions within the Indian government, including Regional Provident Fund Commissioner for Delhi West and Fair Competition Advisor in the Government of the Islamic Republic of Afghanistan. Shri Prakash's academic background includes education from prestigious institutions such as the Lee Kuan Yew School of Public Policy in Singapore, IIM Visakhapatnam, the International Institute of Social Studies in the Netherlands, and Delhi School of Economics. Throughout his career, Shri Prakash has demonstrated a passion for leveraging technology to transform public services and drive inclusive societal development. His strategic vision, coupled with his expertise in programme innovation, policy formulation, and cross-cultural team leadership, has been instrumental in driving positive change and fostering effective public policy implementation. With a proven track record of navigating complex governance challenges and delivering impactful results, Shri Uttam Prakash continues to be a driving force in shaping the future of public governance in India and beyond.

Ms. Vidhy Shethna is a Project Manager at the Entrepreneurship Development Institute of Ahmedabad. Her academic background in economics and policy governance has shaped her perspective on development, allowing her to analyze the process from both humanist and technicist viewpoints. Her role at EDII involves overseeing projects & documenting the best practices of the flagship programmes, the Start-Up Village Entrepreneurship Program of the Ministry of Rural Development (MoRD). In addition to her work on the Start-Up Village Entrepreneurship Program, Vidhy is also committed to developing documents under the Scheme of Funds for Regeneration of Traditional Industries (SFURTI) of the Ministry of Micro, Small and Medium Enterprises (MoSME). She is involved in preparing Detailed Project Reports (DPRs) and progress report of the projects under the National Rural Economic Transformation Project (NRETP) initiated by the National Rural Livelihood Mission (NRLM).